W9-BVL-898

The
Quotable
Jefferson

The Quotable Jefferson

COLLECTED AND EDITED BY
JOHN P. KAMINSKI

PRINCETON UNIVERSITY PRESS
PRINCETON AND OXFORD

Copyright © 2006 by Princeton University Press
Published by Princeton University Press,
41 William Street, Princeton, New Jersey 08540
In the United Kingdom: Princeton University Press,
3 Market Place, Woodstock, Oxfordshire OX20 1SY

Library of Congress Cataloging-in-Publication Data

Jefferson, Thomas, 1743–1826.
The quotable Jefferson / collected and edited by
John P. Kaminski.
p. cm.
Includes bibliographical references and index.
ISBN-13: 978-0-691-12267-0 (cloth : alk. paper)
ISBN-10: 0-691-12267-9 (cloth : alk. paper)
1. Jefferson, Thomas, 1743–1826—Quotations.
2. Quotations, American.   I. Kaminski, John P.
II. Title.
E302.J442 2006b
081—dc22   2005030020

British Library Cataloging-in-Publication Data is available

This book has been composed in PUP Monticello

Printed on acid-free paper. ∞

pup.princeton.edu

Printed in the United States of America

1 3 5 7 9 10 8 6 4 2

This book is dedicated to
the editors, past and present,
of the Jefferson papers and to
Princeton University Press,
their publisher

Contents

✦

Preface

Throughout his life Jefferson had a romance with language. As a youngster growing up on the Virginia Piedmont; as a teenager studying at the College of William and Mary; as a young adult cloistered in his suite at Monticello within his ever expanding library; as a parent and mentor dispensing sage advice to his daughters, grandchildren, and sundry young men studying law with him; as a widower deliciously flirting with beautiful, fashionable, intelligent women in Europe and America; as a diplomat and politician in local, state, national, and international service; as a busy and productive retiree; as a tireless correspondent communicating with old friends, political associates, and learned men in a wide range of scientific fields, and virtually until the day of his death, Jefferson was fascinated with the written word.

This allure of language, however, did not extend to the spoken word. John Adams recalled that in the Second Continental Congress Jefferson "never spoke in public; and during the whole Time I sat with him in Congress, I never heard him utter three Sentences together." Everyone understood that Jefferson had an eloquent pen but could challenge no one "in Elocution and public debate."[1] Jefferson admired great orators, such as Indian chiefs whose natural eloquence captured their listeners' imagination, and Patrick Henry, who according to Jefferson, appeared "to speak as Homer wrote."[2] Unfortunately Jefferson could not transfer his mastery over the written text to the spoken word—his deliveries always fell flat.

Jefferson's love of language was not limited to English. Certainly he praised and glorified Shakespeare "for the enrichment of the language by his free and magical creation of words,"[3] but he enjoyed reading and studying many other languages. He collected samples of Indian languages hoping to trace their common origin. He read Greek, Latin, Italian, French, and Spanish. When purchasing and ordering books for his own library, he always sought editions in the original language. He was ever grateful to his father for instilling in him the love of the ancient Greek and Latin.[4]

Jefferson was also deeply interested in the language of science. He systematically purchased for his library "whatever was rare & valuable in every science."[5] Each science has its own language, and Jefferson became adept in many of these as he read the scientific literature, applied the theories to the particulars, and corresponded with some of the great scholars in the world, using their specialized idiom. He realized that to plumb to the depths of a science, you must become fluent in its own language.

Jefferson was, perhaps above all, a great letter writer. He wrote literally thousands of letters. He delighted in corresponding with old friends, especially Benjamin Rush and, after a rapprochement in 1812, with John Adams. Jefferson also wrote to hundreds of strangers who wrote "civilly" to him, thus making it "hard to refuse them civil answers."[6] Nearly every day he found himself figuratively chained to the writing table—sometimes writing ten or twelve letters in a sitting—a drudgery that kept him from his great love of reading.

Despite encouragement from friends, Jefferson was unable to write a history of his times. His letters, he felt, were "in fact memorials of the transactions with which I have been associated, and may at a future day furnish something to the historian."[7] Jefferson expected that his voluminous correspondence would

> command more conviction than anything I could have written after my retirement; no day having ever passed during that period without a letter to somebody, written too in the moment, and in the warmth and freshness of fact and feeling they will carry internal evidence that what they breathe is genuine. Selections from these after my death, may come out successively as the maturity of circumstances may render their appearance seasonable.[8]

It is from this huge body of correspondence, as well as from Jefferson's official public writings, that this compilation of quotations is taken. It is hoped that these excerpts will serve as a window through which a greater understanding of Jefferson will emerge.

The quotations in this book fall into four general categories. The first and by far the largest section of the book consists of quotations from Jefferson on nearly five hundred different topics. Shorter sections contain (2) descriptions by Jefferson of his contemporaries, (3) descriptions of Jefferson by his contemporaries, and (4) descriptions of Jefferson by himself. These final three biographical sections focus on character, mannerisms, and physical and intellectual stature. The topical quotations extracted from Jefferson's writings fall into three broad categories: (1) entries on government, (2) entries on views of the world, and (3) entries on human nature and interaction.

Entries on Government

Like many of his contemporaries, Jefferson believed in the Enlightenment's concept of the perfectibility of man and government. As a philosopher and a politician, Jefferson searched for the best form of government that would make the most people happy. He examined government in general and its component parts: constitutions, bills of rights, laws, taxes, the politics of governing, the role of the people in governing themselves, and the contribution of the judiciary to a successful or perverted form of government. He ruminated on the role of America in formulating constitutions and the contribution of the American Revolution to the freedom and liberty of mankind. He consistently advocated the separation of church and state. He studied and participated in the protocol and management of foreign affairs. He thought about how to use and control a country's military, how to avoid war, and how to restore and maintain peace. The role of the press in properly balancing government was critical for Jefferson. As much as he deplored "the putrid state into which our newspapers have passed," he understood that it was better to have "newspapers without a government" rather than "a government without newspapers."[9] After his retirement from the presidency, Jefferson looked back to see how his administration applied the theoretical model to the real world of practical and partisan politics. He also took comfort in knowing that in a public career that spanned almost fifty years, he had honorably answered his country's call and done his duty as a citizen.

Entries on Views of the World

Jefferson was always curious about the physical world. He enjoyed reading about different places in the world almost as much as actually traveling to exotic locations. He willingly and eagerly shared his travel expertise with others, especially with young men embarking on Europe's grand tour. He described cities, countries, and regions—their physical environment as well as their climates, populations, and customs. When he traveled, Jefferson studied the economy, the variety of occupations pursued, and above all the region's agriculture. When traveling throughout France, he wrote Lafayette that "I am never satiated with rambling through the fields and farms, examining the culture and cultivators, with a degree of curiosity which makes some take me to be a fool, and others to be much wiser than I am."[10]

Jefferson delighted in reading about nature and the scientific explorations into the earth's flora and fauna. Learning new things about the world and the physical properties that held the universe in equilibrium gave Jefferson's life meaning. It was what he was put on earth to do. Jefferson especially appreciated the practical application of theoretical science in the discovery of inventions to ease the burdens of everyday life.

Entries on Human Nature and Interaction

Jefferson took great satisfaction in analyzing human nature and the interactions of people. Friends and family were foremost in his mind. In the Southern tradition, his home was always open to visitors, whether friends, associates, or strangers. He told his close friend James Monroe that "you shall find with me a room, bed, & plate with a hearty welcome."[11] To a less intimate associate, he wrote, "Call on me in your turn, whenever you come to town: and if it should be about the hour of three, I shall rejoice the more. You will find a bad dinner, a good glass of wine, and a host thankful for your favor, and desirous of encouraging repetitions of it without number, form or ceremony."[12] It was but a natural extension of this hospitality when President Jefferson held informal dinners three or fourth times weekly with members of Congress, the cabinet, and with foreign diplomats. The president used these gatherings to his political advantage.

Jefferson realized how critical education was in perfecting mankind individually and society in general. He readily offered advice to those seeking it and a curriculum for his daughters and for those young men studying law with him. He unsuccessfully advocated a renovation of Virginia's public educational system, but in retirement he fathered a new state university. He loved the arts, frequented museums, and purchased works of paintings and sculpture for his home. He played the violin and encouraged his wife and daughters to develop their musical talent. Music, he said, would "be a companion which will sweeten many hours of life to you."[13] For those tone deaf, he hoped they would eschew music all together.

Jefferson felt that exercise and diet were as important as educating the mind. He loved French cuisine and good wines and often served them in the elaborate French style. Walking and riding were everyday activities for him. As he aged, he felt the diminution of his own senses and abilities and the anguish of life's difficulties—particularly the death of friends and loved ones. He compared the pleasures and pain of life and was thankful for more of the former than of the latter.

He held deep convictions about the condition of oppressed groups in society—the indigent, women, Indians, and African-American slaves.

Sometimes these convictions were neither liberal nor well informed. All too often Jefferson's actions did little to improve the standing of any of these groups.

Jefferson believed that religion was a highly personal thing between each person and God. He steadfastly supported the free exercise of religion without government interference. He lived by a strict moral code regulated by his conscience—the moral compass given to all by God. Early in life he ceased to think about the hereafter. Unable to fathom what lay in store after death, he comfortably reposed his head on "the pillow of ignorance" provided by God. He thought it best to nourish the good passions in his life and try to control the bad so that he might "merit an inheritance in a state of being of which I can know so little, and to trust for the future to him who has been so good for the past."[14]

In gathering the quotations in this book, a number of documentary editions have been invaluable. The modern edition of Jefferson's papers published by Princeton University Press has been my primary source. First edited by Julian P. Boyd, the series has been admirably continued by Charles T. Cullen, John Catanzariti, and now by Barbara B. Oberg. The new retirement series (also published by Princeton University Press) is directed by J. Jefferson Looney at the Robert H. Smith International Center for Jefferson Studies at Monticello. Other valuable editions have been consulted: Merrill Peterson's compilation of Jefferson's writings published by the Library of America in 1984, and the complete Jefferson-Adams correspondence edited by Lester J. Cappon and published by the University of North Carolina Press in 1959. For letters not in these volumes, I relied on the H. A. Washington edition of Jefferson's writings published in the mid-nineteenth century.

Once quotations were selected and transcribed from these documentary editions, the accuracy of the transcriptions was checked against the manuscript whenever possible. I did much of this checking on the Library of Congress's American Memory Web site, from the microfilm of the Jefferson papers in the University of Virginia Library, and from the Jefferson manuscripts in the Massachusetts Historical Society. I am very grateful to Martha J. King, Linda Monaco, and Nancy Taylor for their assistance with this verification.

ᑦᘓᡃᢙᕽᑋ

This book is dedicated to the editors, past and present, of the Jefferson papers and to Princeton University Press, their publisher. They are fulfilling the wish of John Adams, who hoped that Jefferson's letters would be published: "they will exhibit a Mass of Taste, Sense, Literature and Science, presented in a sweet simplicity and a neat elegance of

Style, which will be read with delight in future ages."[15]

John P. Kaminski
Madison, Wis.
May 2005

Notes

1. John Adams, *Autobiography*, 1802, L. H. Butterfield et al., eds., *Diary and Autobiography of John Adams* (4 vols., Cambridge, Mass., 1961), 3:335.

2. Thomas Jefferson, *Autobiography*, 1821, Merrill D. Peterson, ed., *Thomas Jefferson: Writings* (New York, 1984), 6.

3. To Joseph Milligan, Monticello, April 6, 1816, H. A. Washington, ed., *The Writings of Thomas Jefferson* (9 vols., Washington, D.C., 1853–1854), 6:573.

4. To John Brazer, Poplar Forest, August 24, 1819, Peterson, *Jefferson: Writings*, 1423.

5. To Samuel Harrison Smith, Monticello, September 21, 1814, ibid., 1353.

6. To John Adams, Monticello, January 11, 1817, Lester J. Cappon, ed., *The Adams-Jefferson Letters: The Complete Correspondence between Thomas Jefferson and Abigail and John Adams* (Chapel Hill, N.C., 1959), 505.

7. To William Short, Monticello, May 5, 1816, Jefferson Papers, Library of Congress.

8. To William Johnson, Monticello, March 4, 1823, Washington, *Writings of Jefferson*, 7:277.

9. To Walter Jones, Monticello, January 2, 1814, and to Edward Carrington, Paris, January 16, 1787, Peterson, *Jefferson: Writings*, 1317, 880.

10. To the Marquis de Lafayette, Nice, France, April 11, 1787, ibid., 894.

11. To Monroe, Paris, December 10, 1784, Julian P. Boyd et al., eds., *The Papers of Thomas Jefferson* (Princeton, 1950–), 7:563.

12. To Richard Peters, Philadelphia, June 30, 1791, ibid., 20:590.

13. To Martha Jefferson Randolph, New York, April 4, 1790, ibid., 16:300.
14. To Isaac Story, Washington, December 5, 1801, Jefferson Papers, Library of Congress.
15. Adams to Jefferson, Quincy, July 12, 1822, Cappon, *Adams-Jefferson Letters*, 582.

Introduction

Overview

America has been blessed with few Renaissance men. Certainly Thomas Jefferson is among this group, and some would argue that only he and Benjamin Franklin fall into this category. Among his many accomplishments, Jefferson was a statesman, parliamentarian, codifier of laws, antiquarian, historian, surveyor, philosopher, diplomat, scientist, architect, inventor, educator, lawyer, farmer, breeder, manufacturer, scientist, botanist, horticulturist, anthropologist, archaeologist, meteorologist, paleontologist, lexicologist, linguist, ethnologist, biblicist, mathematician, astronomer, geographer, librarian, bibliophile, bibliographer, classicist, scholar and historian of religions, cryptographer, translator, writer, editor, musician, and gastronome and connoisseur of wine.

Jefferson's skill as a writer has accentuated many of his accomplishments. Partly because of his preference for style over a rigid adherence to the rules of grammar, he was perhaps the most eloquent of all American writers. In identifying the thirty-three year old Virginian as the person who should write the Declaration of Independence, Congressman John Adams said that Jefferson had "a masterly Pen" and "a remarkable felicity of expression." The impact of Jefferson's writing has transcended his own era. Abraham Lincoln heavily drew upon Jefferson. The words, phrases, and philosophy of the Declaration of Independence have inspired those seeking equality for minorities, for women, and most recently for oppressed Europeans seeking to shake off their Communist shackles.

More than most of the Founders, Thomas Jefferson is hard to understand, even paradoxical, not only for us today, but also for the people of his own time. Far more a theoretical philosopher than his contemporaries, he repeatedly left the safety and seclusion of his mountaintop retreat to brave the violence and turbulence of revolution and diplomacy, of partisan politics and public service. He served almost continuously, though sometimes reluctantly, in the colonial and state legislatures, the Continental and Confederation congresses, as governor of Virginia, minister to France, secretary of state, political party leader, and as the second vice president and third president of the United States. Jefferson not only wrote the words of the Declaration of Independence, but he thoroughly believed in the revolutionary principles they espoused and consistently attempted to implement those principles in the real world of practical politics.

As a political philosopher, Jefferson was greatly admired and savagely condemned by his contemporaries. Jefferson's political enemies (as well as some later historians) belittled him "as a man of sublimated & paradoxical imagination—cherishing notions incompatible with regular and firm government."[1] Alexander Hamilton saw Jefferson's politics as "tinctured with fanaticism" and believed that he was "too much in earnest in his democracy."[2] The gossipy John Nicholas, clerk of Jefferson's Albemarle County, told George Washington that Jefferson was "one of the most artful, intriguing, industrious and double-faced politicians in all America."[3]

Admirers, however, like James Madison, could readily forgive Jefferson's sometimes impractical ideas because they so admired his commitment to republican principles and his remarkable ability to express those principles with an eloquence that approached poetry. To Margaret Bayard Smith, the matriarch of Washington society, it seemed "impossible, for any one personally to know him & remain his enemy."[4]

Jefferson believed that every man owed his country "a debt of service . . . proportioned to the bounties which nature & fortune have measured to him."[5] Some men were "born for the public. Nature, by fitting them for the service of the human race on a broad scale, has stamped them with the evidences of her destination & their duty."[6] The Revolutionary generation, Jefferson believed, had been "thrown into times of a peculiar character, and to work our way through them has required services & sacrifices from our countrymen generally, and, to their great honor, these have been generally exhibited, by every one in his sphere, & according to the opportunities afforded."[7] Jefferson was convinced that he was "conscientiously called" to his "tour of duty," and he believed that he had faithfully responded.[8]

Early Life

Born on April 13, 1743, on the fringe of the Virginia frontier, Thomas Jefferson was the eldest of seven children—five girls and two boys. Jefferson's father, Peter, was a prosperous, self-made Albemarle County planter/surveyor. His marriage to Jane Randolph, the daughter of a wealthy planter from a distinguished family, not only assisted Peter financially, but also contributed to his rise socially and politically.

Young Thomas Jefferson was truly shaped by his times. He was raised and imbued with the spirit of the Enlightenment, which recognized the perfectibility of both man and government through education and the discovery of well-designed natural laws using man's innate reason. Although always an optimist, Jefferson's immersion in the Whig political writings of seventeenth- and eighteenth-century England instilled in him a pervasive skepticism of government officials who often sought to expand their authority at the expense of the rights of their constituents.

Jefferson acknowledged the influence of several individuals in shaping his character and philosophy of life. His mother, he readily admitted, had little influence, but his father, who died when Jefferson was only fourteen, was a primary influence. At the age of five, Jefferson attended the English School and four years later the Latin School, where he continued until his father's death. For the next two years Jefferson studied with an Anglican minister,

James Maury, concentrating on Latin and Greek, literature, mathematics, and the Bible. Although well trained in the Bible and, like his father, a parish vestryman, Jefferson never accepted the Bible as divine Scripture. He read it more as history and readily embraced the philosophical teachings of Jesus. In this sense, he believed himself a Christian.

When seventeen, Jefferson left Shadwell, the family plantation, and attended the College of William and Mary in Williamsburg, Virginia's provincial capital. For the next three years, the lanky, ruddy, freckle-faced youth with tousled reddish-hair, blue-gray eyes, and a sometimes disheveled appearance, studied with Dr. William Small, the college's professor of mathematics and an immigrant from Scotland, and George Wythe, the college's first professor of law.

In 1762, Jefferson left William and Mary and returned to Shadwell, where he continued reading law under the direction of Wythe, whom Jefferson considered not only his mentor but his foster father. Jefferson expanded his reading and avidly acquired books for his growing library. He was admitted to the bar in 1767, established a successful and growing practice, doubled his estate to five thousand acres, and decided to design and build a new house. (He saw Shadwell as his mother's house.) As it was situated across the Rivanna River on the summit of a mountain with a commanding view of the Blue Ridge Mountains to the west and overlooked the valley village of Charlottesville, Jefferson called his

new home "Monticello," Italian for "little mountain."

In 1770 disaster struck when Shadwell burned
to the ground, and with it, Jefferson's library of almost seven hundred books worth several hundred
pounds. Jefferson wished it had been the money
that had gone up in flames; that would have cost
him not "a sigh." Immediately, however, Jefferson
started reacquiring books, and within three years
his library contained 1,256 volumes.

Although Monticello was far from completed
when Shadwell burned down, it was advanced
enough to convince Jefferson to abandon "some
treasonable thoughts of leaving these my native
hills."[9] In November 1770, Jefferson moved into a
tiny brick cottage at Monticello.

Jefferson spent much of 1771 in Williamsburg,
where the young lawyer tried cases in the general
court and courted Martha Wayles Skelton, a twenty-
three-year-old widow who lived on her father's plantation near Williamsburg. The slender, auburn-haired
beauty had been much courted, but she found herself
most attracted to the gangly young frontier lawyer.
The couple married on January 1, 1772, and jour-
neyed the one hundred miles west to spend their first
winter together in the cozy "honeymoon" cottage on
the mountain. In September 1772 their first child,
Martha (usually called Patsy), was born. In May 1773
Jefferson's father-in-law died, leaving his daughter
about five thousand acres and fifty slaves, but also an
enormous debt that plagued Jefferson for years.

The Revolution

At the age of twenty-six Jefferson was elected to the colonial legislature in 1769. He proposed but failed to get a bill enacted to make it easier for owners to emancipate their slaves. Allied with other young, radical legislators, Jefferson opposed Britain's new imperial policy that attempted to wield greater control over the colonies. The burgesses called for the appointment of committees of correspondence in all of the colonies to coordinate sentiment and activities, and they also called for the appointment of delegates to attend a continental congress. Jefferson prepared a petition to the king for Virginia to submit to Congress, but on the way to take his seat, he was taken ill with dysentery and was unable to attend. He sent copies of his draft petition forward, but the burgesses rejected it as too radical. Most Americans who opposed British policies argued that Parliament could tax Americans if the tax was primarily aimed at regulating commerce. These "external taxes" were constitutional, but "internal taxes" aimed primarily at raising revenue were blatantly unconstitutional. Jefferson went much further, maintaining that Great Britain and the American colonies were totally separate from each other except in loyalty to the same king. Parliament, therefore, had no authority whatsoever to legislate for the colonies.

In March 1775 the Virginia provincial convention added Jefferson to its delegation to the Second Continental Congress. Before Congress assembled, the first shots of the Revolution were fired at Lexington and Concord in Massachusetts.

American petitions, resolutions, and declarations never swayed Parliament, the ministry, or King George. Quite the contrary. The king and Parliament declared the colonists in a state of rebellion. Abandoning efforts at reconciliation, the British attacked with overwhelming military power in an attempt to intimidate Americans into submission. Many Americans now became convinced that reconciliation was impossible. When, in Congress, Richard Henry Lee of Virginia made the proposal for independence on June 7, 1776, most delegates saw the necessity for such a drastic step. Congress consequently appointed a committee to draft a declaration of independence. The committee consisted of John Adams, Benjamin Franklin, Robert R. Livingston, Roger Sherman, and Thomas Jefferson (the only Southerner). The committee chose the thirty-three-year-old Virginian to draft the declaration instead of the more experienced Franklin or Adams. A quarter century later Adams remembered his arguments for choosing Jefferson as the draftsman:

1. That he was a Virginian and I a Massachusettsian. 2. that he was a southern Man and I a northern one. 3. That I had been so obnoxious for my early and constant Zeal in promoting the Measure, that any draft of mine, would undergo a more severe Scrutiny and Criticism in Congress, than one

of his composition. 4thly and lastly and that would
be reason enough if there were no other, I had a
great Opinion of the Elegance of his pen and none
at all of my own. I therefore insisted that no hesitation should be made on his part. He accordingly . . .
in a day or two produced to me his Draft.[10]

The genius of Thomas Jefferson is that he in-
fused the Declaration with "the proper tone and
spirit called for." Jefferson took a huge body of political literature—twenty-two thousand pamphlets
published in Britain in the seventeenth century and
several thousand more published during the eigh-
teenth in Britain and America—and distilled it into
five sentences—fewer than two hundred words—the
introduction to the Declaration of Independence.
Those five sentences constitute arguably what is the
greatest statement in political literature.

We hold these truths to be self-evident, that all
men are created equal, that they are endowed by
their Creator with certain unalienable Rights, that
among these are Life, Liberty and the pursuit of
Happiness,—That to secure these rights, Governments are instituted among Men, deriving their
just powers from the consent of the governed,—
That whenever any Form of Government becomes
destructive of these ends, it is the Right of the People to alter or to abolish it; and to institute new
Government, laying its foundation on such principles and organizing its powers in such form, as to

them shall seem most likely to effect their Safety
and Happiness. Prudence, indeed, will dictate that
Governments long established should not be
changed for light and transient causes; and accordingly all experience hath shewn, that mankind are
more disposed to suffer, while evils are sufferable.
But when a long train of abuses and usurpations,
pursuing invariably the same Object evinces a design to reduce them under absolute Despotism, it is
their right, it is their duty, to throw off such Government, and to provide new Guards for their future security.

Jefferson's truth may be self-evident, but "the
pursuit of Happiness" has baffled many. The sim-
plest explanation is that this phrase is a euphemistic
synonym for "property," similar to John Locke's
"life, liberty, and estate." Jefferson, however, meant
far more than the right to buy, possess, and dispose
of property. He wanted a government that, in the
words of John Adams, "communicates ease, comfort,
[and] security"[11] — a government that would provide
protection from foreign invasion, from assault by
criminals (and attack by Indians in America), and
from oppressive government rule and taxation. Government, according to Jefferson, should provide an
efficient, well-run economic environment as well as a
society where contrary religious and political opinions could exist in harmony — where the majority
ruled but with due deference to the rights of the minority.

The Reformer

Jefferson was elected to the first Virginia House of Delegates that assembled in Williamsburg in October 1776. Embracing the principles espoused in the Declaration of Independence, he hoped to rid Virginia of the last vestiges of feudalism and aristocratic favoritism. In mid-October 1776 Jefferson suggested that the House appoint a committee to revise the state's laws. Two weeks later the House appointed a committee of five, including George Wythe and Jefferson, with Jefferson as its chair. It took the committee three years to submit its final report—a thorough reformation of the law on republican and liberal principles—by which time Jefferson, no longer in the House, was personally unable to shepherd the new laws into being.

The legislature considered some reforms immediately. Jefferson, ever the advocate of republicanism and the widespread ownership of property, successfully campaigned for the abolition of entail, the feudal relic that required inherited property to pass intact to heirs. Later primogeniture (the inheritance of estates by the eldest son) and the system of quitrents were disallowed, thus guaranteeing a broader ownership of land.

Jefferson also supported the complete separation of church and state. Although the Virginia Declaration of Rights provided that "all men are equally entitled to the free exercise of religion, according to the dictates of conscience," and the state constitution discontinued the official establishment of the Anglican Church, Jefferson felt that a more explicit separation of church and state was needed. In 1779 he drafted *A Bill for Establishing Religious Freedom*. Like most of his reforms, it lay dormant. In 1783, Patrick Henry, Edmund Pendleton, and Richard Henry Lee proposed public support for Christian Protestant ministers. James Madison now revived and championed Jefferson's bill in the House of Delegates, and in January 1786 the bill was adopted. It provided

> that the opinions of men are not the object of civil government, nor under its jurisdiction . . . that no man shall be compelled to frequent or support any religious worship, place, or ministry whatsoever, nor shall be enforced, restrained, molested, or burdened in his body or goods, nor shall otherwise suffer, on account of his religious opinions or belief; but that all men shall be free to profess, and by argument to maintain, their opinions in matters of religion, and that the same shall in no wise diminish, enlarge, or affect their civil capacities.[12]

In May 1779 the legislature elected Jefferson governor. He did not want the job but believed that "in a virtuous government, and more especially in times like these, public offices are, what they should be, burdens to those appointed to them which it would be wrong to decline, though foreseen to bring with them intense labor and great private loss."[13] It was the worst time to be governor of a Southern state. The British had abandoned their strategy of separating New England from New York and had transferred their military initiatives to the South, capturing Savannah in December 1778 and Charleston in May 1780. Several amphibious assaults against Virginia took place during this time and the British army commanded by General Charles Cornwallis relentlessly marched northward toward Virginia. On May 20 Cornwallis captured Richmond, Virginia's new capital, forcing the Patriot government to evacuate to Charlottesville. Cornwallis sent a detachment of rangers to capture the government. Warned just in time, government officials hastily fled across the Blue Ridge Mountains to Staunton. At Monticello, Jefferson was also warned and escaped to a nearby mountaintop, where he watched the British in Charlottesville through his telescope.

Although Jefferson's term as governor had expired on June 2, he was blamed by those who looked for a scapegoat. Former governor Patrick Henry, who had led the opposition to Jefferson's reform program, called for an investigation. Finding no evidence of either wrongdoing or cowardice, the House of Delegates passed a resolution affirming "the high opinion which they entertain of Mr. Jefferson's Ability, Rectitude, and Integrity as chief Magistrate of this Commonwealth, and mean by thus publicly avowing their opinion, to obviate and remove all unmerited Censure."[14] The charges against him, however, had done severe damage to Jefferson's reputation and to his attitude about public service. Jefferson vowed never to serve in public office again.

Jefferson and Slavery

Throughout his life Jefferson wrestled with the problem of slavery.[15] He, like most Americans, denounced the foreign slave trade that captured free men, women, and children in Africa, forcibly transported them in the most inhumane fashion to the Western Hemisphere, and sold them as property into lifelong bondage. As a first-year legislator in 1769 and in drafting the Declaration of Independence seven years later, Jefferson had denounced the foreign slave trade. Not until 1782, when Jefferson was temporarily retired from public service, did Virginia prohibit the foreign slave trade. Then, as president in December 1806, Jefferson proposed to Congress that the foreign slave trade be prohibited as of January 1, 1808 (the earliest allowable date for a congressional prohibition under the Constitution). Congress enacted the bill on March 2, 1807, and President Jefferson signed it the next day.

Jefferson also consistently denounced the institution of slavery in principle. In 1781, as the Revolution neared its conclusion, Jefferson denounced the incongruity of fighting a revolution for liberty while keeping a race of people in bondage. "Indeed," Jefferson wrote, "I tremble for my country when I reflect that God is just: that his justice cannot sleep for ever." Jefferson deplored not only the injustice done to blacks, but the unhealthy effect—political, social, moral, and economic—that slavery had on whites: "There must doubtless be an unhappy influence on the manners of our people produced by the existence of slavery among us. The whole commerce between master and slave is a perpetual exercise of the most boisterous passions, the most unremitting despotism on the one part, and degrading submissions on the other."[16]

In the mid-1780s Jefferson saw the institution of slavery as a conflict between "justice" and "avarice & oppression." He looked to the youth of revolutionary America who "have sucked in the principles of liberty as it were with their mother's milk" to abolish the evil institution.[17] After his presidency, Jefferson continued to denounce slavery. But Jefferson also saw many obstacles to emancipation. Metaphorically he described slavery as having "the wolf by the ear, and we can neither hold him, nor safely let him go." Now, instead of justice versus avarice and oppression, Jefferson saw the dilemma as "justice is in one scale, and self-preservation in the other."[18] And he refused either to be an active participant or even a silent, behind-the-scenes supporter of emancipation. That he left for a future generation.

Jefferson hoped for emancipation, but he saw it happening only if three parts of a coordinated plan could be implemented: (1) gradual and compensated emancipation in which slaveowners would be paid from public funds for their financial loss; (2) colonization of free blacks, preferably to Africa, but more likely to some Caribbean island nation; and (3) replacement of the black labor force with a free alternative—most likely Protestant Germans similar to those who had emigrated to Pennsylvania. Jefferson felt that colonization was required because of racism. He had come to believe that blacks were inferior to whites and thus the intermingling of blood should be avoided. Furthermore blacks would forever hate whites for the evils perpetrated against them. Conflict was thus inevitable if the two races lived close together.

Because the practicalities of such a plan prohibited it from being implemented when most slaves remained in the South, Jefferson came to advocate the diffusion of slavery throughout America, especially to the West. Only in this way could a similar nationwide attitude and appreciation for the problem be realized. Until his death, Jefferson hoped that this terrible problem—"this hideous blot" on America—could be obliterated: "The abolition of the evil is not impossible; it ought never therefore to be despaired of. Every plan should be adopted, every experiment tried, which may do something towards the ultimate object."[19] But Jefferson himself would not participate in any such plan.

Home and Escape from Home

Jefferson returned to Monticello in September 1781 "to my farm, my family and books from which I think nothing will evermore separate me."[20] On May 8, 1782, Martha Jefferson gave birth to their sixth child, Lucy Elizabeth. Martha Jefferson never recovered from the childbirth. Perhaps anemia sapped her strength as she steadily weakened before Jefferson's eyes. For four months she languished as Jefferson watched over her almost constantly. Finally, on September 6, she died. Jefferson collapsed in her bedroom. A period of deep mourning followed. He destroyed his entire correspondence with Martha. His three daughters were sent away, and friends feared that Jefferson, too, might die. For weeks he incessantly paced in his library, then started riding around his farms on horseback for hours at a time. A concerned James Madison saw that "perhaps this domestic catastrophe may prove in its operation beneficial to his country by weaning him from those attachments which deprived it of his services."[21] Madison convinced Congress to add Jefferson to the on-going peace negotiations in Paris. Jefferson, who had always wanted to visit Europe, leaped at the chance to leave Monticello. He went to Baltimore to await transport on a French warship, but before they departed, word arrived that a preliminary peace treaty had been signed, and Congress rescinded his appointment. Jefferson went back to Monticello.

In June 1783, the Virginia legislature appointed Jefferson to Congress beginning in November. Immediately Jefferson became a leader, making thirty-one committee reports in Congress's five-month session. One report proposed a radical new national system of coinage, abandoning the familiar English system in favor of a decimal system based upon the dollar. Although the latter was not immediately instituted, the report served as the model for the system that was eventually adopted in 1794.

In 1781 Governor Jefferson had been instrumental in getting Virginia to cede its huge territory north and west of the Ohio River to Congress. Such a cession benefited Congress, placated other states (especially those with no western lands), and, under the prevailing theory of the Baron de Montesquieu that republics could not survive in large territories, would help assure the liberties of Virginians. Now in Congress, Jefferson drafted the Land Ordinance of 1784 that provided for the administration of the Northwest Territory and the admittance of new states into the union on an equal basis with the original thirteen states. Unfortunately, by the vote of a single delegate, Congress removed Jefferson's prohibition of slavery and indentured servitude from the Northwest Territory. (Such prohibitions would be reestablished in the Northwest Ordinance of 1787.)

Jefferson also had an interest in the western lands beyond the borders of the United States. According to the Treaty of Peace, the Mississippi River served as America's western border. Although Spain claimed the territory west of the Mississippi, information had been received that "a very large sum of money" had been raised in England to explore the land between the Mississippi and the Pacific Ocean. Ostensibly the proposed expedition had only scientific goals, but Jefferson feared that the British "have thoughts of colonizing into that quarter." Jefferson and others began raising funds for an American expedition of discovery. Although he feared that Americans did not possess "enough of that kind of spirit to raise the money," he sounded out fellow Virginian George Rogers Clark, the Revolutionary War hero of battles in Illinois and Indiana, to see if he would be willing "to lead such a party."[22] Jefferson's interest in the West never waned. Twenty years would pass before President Jefferson purchased the Louisiana Territory, thus doubling the size of the United States. He then chose Meriwether Lewis and William Clark (George Rogers Clark's brother) to lead an expedition to the Pacific.

Service Abroad

After the war for independence, Congress wanted to establish diplomatic and commercial relations with all countries. It appointed a three-man commission to negotiate commercial treaties with European and North African countries. Benjamin Franklin and John Adams, both still in France, were obvious appointments. Needing a Southerner to round out the commission, Congress appointed Jefferson on May 7, 1784. On July 5 Jefferson and his twelve-year-old daughter, Patsy, set sail from Boston. Despite all the horror stories told about Atlantic crossings, their nineteen-day voyage was uneventful. Patsy likened it to floating down a river. Not so the harrowing thirteen-hour crossing of the tempestuous English Channel.

After arriving in Paris in August 1784, both father and daughter shed their provincial attire and
purchased more fashionable wardrobes for Paris. Patsy, enrolled in an exclusive Catholic convent school in
which religion was excluded from the curriculum,
adjusted easily, but her father struggled. His lack of
conversational French hampered his ability to communicate, and the dampness of the weather and un-
wholesomeness of the water caused him considerable
suffering during the "seasoning" process.[23]

In late February 1785 Congress appointed John
Adams minister plenipotentiary to Great Britain, and
in early May, John and Abigail Adams left France.
Abigail hated to leave "Mr. Jefferson, he is one of the
choice ones of the Earth,"[24] and "the only person
with whom my Companion could associate; with perfect freedom, and unreserve."[25]

In May 1785 Congress approved Benjamin
Franklin's request to return to America and unani-
mously elected Jefferson to replace him as the United States' minister to France. In July Franklin returned to America. Because of the veneration the
French had for Franklin, Jefferson knew that the
transition could be difficult. He described it "as an
excellent school of humility." When presented as the
new American minister, the usual question was
"c'est vous, Monsieur, qui remplace le Docteur
Franklin?" Jefferson generally answered, "no one
can replace him, Sir: I am only his successor."[26]

Jefferson worked tirelessly to improve commercial relations with France, its Caribbean colonies, and

other countries. Treaties were signed with Prussia and Morocco. The Marquis de Lafayette praised Jefferson: "No better minister could be sent to France. He is everything that is good, upright, enlightened, and clever, and is respected and beloved by everyone that knows him."[27]

While in France, Jefferson enjoyed traveling through the countryside observing the people and studying agricultural practices, but he was appalled by the widespread poverty in such a wealthy, fertile country. He wrote Washington, "I was much an enemy to monarchy before I came to Europe. I am ten thousand times more so since I have seen what they are. There is scarcely an evil known in these countries which may not be traced to their king as its source, nor a good which is not derived from the small fibres of republicanism existing among them."[28]

Jefferson was well aware of the shortcomings of the Articles of Confederation, but his loathing for oppressive governments made him tolerant of troubling events going on in America. Divorced from the passion of the unfolding political events in America, Jefferson had few of the anxieties expressed by many of his friends. He saw uprisings like Shays's Rebellion in Massachusetts as nothing to be afraid of and thought that they might even be a good thing:

> They are a proof that the people have liberty enough, and I would not wish them less than they have. If the happiness of the mass of the people can be secured at the expense of a little tempest now & then, or even of

a little blood, it will be a precious purchase. Malo libertatum periculosum quam quietam servitutem [I
prefer dangerous liberty to a quiet servitude].[29]

Jefferson fully supported the efforts in America
to strengthen the Articles of Confederation. He characterized the Constitutional Convention meeting in
Philadelphia in the spring and summer of 1787 as
"an assembly of demi-gods" even though he severely
criticized the delegates for holding their sessions in
secret. Nothing, in Jefferson's opinion, "but the innocence of their intentions, & ignorance of the value
of public discussions" could justify the "tying up of
the tongues of their members."[30] A bit wary of an
overreaction to the political, economic, and social in-
stabilities racking the country, Jefferson warned
that, when making constitutional revisions, "the hole
& the patch should be commensurate."[31]

Jefferson admired much of what was in the
new Constitution, but the lack of both a bill of
rights and term limits for the president and the sen-
ators concerned him greatly. He felt it best to accept
the good in the Constitution and work to amend its
shortcomings. When asked if he was an Anti-
Federalist, Jefferson responded that he was

not a Federalist, because I never submitted the
whole system of my opinions to the creed of any
party of men whatever in religion, in philosophy, in
politics, or in anything else where I was capable of
thinking for myself. Such an addiction is the last
degradation of a free and moral agent. If I could not

> go to heaven but with a party, I would not go there
> at all. Therefore I protest to you I am not of the par-
> ty of Federalists. But I am much farther from that of
> the Antifederalists.[32]

Jefferson was pleased with the outcome of the constitutional revolution in America. There was enough
opposition to do good, but not enough to do bad.

Secretary of State

When Jefferson returned from France he discovered
that President Washington had nominated him to be
secretary of state, and the Senate had confirmed the
appointment. The State Department was to have responsibility not only for foreign affairs but also for
many internal matters, such as copyrights and
patents, coinage, weights and measures, the census,
the federal capital, certification of amendments to the
Constitution, etc. With a budget of $8,000 ($3,500
for the secretary's salary), the secretary was authorized to have four clerks and a half-time translator.

As secretary of state, Jefferson was driven
more by "realpolitik" than by the idealistic theoriz-
ing so characteristic of him otherwise. Two main
controversies permeated Jefferson's tenure as secretary of state—America's attitude toward the French
Revolution and the conflict between Jefferson and
secretary of the treasury Alexander Hamilton over
the kind of government and economy best suited for
the United States.

In January 1793, Jefferson wrote his former personal secretary William Short (who had been elevated to chargé d'affaires to France when Jefferson became secretary of state) to stop sending reports vividly describing the brutality of the Reign of Terror in France. Jefferson believed, as he told Lafayette, "We are not to expect to be translated from despotism to liberty in a feather bed."[33] Short's reports undermined Jefferson in his struggles with Secretary Hamilton, both in foreign affairs and domestic matters. In dramatic language Jefferson told Short how important the French Revolution was to the world in general and to the United States in particular. The unjust deaths of a few must be weighed against the benefits to be derived.

> In the struggle which was necessary, many guilty persons fell without the forms of trial, and with them some innocent. These I deplore as much as any body, & shall deplore some of them to the day of my death. But I deplore them as I should have done had they fallen in battle. It was necessary to use the arm of the people, a machine not quite so blind as balls and bombs, but blind to a certain degree. A few of their cordial friends met at their hands the fate of enemies. But time and truth will rescue & embalm their memories, while their posterity will be enjoying that very liberty for which they would never have hesitated to offer up their lives. The liberty of the whole earth was depending on the issue of the contest, and was ever such a

prize won with so little innocent blood? My own affections have been deeply wounded by some of the
martyrs to this cause, but rather than it should have
failed, I would have seen half the earth desolated.
Were there but an Adam & Eve left in every country, & left free, it would be better than as it is now.[34]

To counteract Hamilton's policies, which Jefferson said had given rise to the formation of a political party, Jefferson and James Madison led the
movement to create an organized opposition: "Our
citizens are divided into two political sects. One
which fears the people most, the other the government."[35] Jefferson justified the creation of the Republican Party and his involvement in it: "The same
political parties which now agitate the U.S. have existed thro' all time. Whether the power of the people, or that of the aristocrats should prevail, were
questions which kept the states of Greece & Rome
in eternal convulsions; as they now schismatize
every people whose minds and mouths are not shut
up by the gag of a despot."[36]

Jefferson also denounced the British and
Spanish policies of arming and inciting the Indians
on America's borders. Jefferson had long believed
that "the two principles on which our conduct towards the Indians should be founded are justice &
fear. After the injuries we have done them, they cannot love us, which leaves us no alternative but that
of fear to keep them from attacking us. But justice is
what we should never lose sight of, & in time it may

recover their esteem."[37] Eventually Jefferson came to believe that the only choice for Indian peoples was to assimilate into the white man's society:

> In truth, the ultimate point of rest & happiness for them is to let our settlements and theirs meet and blend together, to intermix and become one people, incorporating themselves with us as citizens of the U.S. This is what the natural progress of things will of course bring on, and it will be better to promote than to retard it. Surely it will be better for them to be identified with us, and preserved in the occupation of their lands, than be exposed to the many casualties which may endanger them while a separate people.[38]

Soon after Washington was elected to a second term as president, Jefferson announced his intention to resign. He delayed it once, but at the end of 1793, after spending nearly half of his life in public service, the fifty-year-old Jefferson retired to Monticello for a second time, hoping this time to remain forever a private citizen.

The Second Retirement

Although retired from public office, Jefferson could never totally abandon the outside world. He cancelled most of his newspaper subscriptions and read few pamphlets, but national and international news still flowed to Monticello through the rivers of correspondence from abroad and from politically active friends in America who wanted him back in the fray. When in September 1796, President Washington announced his decision to retire after his second term, it became obvious to Republicans that they needed a candidate to run for president who would combat the dangerous tendency of amassing power in the central government and the growing subservience to Great Britain. Jefferson wanted James Madison to run, but everyone knew that only Jefferson stood a chance to defeat John Adams. Jefferson relented.

As was the custom of the day, neither Adams nor Jefferson campaigned. The electoral vote was close: seventy-three for Adams and sixty-eight for Jefferson. Adams would be president and Jefferson vice president. Jefferson was pleased. He hoped that Adams could "be induced to administer the government on its true principles, & to relinquish his bias to an English constitution." Furthermore it might be beneficial for the country if Adams and the Republicans would work together in future elections: "He is perhaps the only sure barrier against Hamilton's getting in."[39]

As vice president, Jefferson believed that he would not be an executive officer. He would not attend cabinet meetings but would only preside over the Senate. Jefferson wrote that "the second office of this government is honorable & easy, the first is but a splendid misery."[40]

With war raging in Europe, many Europeans emigrated to America. Most were sympathetic to the Republicans. In an effort to silence the ever growing criticism of the administration, Congress in 1798 passed and the president signed a new naturalization act, alien acts, and the Sedition Act. The Naturalization Act and the alien acts made it harder to become citizens and easier for the president to deport aliens coming from both friendly and enemy countries. (Adams never used the alien acts.) The Sedition Act provided that anyone who criticized the president or Congress (the vice president was not mentioned) could be prosecuted and, if found guilty, fined and imprisoned. The federal judiciary—all Federalists—enthusiastically enforced the Sedition Act, and several Republican printers and one congressman were imprisoned and fined.

In 1800, Republicans sensed a real opportunity to win control of the presidency and both houses of Congress. The presidential election of 1800 was unbelievably virulent. Jefferson was vilified as a Jacobin who would plunge America into a reign of terror, as an atheist slaveowner who would destroy the country's morals, and as an ally of France who would plunge America into the carnage of European war. Federalists saw Jefferson as "too theoretical & fanciful a statesman to direct with steadiness & prudence the affairs of this extensive & growing confederacy."[41] Hamilton outwardly supported the Federalist ticket of President Adams and Charles Cotesworth Pinckney of South Carolina but secretly campaigned for Pinckney to unseat Adams.

Jefferson and Burr each received seventy-three electoral votes, while Adams received sixty-

five votes and Pinckney sixty-four. But with Jefferson and Burr tied (and having a majority of the
electoral votes), the choice between the two Republican candidates was to be decided by the lame-
duck House of Representatives controlled by Federalists.

The House began voting on February 11, only
three weeks before the anticipated inauguration. Finally, after thirty-six ballots and extensive lobbying
by Hamilton against Burr, a majority of state delega-
tions voted for Jefferson. Years later Jefferson referred to the election as "the revolution of 1800"—"as
real a revolution in the principles of our government
as that of 1776."[42]

President

March 4, 1801, is an important day in American history and in the history of freedom. On this day power
was transferred peacefully from one political party to
an opposing party. The fifty-seven-year-old president-
elect, virtually indistinguishable from his fellow citizens, walked from his boardinghouse to the unfin-
ished Capitol. At Jefferson's request, Chief Justice
John Marshall (a distant cousin and staunch political
opponent) administered the oath of office. The luster
of the event was tarnished only slightly because of the
absence of the outgoing president—John Adams had
left the city at 4 o'clock that morning. Although Jefferson and Adams would live another quarter century,

they would never see each other again. In fact, for the next ten years they remained estranged.

Jefferson's inaugural address, spoken in his soft, somewhat effeminate, almost inaudible voice in the Senate chamber, which was overcrowded with a thousand people, is one of the great speeches in American political literature. Knowing that reconciliation was desperately needed, the new president outstretched a hand. "Every difference of opinion is not a difference of principle. We have called by different names brethren of principle. We are all republicans, we are all federalists." He pleaded with his countrymen to "unite with one heart and one mind" to restore "harmony and affection" to their social intercourse.[43]

Jefferson felt that his most important action as president would be to pay off the federal debt, but foreign affairs threatened Jefferson's austerity program. In 1801 the pasha of Tripoli, one of the Barbary States, again attacked and captured American merchantmen. As in the mid-1780s, Jefferson felt that the best way to handle this aggression was with a show of military force. Unsanctioned by Congress, he sent a small fleet to the Mediterranean with instructions to search for and destroy the enemy's ships and blockade their ports, but after some initial successes the war with Tripoli bogged down. Jefferson's opponents said "It is his war." They blamed the president for, in Jefferson's own words, sending "the least possible competent force." Excessive frugality had, in reality, prolonged the conflict and endangered American lives.[44] By 1805 the pasha realized the war with America was counterproductive and he signed a peace treaty. The United States also signed treaties with Algiers and Tunis.

A more serious diplomatic problem arose when in October 1802 Spain announced the closing of the port of New Orleans to American trade. Under President Washington, a treaty with Spain had formally opened the Mississippi River and the port to American navigation. Unbeknownst to the Americans, Spain and France (now allies fighting Great Britain) had secretly agreed to transfer all of the Louisiana Territory from Spanish to French control. Napoleon dreamed of recreating the French empire in the Western Hemisphere, and the Spanish saw the French possession as an effective buffer separating Spain's lucrative Mexican colonies from the dangerous, ever expanding American settlements. Jefferson viewed the transfer of Louisiana from a weak and ineffective Spanish rule to France as a danger. Writing to Robert R. Livingston, America's new minister to France, without the benefit of secret code, Jefferson indirectly let Napoleon know that a French acquisition of Louisiana would lead to an American alliance with Britain.

Jefferson then authorized Livingston to purchase New Orleans and West Florida for $10 million. As these diplomatic negotiations were transpiring, war fever raged in the American West, and a grand French army sent to protect the new French holdings was decimated by rebellious slaves and fever in Santo Domingo. In need of money to carry on his European wars, Napoleon offered to sell America the entire Louisiana Territory, stretching over a thousand miles from the Mississippi River to the Rocky Mountains, for fifteen million dollars. Uncertain of the constitutionality of buying territory from another country, Jefferson thought about seeking a constitutional amendment to authorize the purchase, but he realized that the opportunity had to be seized. He agreed to the purchase, creating for America an "empire for liberty."

With these major accomplishments, Jefferson was easily reelected. To avoid a repetition of the political and constitutional crisis posed by the election of 1800, the newly adopted Twelfth Amendment to the Constitution provided that candidates for president and vice president would run together as a ticket. With New York's elder statesman George Clinton replacing Aaron Burr as Jefferson's vice president, the Republican ticket resoundingly defeated the Federalist ticket of Charles Cotesworth Pinckney and Rufus King by an electoral vote of 162 to 14.

Jefferson's second administration was nearly as dismal as his first had been triumphal. As the European war intensified, both Britain and France preyed on American shipping. Wanting to avoid war at almost any cost, Jefferson and secretary of state Madison used commerce as diplomatic leverage to moderate French and British naval aggression against neutral shipping. His opponents said that "the President wants nerve—he has not even confidence in himself . . . he has been in the habit of trusting almost implicitly in Mr. Madison."[45] In many ways, the last year of Jefferson's presidency was rudderless as the nation drifted between war and peace. Senator Plumer condemned the president: "Mr. Jefferson is too timid—too irresolute—too fickle—he wants nerve—he wants firmness & resolution. A wavering doubtful hesitating mind joined with credulity is oftentimes as injurious to the nation as a wicked depraved heart."[46]

Retirement

Jefferson looked forward to retirement. On nearly the last day of his presidency, he wrote an old friend about retiring "to my family, my books & farms." Others would now be buffeted by political storms—he would not envy them. "Never," he wrote, "did a prisoner, released from his chains, feel such relief as I shall on shaking off the shackles of power. Nature intended me for the tranquil pursuits of science, by rendering them my supreme delight. But the enormities of the times in which I have lived, have forced me to take a part in resisting them, and to commit myself on the boisterous ocean of political passions."[47]

Supervising his gardens and fields and rearing his grandchildren took up much of Jefferson's time. He established a large vegetable garden and enjoyed planting flowers and trees, the latter not for his own "gratification" but for "posterity."[48] "A Septuagenary," he wrote, "has no right to count on anything beyond annuals."[49] The former president loved trees. During his tenure as secretary of state in Philadelphia, his house was "entirely embosomed in high plane trees, with good grass below, & under them I breakfast, dine, write, read, & receive my company. What would I not give that the trees planted nearest round the house at Monticello were full grown."[50] While hosting one of his dinner parties as president, Jefferson exclaimed, "How I wish that I possessed the power of a despot." The guests sat astonished, before Jefferson finished his idea. "Yes, I wish I was a despot that I might save the noble, the beautiful trees that are daily falling sacrifices to the cupidity of their owners, or the necessity of the poor."[51] Now that he was retired, he would replant trees on his own mountain.

Jefferson loved to work in the garden. If he were to relive his life

it should have been on a rich spot of earth, well watered, and near a good market for the productions of the garden. No occupation is so delightful to me as the culture of the earth, & no culture comparable to that of the garden. Such a variety of subjects, some one always coming to perfection, the failure of one thing repaired by the success of another, & instead of one harvest, a continued one thro' the year. Under a total want of demand except for our family table. I am still devoted to the garden. But tho' an old man, I am but a young gardener.[52]

Jefferson found "delight" in corresponding with old and intimate friends, especially Benjamin Rush, and with John Adams, with whom Rush arranged a reconciliation in 1812. On hearing that the two friends had started corresponding, Rush wrote Adams that "I rejoice in the correspondence which has taken place between you and your old friend Mr. Jefferson. I consider you and him as the North and South Poles of the American Revolution. Some talked, some wrote, and some fought to promote and establish it, but you and Mr. Jefferson thought for us all."[53]

As the years passed, Jefferson experienced the pain of seeing friends die. He wondered whether it was desirable "to witness the death of all our companions, and merely be the last victim?" He doubted it. Why he asked, would one choose to remain "as a solitary trunk in a desolate field, from which all its former companions have disappeared?"[54] But the survivors have "the traveller's consolation. Every step shortens the distance we have to go; the end of our journey is in sight."[55] He wrote to John Adams that "there is a ripeness of time for death, regarding others as well as ourselves, when it is reasonable we should drop off, and make room for another growth. When we have lived our generation out, we should not wish to encroach on another."[56] In 1818 Abigail Adams died. Jefferson wrote the grief-stricken widower a tender letter of condolence:

Tried myself, in the school of affliction, by the loss of every form of connection which can rive the human heart, I know well, and feel what you have lost, what you have suffered, are suffering, and have yet to endure. The same trials have taught me that, for ills so immeasurable, time and silence are the only medicines. I will not therefore, by useless condolences, open afresh the sluices of your grief nor, altho' mingling sincerely my tears with yours, will I say a word more, where words are vain, but that it is of some comfort to us both that the term is not very distant at which we are to deposit, in the same cerement, our sorrows and suffering bodies, and to ascend in essence to an ecstatic meeting with the friends we have loved and lost and whom we shall still love and never lose again. God bless you and support you under your heavy affliction.[57]

When facing their own mortality in 1820, Jefferson wrote Adams.

We . . . have done for our country the good which has fallen in our way, so far as commensurate with the faculties given us. That we have not done more than we could cannot be imputed to us as a crime before any tribunal. I look therefore to that crisis, as I am sure you also do, as one "qui summum nec metuit diem nec optat" [who neither fears the final day nor hopes for it].[58]

In one of the great unbelievable coincidences of history, Jefferson and Adams both died only hours apart on July 4, 1826—the fiftieth anniversary of the Declaration of Independence. Recognizing the importance of the symbolism for the new country, both men valiantly held on to life until that glorious anniversary arrived. It was their final gift to a grateful country. On hearing of Jefferson's death, James Madison, Jefferson's friend for fifty years, wrote that "he lives and will live in the memory and gratitude of the wise & good, as a luminary of Science, as a votary of liberty, as a model of patriotism, and as a benefactor of the human kind."[59]

Notes

1. Alexander Hamilton to John Steele, Philadelphia, October 15, 1792, Harold C. Syrett, ed., *The Papers of Alexander Hamilton* (27 vols., New York, 1961–1987), 12:569.

2. Hamilton to James A. Bayard, New York, January 16, 1801, ibid., 25:319.

3. February 22, 1798, Donald Jackson et al., eds., *The Papers of George Washington: Retirement Series* (Charlottesville, Va., 1976–), 2:101.

4. Smith's account of her visit to Monticello, J. Jefferson Looney, ed., *The Papers of Thomas Jefferson* (Retirement Series, Princeton, 2004), 1:393.

5. To Edward Rutledge, Monticello, December 27, 1796, Julian P. Boyd et al., eds., *The Papers of Thomas Jefferson* (Princeton, 1950–), 29:233.

6. To James Monroe, Washington, January 13, 1803, Merrill D. Peterson, ed., *Thomas Jefferson: Writings* (New York, 1984), 1112.

7. To James Fishback, Monticello, September 27, 1809, Looney, *Jefferson*, 1:565.

8. To Horatio Gates, Monticello, February 3, 1794, and to Ferdinando Fairfax, Monticello, April 25, 1794, Boyd, *Jefferson Papers*, 28:14, 58.

9. To John Page, Charlottesville, February 21, 1770, ibid., I, 35.

10. John Adams, *Autobiography*, 1802, L. H. Butterfield et al., eds., *Diary and Autobiography of John Adams* (4 vols., Cambridge, Mass., 1961), 3:335–37.

11. John Adams, *Thoughts on Government . . .* (1776), Robert J. Taylor et al., eds., *Papers of John Adams* (Cambridge, Mass., 1977–), 4:86.

12. Peterson, *Jefferson: Writings*, 346–48.

13. Quoted in Norman K. Risjord, *Thomas Jefferson* (Madison, Wis., 1994), 42.

14. Ibid., 47.

15. For more on Jefferson's attitude toward slavery, see John P. Kaminski, ed., *A Necessary Evil?: Slavery and the Debate over the Constitution* (Madison, Wis., 1995).

16. *Notes on the State of Virginia*, 1782, Peterson, *Jefferson: Writings*, 289, 288.

17. To Richard Price, Paris, August 7, 1785, Boyd, *Jefferson Papers*, 8:357.

18. To John Holmes, Monticello, April 22, 1820, Peterson, *Jefferson: Writings*, 1434.

19. To Frances Wright, Monticello, August 7, 1825, H. A. Washington, ed., *The Writings of Thomas Jefferson* (9 vols., Washington, D.C., 1853–1854), 7:408.

20. To Edmund Randolph, Monticello, September 16, 1781, Boyd, *Jefferson Papers*, 6:118.

21. Madison to Edmund Randolph, September 30, 1782, William T. Hutchinson et al., eds., *The Papers of James Madison* (Chicago and Charlottesville, 1962–91), 5:120.

22. To Clark, Annapolis, December 4, 1783, Peterson, *Jefferson: Writings*, 783.

23. To James Monroe, Paris, March 18, 1785, Boyd, *Jefferson Papers*, 8:43.

24. Abigail Adams to Mary Cranch, May 8, 1785, L. H. Butterfield et al., eds., *Adams Family Correspondence* (Cambridge, Mass., 1963–), 6:119.

25. Abigail Adams to Thomas Jefferson, London, June 6, 1785, ibid., 6:169.

26. To the Rev. William Smith, Philadelphia, February 19, 1791, Peterson, *Jefferson: Writings*, 975.

27. The Marquis de Lafayette to James McHenry, Paris, December 3, 1785, Stanley J. Idzerda et al., eds., *Lafayette in the Age of the American Revolution: Selected Letters and Papers, 1776–1790* (5 vols., Ithaca, N.Y., 1977–1983), 5:355.

28. To Washington, Paris, May 2, 1788, W. W. Abbot and Dorothy Twohig, eds., *The Papers of George Washington: Confederation Series* (Charlottesville, Va., 1992), 6:256.

29. To Ezra Stiles, Paris, December 24, 1786, Boyd, *Jefferson Papers*, 10:629.

30. To John Adams, Paris, August 30, 1787, Peterson, *Jefferson: Writings*, 908–9.

31. To James Madison, Paris, June 20, 1787, Robert A. Rutland and Charles F. Hobson, eds., *Madison Papers*, 10:64.

32. To Francis Hopkinson, Paris, March 13, 1789, Peterson, *Jefferson: Writings*, 940–41.

33. To the Marquis de Lafayette, New York, April 2, 1790, Boyd, *Jefferson Papers*, 16:293.

34. To Short, Philadelphia, January 3, 1793, Peterson, *Jefferson: Writings*, 1004.

35. To the Comte de Volney, Monticello, December 9, 1795, Boyd, *Jefferson Papers*, 28:551.

36. To John Adams, Monticello, June 27, 1813, Lester J. Cappon, ed., *The Adams-Jefferson Letters: The Complete Correspondence between Thomas Jefferson and Abigail and John Adams* (Chapel Hill, N.C., 1959), 335.

37. To Benjamin Hawkins, Paris, August 13, 1786, Boyd, *Jefferson Papers*, 10:240.

38. To Benjamin Hawkins, Washington, February 18, 1803, Peterson, *Jefferson: Writings*, 1115.

39. To James Madison, Monticello, January 1, 1797, ibid., 1039.

40. To Elbridge Gerry, Philadelphia, May 13, 1797, Boyd, *Jefferson Papers*, 29:362.

41. Charles Carroll of Carrollton to Alexander Hamilton, Annapolis, April 18, 1800, Syrett, *Hamilton Papers*, 24:412.

42. To Spencer Roane, Poplar Forest, September 6, 1819, Peterson, *Jefferson: Writings*, 1425.

43. March 4, 1801, ibid., 492–96.

44. Plumer memorandum, December 31, 1804, Everett Somerville Brown, ed., *William Plumer's Memorandum of Proceedings in the*

Senate, 1803–1807 (New York, 1923), 234–35. Jefferson's actual words in his second annual address to Congress on December 15, 1802, were that "the smallest force competent" was sent "to secure our commerce in that sea."

45. Plumer memorandum, April 8, 1806, 478.

46. Ibid., March 16, 1806, 455.

47. To Pierre Samuel Dupont de Nemours, Washington, March 2, 1809, Peterson, *Jefferson: Writings*, 1203.

48. To Andrew Ellicott, Monticello, June 24, 1812, Thomas Jefferson Papers, Library of Congress, Washington D.C.

49. To Samuel Brown, Monticello, April 17, 1813, ibid.

50. To Martha Jefferson, Philadelphia, July 7, 1793, ibid.

51. Margaret Bayard Smith, Reminiscences, Gaillard Hunt, ed., *The First Forty Years of Washington Society in the Family Letters of Margaret Bayard Smith* (New York, 1906; repr., New York, 1965), 11.

52. To Charles Willson Peale, Poplar Forest, August 20, 1811, Peterson, *Jefferson: Writings*, 1249.

53. Rush to Adams, Philadelphia, February 17, 1812, L. H. Butterfield, ed., *Letters of Benjamin Rush* (2 vols., Princeton, 1951), 2:1127.

54. To Maria Cosway, Monticello, December 27, 1820, Thomas Jefferson Papers, Massachusetts Historical Society, Boston.

55. To John Page, Washington, June 25, 1804, Washington, *Jefferson Writings*, 4:547.

56. To Adams, Monticello, August 1, 1816, *Cappon, Adams-Jefferson Letters*, 484.

57. To Adams, Monticello, November 13, 1818, ibid., 529.

58. To Adams, Monticello, March 14, 1820, ibid., 562–63.

59. To Nicholas P. Trist, Montpelier, July 6, 1826, Jack N. Rakove, ed., *James Madison: Writings* (New York, 1999), 812.

Thomas Jefferson Chronology

1743	Born at Shadwell, Va. (April 13)
1757	Father, Peter Jefferson, dies
1760–1762	Student at the College of William and Mary
1762–1767	Self-educates and also prepares for the law
1769	Begins building Monticello
1769–1774	Delegate to Virginia House of Burgesses
1772	Marries Martha Wayles Skelton (January 1)
1774	Writes *A Summary View of the Rights of British America*
1775–1776	Delegate to Second Continental Congress
1776	Drafts Declaration of Independence
1776–1779	Delegate to Virginia House of Delegates
1779	Submits A *Bill for Establishing Religious Freedom*
1779–1781	Governor of Virginia (elected June 1)
1780	Elected a member of the American Philosophical Society
1781–1782	Writes *Notes on the State of Virginia*
1782	Wife dies (September 6)
1783–1784	Delegate to Confederation Congress
1784	Minister plenipotentiary to negotiate treaties
1785–1789	Minister plenipotentiary to France
1790–1793	U.S. secretary of state
1797–1801	Vice president of the United States
1798	Drafts Kentucky Resolutions opposing Alien and Sedition laws
1801–1809	President of the United States
1814–1826	Establishes the University of Virginia
1826	Dies at Monticello (July 4)

The
Quotations

The Thoughts and Words of Thomas Jefferson

Advice

You will perceive by my preaching that I am grow-ing old: it is the privilege of years, and I am sure you will pardon it from the purity of its motives.

To Thomas Mann Randolph, Jr., Paris,
November 25, 1785

The greatest favor which can be done me is the communication of the opinions of judicious men, of men who do not suffer their judgments to be biased by either interest or passions.

To Chandler Price, Washington, February 28, 1807

Your situation, thrown at such a distance from us, & alone, cannot but give us all great anxieties for you. As much has been secured for you, by your particular position and the acquaintance to which you have been recommended, as could be done to-wards shielding you from the dangers which sur-round you. But thrown on a wide world, among entire strangers, without a friend or guardian to ad-vise, so young too, & with so little experience of mankind, your dangers are great, & still your safety must rest on yourself. A determination never to do what is wrong, prudence and good humor, will go far towards securing to you the estimation of the world.

To Thomas Jefferson Randolph, Washington, November 24, 1808

How easily we prescribe for others a cure for their difficulties, while we cannot cure our own.

To John Adams, Monticello, January 22, 1821

Adore God. Reverence and cherish your parents. Love your neighbor as yourself, and your country more than yourself. Be just. Be true. Murmur not at the ways of Providence.

To Thomas Jefferson Smith, Monticello, February 21, 1825

Consultation

I have found in the course of our joint services that I think right when I think with you.

To John Adams, Paris, July 7, 1785

Setting an Example

View, in those whom you see, patients to be cured of what is amiss by your example, encourage in them that simplicity which should be the ornament of their country; in fine, follow the dispositions of your own native benevolence & sweetness of temper, and you will be happy & make them so.

To Madame de Bréhan, Paris, May 9, 1788

I have ever deemed it more honorable, & more prof-itable too, to set a good example than to follow a bad one. The good opinion of mankind, like the lever of Archimedes, with the given fulcrum, moves the world.

To José Correa da Serra, Monticello, December 27, 1814

Suggestions

Suggestion and fact are different things.

To the Marquis de Lafayette, Monticello, August 4, 1781

As I know from experience that profitable suggestions sometimes come from lookers on, they may be usefully tolerated, provided they do not pretend to the right of an answer.

To Unknown, 1813

Ten Canons for Practical Life

Decalogue of Canons for Observation in Practical Life

1. Never put off till tomorrow what you can do to-day.

2. Never trouble another for what you can do yourself.

3. Never spend your money before you have it.

4. Never buy what you do not want, because it is cheap; it will be dear to you.

5. Pride costs us more than hunger, thirst and cold.

6. We never repent of having eaten too little.

7. Nothing is troublesome that we do willingly.

8. How much pain have cost us the evils which have never happened.

9. Take things always by their smooth handle.
10. When angry, count ten, before you speak; if very angry, an hundred.

To Thomas Jefferson Smith, Monticello,
February 21, 1825

Agriculture

I am never satiated with rambling through the fields and farms, examining the culture and cultivators, with a degree of curiosity which makes some to take me for a fool and others to be much wiser than I am.

To the Marquis de Lafayette, April 11, 1787

A steady application to agriculture with just trade enough to take off its superfluities is our wisest course.

To Wilson Miles Cary, Paris, August 12, 1787

The pursuits of Agriculture [are] the surest road to affluence and best preservative of morals.

To John Blair, Paris, August 13, 1787

Agriculture . . . is our wisest pursuit, because it will in the end contribute most to real wealth, good morals & happiness. . . . The moderate & sure income of husbandry begets permanent improvement, quiet life, and orderly conduct both public and private. We have no occasion for more commerce than to take off our superfluous produce.

To George Washington, Paris, August 14, 1787

I return to farming with an ardor which I scarcely knew in my youth, and which has got the better entirely of my love of study. Instead of writing 10 or 12 letters a day, which I have been in the habit of doing as a thing of course, I put off answering my letters now, farmer-like, till a rainy day, & then find it sometimes postponed by other necessary occupations.

To John Adams, Monticello, April 25, 1794

This first & most precious of all the arts.

To Robert R. Livingston, Philadelphia, April 30, 1800

The class principally defective is that of agriculture. It is the first in utility & ought to be the 1st in respect. The same artificial means which have been used to produce a competition in learning may be equally successful in restoring agriculture to its primary dignity in the eyes of men. It is a science of the very first order. It counts among its handmaids the most respectable sciences, such as chemistry, natural philosophy, mechanics, mathematics generally, natural history, botany. In every college & university, a professorship of Agriculture, & the class of its students, might be honored as the first.

To David Williams, Washington, November 14, 1803

Attached to agriculture by inclination as well as by a conviction that it is the most useful of the occupations of man, my course of life has not permitted me to add to its theories the lessons of practice.

To M. Silvestre, secretary of the Agricultural Society of Paris, Washington, May 29, 1807

About to be relieved from this corvée* by age and the fulfillment of the quadragena stipendia,** what remains to me of physical activity will chiefly be employed in the amusements of agriculture. Having little practical skill, I count more on the pleasures than the profits of that occupation.

*servitude; forced labor

**forty years' service

To Charles Philbert Lasteryrie-du Saillant, Washington, July 15, 1808

No sentiment is more acknowledged in the family of Agriculturalists than that the few who can afford it should incur the risk & expense of all new improvements, & give the benefit freely to the many of more restricted circumstances.

To President James Madison, Monticello, May 13, 1810

The spontaneous energies of the earth are a gift of nature, but they require the labor of man to direct their operation. And the question is so to husband his labor as to turn the greatest quantity of the earth to his benefit. Ploughing deep, your recipe for killing weeds is also the recipe for almost every good thing in farming.

The plow is to the farmer what the wand is to the sorcerer. Its effect is really like sorcery. In the country wherein I live, we have discovered a new use for it, equal in value to its services before known. Our country is hilly and we have been in the habit of ploughing in strait rows whether up or down hill, in oblique lines, or however they lead, and our soil was all rapidly running into the rivers. We now plough horizontally following the curvatures of the hills and hollows on the dead level, however crooked the lines may be. Every furrow thus acts as a reservoir to receive and retain the waters, all of which go to the benefit of the growing plant instead of running off into streams.

To Charles Willson Peale, March 17, 1813

Farmers

Those who labor in the earth are the chosen people of god, if ever he had a chosen people, whose breasts he has made his peculiar deposit for substantial and genuine virtue.

Notes on the State of Virginia, 1782

Cultivators of the earth are the most valuable citizens. They are the most vigorous, the most independent, the most virtuous, & they are tied to their country & wedded to its liberty & interests by the most lasting bands.

To John Jay, Paris, August 23, 1785

The cultivators of the earth are the most virtuous citizens and possess most of the amor patriae.*

Merchants are the least virtuous, and possess the least of the amor patriae.

*love of one's country; patriotism

To Jean Nicolas Démeunier, January 24, 1786

Ours are the only farmers who can read Homer.

To St. John de Crèvecoeur, Paris, January 15, 1787

Have you become a farmer? Is it not pleasanter than to be shut up within 4 walls and delving eternally with the pen? I am become the most ardent farmer in the state. I live on my horse from morning to night almost.

To Henry Knox, Monticello, June 1, 1795

I am entirely a farmer, soul and body, never scarcely admitting a sentiment on any other subject.

To Thomas Pinckney, Monticello, September 8, 1795

If a debt is once contracted by a farmer, it is never paid but by a sale.

To Mary Jefferson Eppes, Philadelphia, January 7, 1798

The truth is that farmers, as we all are, have no command of money. Our necessaries are all supplied either from our farms, or a neighboring store. Our produce, at the end of the year, is delivered to the merchant & thus the business of the year is done by barter, without the intervention of scarcely a dollar: and thus also we live with a plenty of every thing except money.

To William Duane, Monticello, March 28, 1811

So that in the lotteries of human life you see that even farming is but gambling.

To Unknown, no date [1813?]

Gardening

I have often thought that if heaven had given me choice of my position & calling, it should have been on a rich spot of earth, well watered, and near a good market for the productions of the garden. No occupation is so delightful to me as the culture of the earth, & no culture comparable to that of the garden. Such a variety of subjects, some one always coming to perfection, the failure of one thing repaired by the success of another, & instead of one harvest, a continued one thro' the year. Under a total want of demand except for our family table. I am still devoted to the garden. But tho' an old man, I am but a young gardener.

To Charles Willson Peale, Poplar Forest, August 20, 1811

Introducing New Crops

One service of this kind rendered to a nation is worth more to them than all the victories of the most splendid pages of their history, and becomes a source of exalted pleasure to those who have been instrumental to it.

To Alexandre Giroud, Philadelphia, May 22, 1797

Natural Fertilizing

The atmosphere is certainly the great workshop of nature for elaborating the fertilizing principles, & insinuating them into the soil.

To William Strickland, Philadelphia, March 23, 1798

America

I sincerely wish you may find it convenient to come here. The pleasure of the trip will be less than you expect but the utility greater. It will make you adore your own country, its soil, its climate, its equality, liberty, laws, people and manners. My god! How little do my countrymen know what precious blessings they are in possession of, and which no other people on earth enjoy. I confess I had no idea of it myself.

To James Monroe, Paris, June 17, 1785

You have properly observed that we can no longer be called Anglo-Americans. That appellation now describes only the inhabitants of Nova Scotia, Canada, &c. I had applied that of Federo-Americans to our citizens, as it would not be so decent for us to assume to ourselves the flattering appellation of Free-Americans.

To Brissot de Warville, Paris, August 16, 1786

Head. When you reflect that all Europe is made to believe we are a lawless banditti, in a state of absolute anarchy, cutting one another's throats, & plundering without distinction, how can you expect that any reasonable creature would venture among us?

Heart. But you & I know that all this is false: that there is not a country on earth where there is greater tranquility, where the laws are milder, or better obeyed: where every one is more attentive to his own business, or meddles less with that of others: where strangers are better received, more hospitably treated, & with a more sacred respect.

To Maria Cosway, Paris, October 12, 1786

Nothing in Europe can counterbalance the freedom, the simplicity, the friendship & the domestic felicity we enjoy in America.

To Johann Ludwig de Unger, Paris, February 16, 1788

[America] is made on an improved plan. Europe is a first idea, a crude production, before the maker knew his trade, or had made up his mind as to what he wanted.

To Angelica Schuyler Church, Paris, February 17, 1788

I know no country where . . . public esteem is so attached to worth, regardless of wealth.

To Angelica Schuyler Church, Germantown, Pa.,
November 27, 1793

Our geographical distance is insensible still to foreigners.

To John Adams, Monticello, May 27, 1796

American Character
It is a part of the American character to consider nothing as desperate; to surmount every difficulty by resolution and contrivance. In Europe there are

shops for every want. Its inhabitants therefore have no idea that their wants can be furnished otherwise. Remote from all other aid, we are obliged to invent and to execute; to find means within ourselves, and not to lean on others.

To Martha Jefferson, Aix en Provence, March 28, 1787

There is a modesty often which does itself injury. Our countrymen possess this. They do not know their own superiority.

To John Rutledge, Jr., Paris, February 2, 1788

The steady character of our countrymen is a rock to which we may safely moor.

To Elbridge Gerry, Washington, March 29, 1801

In our cities he will find distant imitations of the cities of Europe. But if he wishes to know the nation, its occupations, manners, & principles, they reside not in the cities; he must travel through the country, accept the hospitalities of the country gentlemen, and visit with them the school of the people.

To Madame de Stael de Holstein, Washington,
July 16, 1807

America's Future
Our confederacy must be viewed as the nest from which all America, North & South is to be peopled.

To Archibald Stuart, Paris, January 25, 1786

I carry with me the consolation of a firm persuasion
that heaven has in store for our beloved country,
long ages to come of prosperity and happiness.

Eighth (and final) Annual Message to Congress,
November 8, 1808

As the Hope of the World

Happy for us that abuses have not yet become patri-
monies, and that every description of interest is in
favor of rational & moderate government. That we
are yet able to send our wise & good men together
to talk over our form of government, discuss its
weaknesses, and establish its remedies with the
same sang-froid,* as they would a subject of agriculture. The example we have given to the world is single, that of changing the form of government under
the authority of reason only, without bloodshed.

*composure; determination

To Ralph Izard, Paris, July 17, 1788

We can surely boast of having set the world a beautiful example of a government reformed by reason
alone without bloodshed.

To Edward Rutledge, Paris, July 18, 1788

Never was a finer canvas presented to work on than
our countrymen. All of them engaged in agriculture
or the pursuits of honest industry, independent in
their circumstances, enlightened as to their rights,
and firm in their habits of order & obedience to the
laws. This I hope will be the age of experiments in

government, and that their basis will be founded in principles of honesty, not of mere force. We have seen no instance of this since the days of the Roman republic, nor do we read of any before that.

To John Adams, Monticello, February 28, 1796

A just & solid republican government maintained here, will be a standing monument & example for the aim & imitation of the people of other countries; and I join with you in the hope and belief that they will see from our example that a free government is of all others the most energetic; that the inquiry which has been excited among the mass of mankind by our revolution & its consequences will ameliorate the condition of man over a great portion of the globe.

To John Dickinson, Washington, March 6, 1801

It is impossible not to be sensible that we are acting for all mankind: that circumstances denied to others, but indulged to us, have imposed on us the duty of proving what is the degree of freedom and self-government in which a society may venture to leave its individual members.

To Joseph Priestley, Washington, June 19, 1802

The station which we occupy among the nations of the earth is honorable, but awful. Trusted with the destinies of this solitary republic of the world, the only monument of human rights, & the sole depository of the sacred fire of freedom & self-government from hence it is to be lighted up in other regions of

the earth, if other regions of the earth shall ever become susceptible of its benign influence. All
mankind ought then, with us, to rejoice in its prosperous, & sympathize in its adverse fortunes, as in-
volving every thing dear to man.

To the citizens of Washington, March 4, 1809

The last hope of human liberty in this world rests
on us.

To William Duane, Monticello, March 28, 1811

The eyes of the virtuous, all over the earth, are
turned with anxiety on us, as the only depositories
of the sacred fire of liberty, and that our falling
into anarchy would decide forever the destinies of
mankind, and seal the political heresy that man is
incapable of self-government.

To John Hollins, Monticello, May 5, 1811

I hope & firmly believe that the whole world will,
sooner or later, feel benefit from the issue of our assertion of the rights of man.

To Benjamin Galloway, Monticello, February 2, 1812

We are destined to be a barrier against the returns
of ignorance and barbarism.

To John Adams, Monticello, August 1, 1816

I will not believe our labors are lost. I shall not die
without a hope that light and liberty are on steady
advance. . . . And even should the cloud of barbarism

and despotism again obscure the science and liberties of Europe, this country remains to preserve and restore light and liberty to them. In short, the flames kindled on the 4th of July 1776 have spread over too much of the globe to be extinguished by the feeble engines of despotism. On the contrary they will consume those engines, and all who work them.

To John Adams, Monticello, September 12, 1821

The American Revolution

The Declaration of Independence
I turned to neither book nor pamphlet while writing it. I did not consider it as any part of my charge to invent new ideas altogether, & to offer no sentiment which had ever been expressed before.

To James Madison, Monticello, August 30, 1823

The Declaration [was] the genuine effusion of the soul of our country at that time.

To James Madison, Monticello, September 16, 1825

May it be to the world what I believe it will be, (to some parts sooner, to others later, but finally to all,) the Signal of arousing men to burst the chains, under which Monkish ignorance and superstition had persuaded them to bind themselves, and to assume

Jefferson's draft of the first page of the Declaration of Independence. (Jefferson Papers, Library of Congress.)

the blessings & security of self-government. That form which we have substituted, restores the free right to the unbounded exercise of reason and freedom of opinion. All eyes are opened, or opening, to the rights of man. The general spread of the light of science has already laid open to every view the palpable truth that the mass of mankind has not been born, with saddles on their backs, nor a favored few booted and spurred, ready to ride them legitimately, by the grace of god. These are grounds of hope for others. For ourselves, let the annual return of this day forever refresh our recollections of these rights, and an undiminished devotion to them.

To Roger C. Weightman, Monticello, June 24, 1826

Purpose

The approbation of my ancient friends is, above all things, the most grateful to my heart. They know for what objects we relinquished the delights of domestic society, tranquility & science, & committed ourselves to the ocean of revolution, to wear out the only life god has given us here in scenes the benefits of which will accrue only to those who follow us. Surely we had in view to obtain the theory & practice of good government; and how any, who seemed so ardent in this pursuit, could as shamelessly have apostatized, and supposed we meant only to put our government into other hands, but not other forms, is indeed wonderful. The lesson we have had will probably be useful to the people at large, by showing to them how capable they are of being made the instruments of their own bondage.

To John Dickinson, Washington, December 19, 1801

The Arts

You see I am an enthusiast on the subject of the arts. But it is an enthusiasm of which I am not ashamed, as its object is to improve the taste of my countrymen, to increase their reputation, to reconcile to them the respect of the world & procure them its praise.

To James Madison, Paris, September 20, 1785

One who loves the arts must be well disposed to those who practice them.

To Francis Hopkinson, Paris, September 18, 1787

Painters of high reputation are either above copying, or ask extravagant prices. But there are always men of good talents, who being kept in obscurity by untoward circumstances, work cheap, & work well. Copies by such hands as these might probably be obtained at such prices as I would be willing to give.

To Philip Mazzei, Paris, October 17, 1787

I am but a son of natu re, loving what I see and feel, without being able to give a reason, nor caring much whether there be one.

To Maria Cosway, Paris, April 24, 1788

Architecture

This is the second time I have been in love since I left Paris. The first was with a Diana at the Chateau de Laye Epinaye in Beaujolais, a delicious morsel of sculpture, by M[ichael] A[ngelo] Slodtz. This you will say, was in rule, to fall in love with a female beauty: but, with a house! It is out of all precedent. No, madam, it is not without a precedent, in my own history. While at Paris, I was violently smitten with the Hotel de Salm, and used to go to the Thuileries* almost daily to look at it. The loueuse des chaises,** inattentive to my passion, never had the complaisance to place a chair there; so that, sitting on the parapet, and twisting my neck round to see the object of my admiration, I generally left it with a torticollis.***

> *The gardens of Thuileries Palace in the center of Paris had become almost public. Chairs could be rented. From here, Jefferson observed the construction of the Hotel de Salm across the Seine.
>
> **renters of chairs
>
> ***stiff neck

To Madame de Tessé, Nismes, France, March 20, 1787

Literature

Literature is not yet a distinct profession with us. Now and then a strong mind arises, and at its intervals of leisure from business, emits a flash of light.

To J. Evelyn Denison, Monticello, November 9, 1825

Music

If there is a gratification which I envy any people in this world it is to your country its music. This is the favorite passion of my soul, & fortune has cast my lot in a country where it is in a state of deplorable barbarism.

To Giovanni Fabbroni, Williamsburg, June 8, 1778

[The Harmonica] However imperfect this instrument is for the general mass of musical compositions, yet for those of a certain character it is delicious.

To Charles Burney, Paris, February 12, 1787

[Music] will be a companion which will sweeten many hours of life to you.

To Martha Jefferson Randolph, New York, April 4, 1790

Music is invaluable where a person has an ear. Where they have not, it should not be attempted. It furnishes a delightful recreation for the hours of respite from the cares of the day, and lasts us through life.

To Nathaniel Burwell, Monticello, March 14, 1818

Poetry

Misery is often the parent of the most affecting touches in poetry. . . . Love is the peculiar oestrum* of the poet.

*inspiration

Notes on the State of Virginia, 1782

It is not for a stranger to decide on the merit of poetry in a language foreign to him.

To Hilliard d'Auberteuil, Paris, January 27, 1787

A poet is as much the creature of climate as an orange or palm tree.

To William Short, Paris, May 21, 1787

I subscribe with pleasure to the publication of your volumes of poems. I anticipate the same pleasure from them which the perusal of those heretofore published has given me. . . . Under the shade of a tree one of your volumes will be a pleasant pocket companion.

To Philip Freneau, Monticello, May 22, 1809

Books

An honest heart being the first blessing, a knowing head is the second. It is time for you now to begin to be choice in your reading, to begin to pursue a regular course in it, & not to suffer yourself to be turned to the right or left by reading any thing out of that course.

To Peter Carr, Paris, August 19, 1785

Books, really good, acquire just reputation in that time, & so become known to us & communicate to us all their advances in knowledge.

To Charles Bellini, Paris, September 30, 1785

Read good books because they will encourage as well as direct your feelings.

To Peter Carr, Paris, August 10, 1787

When I name a particular edition of a book, send me that edition and no other.

When I do not name the edition, never send a folio or quarto if there exists an 8vo. or small edition. I like books of a handy size.

To Thomas Paine, Paris, October 2, 1788

[Hopes to have Wythe visit Monticello] and of gratifying your taste for books, by introducing you to a collection now certainly the best in America.

To George Wythe, Monticello, October 23, 1794

I cannot live without books.

To John Adams, Monticello, June 10, 1815

My repugnance to the writing table becomes daily & hourly more deadly & insurmountable. In place of this has come on a canine appetite for reading. And I indulge it because I see in it a relief against the taedium senectutis,* a lamp to lighten my path thro' the dreary wilderness of time before me, whose bourne I

Jefferson's Cabinet in Monticello. (Robert C. Lautman/
Thomas Jefferson Foundation, Inc.)

see not. Losing daily all interest in the things around
us, something else is necessary to fill the void. With
me it is reading, which occupies the mind without
the labor of producing ideas from my own stock.

*weariness of old age

To John Adams, Monticello, May 17, 1818

I was a hard student until I entered on the business of life, the duties of which leave no idle time to those disposed to fulfill them; & now, retired and at the age of 76, I am again a hard student. Indeed, my fondness for reading and study revolts me from the drudgery of letter writing. . . . I never go to bed without an hour, or half hour's previous reading of something moral, whereon to ruminate in the intervals of sleep.

To Vine Utley, Monticello, March 21, 1819

Books constitute capital. A library book lasts as long as a house, for hundreds of years. It is not then an article of mere consumption but fairly of capital.

To James Madison, Monticello, September 16, 1821

Dictionaries

Your idea is an excellent one in producing authorities for the meanings of words, "to select the prominent passages in our best writers, to make your dictionary a general index to English literature and thus intersperse with verdure and flowers the barren deserts of Philology." And I believe with you that "wisdom, morality, religion, thus thrown down, as if without intention, before the reader, in quotations, may often produce more effect than the very passages in the books themselves."

To Sir Herbert Croft, Monticello, October 30, 1798

Jefferson's Library

I learn from the newspapers that the vandalism of our enemy has triumphed at Washington over science as well as the Arts, by the destruction of the public library with the noble edifice in which it was deposited. . . . I presume it will be among the early objects of Congress to recommence their collection. This will be difficult while the war continues and intercourse with Europe is attended with so much risk. You know my collection, its condition and extent. I have been 50 years making it & have spared no pains, opportunity or expense to make it what it is. While residing in Paris, I devoted every afternoon I was disengaged, for a summer or two, in examining all the principal book stores, turning over every book with my own hands and putting by everything which related to America, and indeed whatever was rare & valuable in every science. Besides this, I had standing orders, during the whole time I was in Europe, in its principal book-marts, particularly Amsterdam, Frankfort, Madrid, and London, for such works relating to America as could not be found in Paris. So that, in that department particularly, such a collection was made as probably can never again be effected; because it is hardly probable that the same opportunities, the same time, industry, perseverance, and expense, with some knowledge of the bibliography of the subject would again happen to be in concurrence. During the same period, and after my return to America, I was led to procure also whatever related to the duties of those in the high concerns of the nation. So that the collection, which I suppose is between 9 and 10,000 volumes, while it includes what is chiefly valuable in science and literature generally, extends more particularly to whatever belongs to the American statesman. In the diplomatic and Parliamentary branches, it is particularly full. It is long since I have been sensible it ought not to continue private property, and had provided that at my death, Congress should have the refusal of it, at their own price. But the loss they have now incurred makes the present the proper moment for their accommodation, without regard to the small remnant of time and the barren use of my enjoying it.

To Samuel Harrison Smith, Monticello,
September 21, 1814

Libraries

I have often thought that nothing would do more extensive good at small expense than the establishment of a small circulating library in every county, to consist of a few well-chosen books, to be lent to the people of the county under such regulations as would secure their safe return in due time. These should be such as would give them a general view of that of other history & particular view of their own country, a tolerable knowledge of geography, the elements of Natural philosophy, of agriculture & mechanics.

To John Wyche, Monticello, May 19, 1809

You are pleased to ask my opinion on the subject of the arrangement of libraries. I shall communicate with pleasure what occurs to me on it. Two methods offer themselves, the one Alphabetical, the other according to the subject of the book. The former is very unsatisfactory, because of the medley it presents to the mind, the difficulty sometimes of recalling the author's name, and the greater difficulty, where the name is not given of selecting the word in the title which shall determine its Alphabetical place. The arrangement according to subject is far preferable, altho' sometimes presenting difficulty also, for it is often doubtful to what particular subject a book should be ascribed.

To George Watterston, Monticello, May 7, 1815

Reviewers

A Reviewer can never let a work pass uncensured. He must always make himself wiser than his author. He would otherwise think it an abdication of his office of Censor.

To William Johnson, Monticello, March 4, 1823

For the functions of a Reviewer I have neither time, talent, nor inclination, and I trust that, on reflection, your indulgence will not think unreasonable my unwillingness to embark in an office of so little enticement.

To Thomas Earle, Monticello, September 24, 1823

I make it an invariable rule to decline ever giving opinions on new publications in any case whatever. No man on earth has less taste or talent for criticism than myself.

To Alexander Smyth, Monticello, January 17, 1825

Cities, Countries, and Regions

Cities

The mobs of great cities add just so much to the support of pure government, as sores do to the strength of the human body.

Notes on the State of Virginia, 1782

I am constantly roving about to see where I have never seen before and shall never see again. In the great cities, I go to see what travelers think alone worthy of being seen, but I make a job of it and generally gulp it all down in a day.

To the Marquis de Lafayette, April 11, 1787

I think our governments will remain virtuous for many centuries; as long as they are chiefly agricultural; and this will be as long as there shall be vacant lands in any part of America. When they get piled upon one another in large cities, as in Europe, they will become corrupt as in Europe.

To James Madison, Paris, December 20, 1787

As soon as I am fixed in Philadelphia, I shall be in hopes of receiving Jack.* Load him, on his departure, with charges not to give his heart to any object he will find there. I know no such useless bauble in a house as a girl of mere city education. She would finish by fixing him there and ruining him. I will enforce on him your charges, and all others which shall be for his good.

> *Jefferson had offered to assist his nephew, John Eppes, with his studies in Philadelphia and even to hire him as a copyist. Eppes spent two years in Philadelphia and studied law under Jefferson's tutelage. Jefferson gave Eppes the extremely important job of secretly copying James Madison's notes of the debates in the Federal Convention of 1787. Eppes and Jefferson's daughter, Polly, were married in October 1797.

To Elizabeth Wayles Eppes, Monticello, October 31, 1790

I view great cities as pestilential to the morals, the health and the liberties of man. True, they nourish some of the elegant arts, but the useful ones can thrive elsewhere, and less perfection in the others, with more health, virtue & freedom, would be my choice.

To Benjamin Rush, Monticello, September 23, 1800

But the great mass of our people are agricultural; and the commercial cities, tho' by the command of newspapers they make a great deal of noise, have little effect in the direction of the government. They are as different in sentiment & character from the country people as any two distinct nations, and are clamorous against the order of things established by the agricultural interest.

To Marc Auguste Pictet, Washington, February 5, 1803

The general desire of men to live by their heads rather than their hands & the strong allurements of great cities to those who have any turn for dissipation, threaten to make them here, as in Europe, the sinks of voluntary misery.

To David Williams, Washington, November 14, 1803

A city life offers you indeed more means of dissipating time, but more frequent also, and more painful objects of vice and wretchedness.

To William Short, Monticello, September 8, 1823

Cuba

I shall sincerely lament Cuba's falling into any hands but those of its present owners. Spanish America is at present in the best hands for us, & "chi sta bene, non si muove"* should be our motto.

*Whoever is in a good position, does not move.

To Albert Gallatin, Monticello, May 17, 1808

That he [Napoleon] would give us the Floridas to withhold intercourse with the residue of those colonies cannot be doubted. But that is no price, because they are ours in the first moment of the first war; & until a war they are of no particular necessity to us. But, altho' with difficulty, he will consent to our receiving Cuba into our union to prevent our aid to Mexico & the other provinces. That would be a price, & I would immediately erect a column on the Southernmost limit of Cuba & inscribe on it a Ne plus ultra* as to us in that direction.

We should then have only to include the North in our confederacy, which would be of course in the first war, and we should have such an empire for liberty as she has never surveyed since the creation & I am persuaded no constitution was ever before so well calculated as ours for extensive empire & self government.

*not more beyond

To President James Madison, Monticello, April 27, 1809

It will be objected to our receiving Cuba, that no limit can then be drawn to our future acquisitions. Cuba can be defended by us without a navy & this develops the principle which ought to limit our views. Nothing should ever be accepted which would require a navy to defend it.

To President James Madison, Monticello, April 27, 1809

Cuba alone seems at present to hold up a speck of war to us. Its possession by Great Britain would indeed be a great calamity to us. Could we induce her [Britain] to join us in guaranteeing its independence against all the world, except Spain, it would be nearly as valuable to us as if it were our own. But, should she [Britain] take it, I would not immediately go to war for it; because the first war on other accounts will give it to us; or the island will give itself to us, when able to do so.

To President James Monroe, Monticello, June 11, 1823

Her addition to our confederacy is exactly what is wanting to round our power as a nation to the point of its utmost interest.

To President James Monroe, Monticello, June 23, 1823

But we have first to ask ourselves a question. Do we wish to acquire to our own confederacy any one or more of the Spanish provinces? I candidly confess that I have ever looked on Cuba as the most interesting addition which could ever be made to our system of states. The control which with Florida point, this island would give us over the Gulf of Mexico and the countries, and the isthmus bordering on it, as well as all those whose waters flow into it, would fill up the measure of our political well-being. Yet, as I am sensible that this can never be obtained even with her own consent, but by war; and its independence, which is our second interest (and especially its independence of England) can be secured without it, I have no hesitation in abandoning my first wish to future chances, and accepting its independence with peace & the friendship of England, rather than its association at the expense of war and her enmity.

To President James Monroe, Monticello, October 24, 1823

Europe

I can scarcely withhold myself from joining in the wish of Silas Deane that there were an ocean of fire between us & the old world.

To Elbridge Gerry, Philadelphia, May 13, 1797

I consider Europe at present as a world apart from us, about which it is improper for us even to form opinions, or to indulge any wishes but the general one that whatever is to take place in it, may be for its happiness.

> To Julien Niemcewicz, Monticello, April 22, 1807

We especially ought to pray that the powers of Europe may be so poised & counterpoised among themselves that their own safety may require the presence of all their force at home, leaving the other quarters of the globe in undisturbed tranquility.

> To John Crawford, Monticello, January 2, 1812

European Education

But why send an American youth to Europe for education? What are the objects of an useful American education? Classical knowledge; modern languages & chiefly French, Spanish, & Italian; Mathematics; Natural philosophy, Natural history; Civil History; Ethics. In Natural philosophy I mean to include Chemistry & Agriculture, and in Natural history to include Botany as well as the other branches of those departments. It is true that the habit of speaking the modern languages cannot be as well acquired in America, but every other article can be as well acquired at William & Mary College as at any place in Europe.

> To John Bannister, Jr., Paris, October 15, 1785

There is a great deal of ill to be learnt here by young people, and no good but what can be better learnt with us.

To Henry Skipwith, Paris, May 6, 1786

He [John Rutledge, Jr.] is likely to be as much improved by this tour, as any person can be, and to return home charged, like a bee, with the honey gathered on it.

To John Rutledge, Sr., Paris, July 17, 1788

France

She is the wealthiest but worst governed country on earth.

To Joseph Jones, Paris, June 19, 1785

I consider your boasts of the splendor of your city [London] and of its superb hackney coaches as a flout, and declaring that I would not give the polite, self-denying, feeling, hospitable, good humored people of this country & their amiability in every point of view (tho' it must be confessed our streets are somewhat dirty, & our fiacres* rather indifferent) for ten such races of rich, proud, hectoring, swearing, squibbing, carnivorous animals as those among whom you are; and that I do love this people with all my heart, and think that with a better religion, a better form of government and their present governors their condition & country would be most enviable.

*coaches for hire

To Abigail Adams, Paris, June 21, 1785

[Frenchmen] have as much happiness in one year as an Englishman in ten.

To Abigail Adams, Paris, August 9, 1786

The only nation on earth on whom we can solidly rely for assistance till we can stand on our own legs.

To Ralph Izard, Paris, November 18, 1786

It is impossible to be among a people who wish more to make one happy, a people of the very best character it is possible for one to have. We have no idea in America of the real French character. With some true samples, we have had many false ones.

To Eliza House Trist, Paris, December 15, 1786

A Frenchman never says No: and it is difficult for a stranger to know when he means it. Perhaps it is the longest to be learnt of all the particularities of the nation.

To Thomas Paine, Paris, July 3, 1788

The cutting off heads is become so much à la mode,* that one is apt to feel of a morning whether their own is on their shoulders.

*the fashion

To Maria Cosway, Paris, July 25, 1789

Of all nations of any consideration France is the one which, hitherto has offered the fewest points on which we could have any conflict of right, and the most points of a communion of interests. From these causes we have ever looked to her as our natural friend, as one with which we never could have an occasion of difference. Her growth therefore we viewed as our own, her misfortunes ours.

To Robert R. Livingston, Washington, April 18, 1802

While I freely admit the right of a nation to change its political principles & constitution at will, and the impropriety of any but its own citizens censuring that change, I expect your lordship has been disappointed, as I acknowledge I have been in the issue of the convulsions on the other side the channel. This has certainly lessened the interest which the philanthropist warmly felt in those struggles. Without befriending human liberty a gigantic force has risen up which seems to threaten the world.

To the Earl of Buchan, Washington, July 10, 1803

No people on earth retain their national adherence longer or more warmly than the French.

To William C. C. Claiborne, Monticello,
September 10, 1809

Ask the traveled inhabitant of any nation, In what country on earth would you rather live?—Certainly in my own, where all my friends, my relations, and the earliest & sweetest affections and recollections of my life. Which would be your second choice? France.

Autobiography, 1821

Great Britain

During the late war I had an infallible rule for decid-
ing what that nation would do on every occasion. It
was, to consider what they ought to do, and to take
the reverse of that as what they would assuredly do,
and I can say with truth that I was never deceived.

To William Stephens Smith, Paris, June 22, 1785

His obstinacy of character we know; his hostility we
have known, and it is embittered by ill success.

To Richard Henry Lee, London, April 22, 1786

That nation hates us, their ministers hate us, and
their king more than all other men.

To John Page, Paris, May 4, 1786

We have a blind story here of somebody attempting
to assassinate your king. No man upon earth has my
prayers for his continuance in life more sincerely
than him. He is truly the American Messiah. The
most precious life that ever god gave, and may god
continue it. Twenty long years has he been laboring
to drive us to our good and he labors and will labor
still for it if he can be spared. We shall have need of
him for twenty more. The Prince of Wales on the
throne, Lansdowne & Fox in the ministry, & we are
undone! We become chained by our habits to the
tails of those who hate & despise us. I repeat it then
that my anxieties are all alive for the health & long
life of the king. He has not a friend on earth who
would lament his loss so much & so long as I should.

To Abigail Adams, Paris, August 9, 1786

The people of England, I think, are less oppressed than here. But it needs but half an eye to see, when among them, that the foundation is laid in their dispositions, for the establishment of a despotism. Nobility, wealth, and pomp are the objects of their adoration. They are by no means the free-minded people we suppose them in America. Their learned men too are few in number, and are less learned and infinitely less emancipated from prejudice than those of this country.

To George Wythe, Paris, August 13, 1786

Our friend George is rather remarkable for doing exactly what he ought not to do.

To David Ramsay, Paris, August 4, 1787

I never yet found any other general rule for foretelling what they will do, but that of examining what they ought not to do.

To John Adams, Paris, September 28, 1787

Of all nations on earth they require to be treated with the most hauteur.* They require to be kicked into common good manners.

*haughtiness; arrogance

To William Stephens Smith, Paris,
September 28, 1787

Since the accession of their present monarch, has it not been passion, & not reason, which, nine times out of ten, has dictated her measures? Has there been a better role of prognosticating what he would do, than to examine what he ought not to do?

To John Jay, Paris, October 8, 1787

We know little of what is passing in that country, for I would not call knowledge the misinformation we get thro' the English papers. We know from our own experience that they say of their enemies, not what is true, or what they believe to be true, but what they would wish the world to believe of them.

To Madame de Tessé, Monticello, September 8, 1795

Theirs is the workshop to which we go for all we want.

To Elbridge Gerry, Philadelphia, May 13, 1797

As we have employed some of the best materials of the British constitution in the construction of our own government, a knowledge of British history becomes useful to the American politician.

To John Norvell, Washington, June 11, 1807

Our laws, language, religion, politics, & manners are so deeply laid in English foundations, that we shall never cease to consider their history as a part of ours, and to study ours in that as its origin.

To William Duane, Monticello, August 12, 1810

I am sorry for her people, who are individually as respectable as those of other nations. It is her government which is so corrupt, and which has destroyed the nation. It was certainly the most corrupt and un-principled government on earth. I should be glad to see their farmers and mechanics come here, but I hope their nobles, priests, and merchants will be kept at home to be moralized by the discipline of the new government.

To William Duane, Monticello, November 13, 1810

As for France & England, with all their preemi-nence in science, the one is a den of robbers, & the other of pirates.

To John Adams, Monticello, January 21, 1812

We concur in considering the government of En-gland as totally without morality, insolent beyond bearing, inflated with vanity and ambition, aiming at the exclusive dominion of the sea, lost in corrup-tion, of deep-rooted hatred towards us, hostile to liberty wherever it endeavors to show its head, and the eternal disturber of the peace of the world.

To Thomas Leiper, Monticello, June 12, 1815

No nation on earth can hurt us so much as yours; none be more useful to you than ours.

To William Roscoe, Monticello, December 27, 1820

Great Britain is the nation which can do us the most harm of any one, or all, on earth; and with her on our side we need not fear the whole world.

To President James Monroe, Monticello,
October 24, 1823

In England the constitution may be altered by a single act of the legislature, which amounts to the having no constitution at all.

To Adamantios Coray, Monticello, October 31, 1823

Gr. Britain, the land of our own language, habits and manners.

To Richard Rush, Monticello, April 26, 1824

Greece

I cannot help looking forward to the reestablishment of the Greeks as a people, and the language of Homer becoming again a living language as among possible events.

To George Wythe, Paris, September 16, 1787

Italy

I wish your Italy lay only on the other side of Chesapeake bay, that I might go and see it: if I were to take another voyage on this side the Styx, it would certainly be to see that.

To Philip Mazzei, Monticello, September 8, 1795

Lake George and Lake Champlain

Lake George is, without comparison, the most beautiful water I ever saw; formed by a contour of mountains into a basin thirty-five miles long, and from two to four miles broad, finely interspersed, with islands, its water limpid as crystal, and the mountain sides covered with rich groves of thuja, silver fir, white pine, aspen, and paper birch down to the water-edge; here and there precipices of rock to checker the scene and save it from monotony. An abundance of speckled trout, salmon trout, bass, and other fish, with which it is stored, have added, to our other amusements, the sport of taking them. Lake Champlain, though much larger, is a far less pleasant water. It is muddy, turbulent, and yields little game. After penetrating into it about twenty-five miles, we have been obliged, by a head wind and high seas, to return, having spent a day and a half in sailing on it.

To Martha Jefferson Randolph, Lake Champlain, May 31, 1791

New England

Seeing therefore that an association of men who will not quarrel with one another is a thing which never yet existed, from the greatest confederacy of nations down to a town meeting or a vestry, seeing that we must have somebody to quarrel with, I had rather keep our New-England associates for that purpose than to see our bickerings transferred to others. They are circumscribed within such narrow limits, & their population so full, that their numbers will ever be the minority, and they are marked, like the Jews, with such a peculiarity of character, as to constitute from that circumstance the natural division of our parties.

To John Taylor, Philadelphia, June 4, 1798

Panama Canal

Were they to make an opening thro' the isthmus of Panama, a work much less difficult than some even of the inferior canals of France, however small this opening should be in the beginning, the tropical current, entering it with all its force, would soon widen it sufficiently for its own passage, & thus complete in a short time that work which otherwise will still employ it for ages. Less country too would be destroyed by it in this way.

To Jean Baptiste Le Roy, Paris, November 13, 1786

Pennsylvania

Pennsylvania, the cradle of toleration and freedom of religion.

To Thomas Cooper, Monticello, November 2, 1822

Russia

Russia (while her present monarch* lives) is the most cordially friendly to us of any power on earth, will go furthest to serve us, & is most worthy of conciliation.

*Alexander

To William Duane, Washington, July 20, 1807

I pray you to place me rectus in curia* in this business with the emperor, and to assure him that I carry into my retirement the highest veneration for his virtues, and fondly cherish the belief that his dispositions and power are destined by heaven to better,

in some degree at least, the condition of oppressed
man.

　　*blameless
　To William Short, Washington, March 8, 1809

Alexander is unquestionably a man of an excellent
heart, and of very respectable strength of mind; and
he is the only sovereign who cordially loves us. . . .
Of Alexander's sense of the merits of our form of
government, of its wholesome operation on the condition of the people, and of the interest he takes in
the success of our experiment, we possess the most
unquestionable proofs; and to him we shall be indebted if the rights of neutrals, to be settled whenever peace is made, shall be extended beyond the
present belligerents.

　To William Duane, Monticello, November 13, 1810

South America

You ask me if any thing transpires here on the subject of S. America? Not a word. I know that there
are combustible materials there, and that they wait
the torch only. But this country [France] probably
will join the extinguishers.

　To William Stephens Smith, Paris, November 13, 1787

Behold! another example of man rising in his might
and bursting the chains of his oppressor, and in the
same hemisphere. Spanish America is all in revolt.
The insurgents are triumphant in many of the
States, and will be so in all. But there the danger is

that the cruel arts of their oppressors have enchained their minds, have kept them in the ignorance of children, and as incapable of self-government as children. If the obstacles of bigotry and priest-craft can be surmounted, we may hope that common-sense will suffice to do everything else. God send them a safe deliverance.

To Tadeusz Kosciusko, Monticello, April 13, 1811 [1816?]

I fear too that the Spaniards [i.e., South Americans] are too heavily oppressed by ignorance & superstition for self-government, and whether a change from foreign to domestic despotism will be to their advantage remains to be seen.

To Samuel Brown, Monticello, July 14, 1813

That they will throw off their European dependence I have no doubt; but in what kind of government their revolution will end is not so certain. History, I believe furnishes no example of a priest-ridden people maintaining a free civil government. . . . I fear [that South America] must end in military despotisms. The different casts of their inhabitants, their mutual hatreds and jealousies, their profound ignorance & bigotry, will be played off by cunning leaders, and each be made the instrument of enslaving the others. . . . But in whatever governments they end, they will be American governments, no longer to be involved in the never-ceasing broils of Europe.

To Alexander von Humboldt, December 6, 1813

What a Colossus shall we be when the Southern continent comes up to our mark! What a stand will it secure as an alliance for the reason & freedom of the globe!

To John Adams, Monticello, August 1, 1816

Spain

Our connections with the Spaniards and Portuguese must become every day more & more interesting, and I should think, the knowledge of their language, manners, and situation, might eventually and even probably become more useful to yourself & country than that of any other place you will have seen. The womb of time is big with events to take place between us & them, and a little knowledge of them will give you great advantages over those who have none at all.

To John Rutledge, Jr., Paris, July 13, 1788

Tennessee

I have no doubt that Tanissee is a good field for a man of industry, integrity and talents: and it is a good country to lay out advantageously the profits of business.

To John Garland Jefferson, Monticello, December 17, 1796

The West

I find they have subscribed a very large sum of money in England for exploring the country from the Mississippi to California. They pretend it is only to promote knowledge. I am afraid they have thoughts of colonizing into that quarter. Some of us have been talking here in a feeble way of making the attempt to search that country. But I doubt whether we have enough of that kind of spirit to raise the money. How would you like to lead such a party? Tho I am afraid our prospect is not worth asking the question.

To George Rogers Clark, Annapolis, December 4, 1783

The Constitution

There is a general disposition through the states to adopt what they shall propose, and we may be assured their propositions will be wise, as a more able assembly never sat in America. Happy for us, that when we find our constitutions defective & insufficient to secure the happiness of our people, we can assemble with all the coolness of philosophers & set it to rights, while every other nation on earth must have recourse to arms to amend or to restore their constitutions.

To C.W.F. Dumas, Paris, September 10, 1787

The constitution, to which we are all attached, was meant to be republican, and we believe to be republican according to every candid interpretation. Yet we have seen it so interpreted and administered, as to be truly what the French have called, a monarchie

masque.* Yet so long has the vessel run on in this
way and been trimmed to it, that to put her on her
republican tack as will require all the skill, the firmness & the zeal of her ablest & best friends.

*a masked monarchy

To Robert R. Livingston, Washington, December 14, 1800

I join cordially in admiring and revering the Constitution of the United States, the result of the collected
wisdom of our country. That wisdom has committed
to us the important task of proving by example that a
government, if organized in all its parts on the Representative principle unadulterated by the infusion
of spurious elements, if founded, not in the fears &
follies of man, but on his reason, on his sense of
right, on the predominance of the social over his dis-
social passions, may be so free as to restrain him in
no moral right, and so firm as to protect him from
every moral wrong.

To Amos Marsh, Washington, November 20, 1801

[On releasing printers imprisoned under the Sedition Law of 1798] I have been actuated by a zealous
devotion to that instrument. It is the ligament which
binds us into one nation.

First Annual Message to Congress, December 8, 1801

When our present government was in the mew, passing from Confederation to Union, how bitter was the
schism between the Feds & Antis. Here you & I were
together again. For altho, for a moment separated by

the Atlantic from the scene of action, I favored the
opinion that 9 states should confirm the constitution
in order to secure it, & the others hold off until certain amendments, deemed favorable to freedom
should be made, I rallied in the first instant to the
wiser proposition of Massachusetts, that all should
confirm, & then all instruct their delegates to urge
those amendments. The amendments were made,
and all were reconciled to the government.

To John Adams, Monticello, June 27, 1813

A constitution has been acquired which, tho neither
of us think perfect, yet both consider as competent
to render our fellow-citizens the happiest and the
securest on whom the sun has ever shone.

To John Adams, Monticello, October 28, 1813

The radical idea of the character of the constitution
of our government, which I have adopted as a key in
cases of doubtful construction is that the whole field
of government is divided into two departments, Domestic and Foreign, (the states in their mutual relations being of the latter) that the former department
is reserved exclusively to the respective states within
their own limits, and the latter assigned to a separate set of functionaries, constituting what may be
called the Foreign branch, which, instead of a federal
basis, is established as a distinct government quoad
hoc,* acting as the domestic branch does on the citizens directly and coercively. That these departments
have distinct Directories, coordinate, and equally

independent and supreme, each within its own sphere of action. Whenever a doubt arises to which of these branches a power belongs, I try it by this test. I recollect no cases where a question simply between citizens of the same state has been transferred to the foreign department, except that of inhibiting tenders but of metallic money, and ex post facto** legislation. The causes of these singularities are well remembered.

*so far as

**having retroactive effect

To Edward Livingston, Monticello, April 4, 1824

With respect to our state and federal governments, I do not think their relations correctly understood by foreigners. They generally suppose the former subordinate to the latter. But this is not the case. They are co-ordinate departments of one simple, and integral whole. To the State governments are reserved all legislation and administration in affairs which concern their own citizens only, and to the federal government is given whatever concerns foreigners, or the citizens of other states; these functions alone being made federal. The one is the domestic, the other the foreign branch of the same government; neither having control over the other, but within its own department. There are one or two exceptions only to this partition of power. But, you may ask, if the two departments should claim each the same subject of power, where is the common umpire to decide ultimately between them? In cases of little importance or urgency, the prudence of both parties will keep them aloof from the questionable ground: but if it can neither be avoided nor compromised, a Convention of the states must be called, to ascribe the doubtful power to that department which they may think best. You will perceive by these details, that we have not yet so far perfected our constitutions as to venture to make them unchangeable. But still, in their present state, we consider them not otherwise changeable than by the authority of the people, on a special election of representatives for that purpose expressly: they are until then the lex legum.*

*the law of laws

To John Cartwright, Monticello, June 5, 1824

Amendments to the Constitution

I am glad to hear that our new constitution is pretty sure of being accepted by states enough to secure the good it contains, & to meet such opposition in some others as to give us hopes it will be accommodated to them by the amendment of its most glaring faults, particularly the want of a declaration of rights.

To John Rutledge, Jr., Paris, February, 2, 1788

We must be contented with the ground which this constitution will gain for us, and hope that a favorable moment will come for correcting what is amiss in it.

To the Comte de Moustier, Paris, May 17, 1788

Implied Powers

[Satirically speaking] We are here engaged in improving our constitution by construction, so as to make it what the majority thinks it should have been.

To Robert R. Livingston, Philadelphia, April 30, 1800

When an instrument admits two constructions, the one safe, the other dangerous, the one precise, the other indefinite, I prefer that which is safe & precise. I had rather ask an enlargement of power from the nation, where it is found necessary, than to assume it by a construction which would make our powers boundless.

To Wilson Cary Nicholas, Monticello, September 7, 1803

I hope our courts will never countenance the sweeping pretensions which have been set up under the words "general defense and public welfare." These words only express the motives which induced the Convention to give to the ordinary legislature certain specified powers which they enumerate, and which they thought might be trusted to the ordinary legislature, and not to give them the unspecified also; or why any specification? They could not be so awkward in language as to mean, as we say, "all and some." And should this construction prevail, all limits to the federal government are done away. This opinion, formed on the first rise of the question, I have never seen reason to change, whether

in or out of power; but on the contrary find it
strengthened and confirmed by five & twenty years
of additional reflection and experience: and any
countenance given to it by any regular organ of the
government, I should consider more ominous than
any thing which has yet occurred.

To Spencer Roane, Monticello, October 12, 1815

Infractions of the Constitution

Infractions of it may sometimes be committed from
inadvertence, sometimes from the panic or passions
of a moment. To correct these with good faith as
soon as discovered will be an assurance to the states
that, far from meaning to impair that sacred charter
of its authorities, the General government views it
as the principle of its own life.

First Annual Message to Congress, December 8, 1801

The utility of the thing has sanctioned the infraction. But if on that infraction we build a 2d, on that
2d a 3d, &c., any one of the powers in the constitution may be made to comprehend every power of
government.

To Albert Gallatin, Washington, October 13, 1802

Original Intent of the Founders

The constitution on which our Union rests, shall be
administered by me according to the safe and honest
meaning contemplated by the plain understanding of
the people of the United States, at the time of its
adoption: a meaning to be found in the explanations

of those who advocated, not of those who opposed it, and who opposed it merely lest the constructions should be applied which they denounced as possible. These explanations are preserved in the publications of the time, and are too recent in the memories of most men to admit of question.

To Messrs. Eddy, Russel, Thurber, Wheaton, and Smyth, Washington, March 27, 1801

Some men look at Constitutions with sanctimonious reverence; & deem them, like the ark of the covenant, too sacred to be touched. They ascribe to the men of the preceding age a wisdom more than human, and suppose what they did to be beyond amendment. I knew that age well: I belonged to it, and labored with it. It deserved well of its country. It was very like the present, but without the experience of the present: and 40 years of experience in government is worth a century of book-reading: and this they would say themselves, were they to rise from the dead. I am certainly not an advocate for frequent & untried changes in laws and constitutions. I think moderate imperfections had better be borne with; because when once known, we accommodate ourselves to them, and find practical means of correcting their ill effects. But I know also that laws and institutions must go hand in hand with the progress of the human mind. As that becomes more developed, more enlightened, as new discoveries are made, new truths disclosed, and manners and opinions change with the change of circumstances, institutions must advance also, and keep pace with the times. We might as well require a man to wear still the coat which fitted him when a boy, as civilized society to remain ever under the regimen of their barbarous ancestors.

To Samuel Kercheval, Monticello, July 12, 1816

It may be impracticable to lay down any general formula of words which shall decide at once, and with precision in every case, this limit of jurisdiction. But there are two Canons which will guide us safely in most of the cases. 1. The capital and leading object of the Constitution was to leave with the States all authorities which respected their own citizens only, and to transfer to the U.S. those which respected citizens of foreign or other states: to make us several as to ourselves, but one as to all others. In the latter case then constructions should lean to the general jurisdiction, if the words will bear it; and in favor of the states in the former, if possible to be so construed. And indeed, between citizen and citizen of the same state, and under their own laws, I know but a single case in which a jurisdiction is given to the General Government. That is, where any thing but gold or silver is made a lawful tender, or the obligation of contracts is any otherwise impaired. The separate legislatures had so often abused that power, that the citizens themselves chose to trust it to the general, rather than to their own special authorities. 2. On every question of construction, carry ourselves back to the time when the constitution was adopted, recollect the spirit manifested in the debates, & instead of trying what meaning may be squeezed out of the text, or invented against it, conform to the probable one in which it was passed.

   . . . I ask for no straining of words against the General Government, nor yet against the States. I believe the States can best govern our home concerns, and the general government our foreign ones. I wish, therefore, to see maintained that wholesome distribution of powers established by the constitution for the limitation of both; and never to see all offices transferred to Washington, where, further withdrawn from the eyes of the people they may more secretly be bought and sold as at market.

   To William Johnson, Monticello, June 12, 1823

Written Constitutions

It is still certain that tho' written constitutions may be violated in moments of passion or delusion, yet they furnish a text to which those who are watchful may again rally & recall the people; they fix too for the people the principles of their political creed.

   To Joseph Priestley, Washington, June 19, 1802

Our peculiar security is in possession of a written constitution. Let us not make it a blank paper by construction.

   To Wilson Cary Nicholas, Monticello, September 7, 1803

Death

When you and I look back on the country over which we have passed, what a field of slaughter does it exhibit! Where are all the friends who entered it with us, under all the inspiring energies of health and hope? As if pursued by the havoc of war, they are strewed by the way, some earlier, some later, and scarce a few stragglers remain to count the numbers fallen, and to mark yet, by their own fall, the last footsteps of their party. Is it a desirable thing to bear up thro' the heat of the action, to witness the death of all our companions, and merely be the last victim? I doubt it. We have however the traveller's consolation. Every step shortens the distance we have to go; the end of our journey is in sight, the bed wherein we are to rest, and to rise in the midst of the friends we have lost. "We sorrow not then at others who have no hope"; but look forward to the day which "joins us to the great majority." But whatever is to be our destiny, wisdom, as well as duty, dictates that we should acquiesce in the will of him whose it is to give and to take away, and be contented in the enjoyment of those who are still permitted to be with us. Of those connected by blood the number does not depend on us. But friends we have, if we have merited them. Those of our earliest years stand nearest in our affections, but in this too you and I have been unlucky. Our college friends (and they are the dearest) how few have stood with us.

To John Page, Washington, June 25, 1804

There is a fullness of time when men should go, & not occupy too long the ground to which others have a right to advance.

To Benjamin Rush, Monticello, August 17, 1811

Time is drawing her curtain on me.

To James Maury, Monticello, June 15, 1815

I shall pass willingly to that eternal sleep which, whether with, or without, dreams, awaits us hereafter.

To William Short, Monticello, May 5, 1816

There is a ripeness of time for death, regarding others as well as ourselves, when it is reasonable we should drop off, and make room for another growth. When we have lived our generation out, we should not wish to encroach on another.

To John Adams, Monticello, August 1, 1816

[Responding to Abigail Adams's wish to visit Jefferson at Monticello, if only she were twenty years younger.] But those 20 years, alas! where are they? With those beyond the flood. Our next meeting must then be in the country to which they have flown, a country, for us, not now very distant. For this journey we shall need neither gold nor silver in our purse, nor scrip, nor coats, nor staves.* Nor is the provision for it more easy than the preparation has been kind. Nothing proves more than this that the being who presides over the world is essentially benevolent, stealing from us, one by one, the faculties of enjoyment, searing our sensibilities, leading us, like the horse in his mill, round and round the same beaten circle. . . .

Until satiated and fatigued with this leaden iteration, we ask our own Congé.** I heard once a very old friend, who had troubled himself with neither poets nor philosophers, say the same thing in plain prose, that he was tired of pulling off his shoes & stockings at night, and putting them on again in the morning. The wish to stay here is thus gradually extinguished: but not so easily that of returning once in a while to see how things have gone on. Perhaps however one of the elements of future felicity is to be a constant and unimpassioned view of what is passing here. If so, this may well supply the wish of occasional visits.

*walking sticks
**discharge; leave; furlough

To Abigail Adams, Monticello, January 11, 1817

We have so lived as to fear neither horn of the dilemma. We have, willingly, done injury to no man; and have done for our country the good which has fallen in our way, so far as commensurate with the faculties given us. That we have not done more than we could cannot be imputed to us as a crime before any tribunal. I look therefore to that crisis, as

I am sure you also do, as one "qui summum nec metuit diem nec optat."* In the mean time be our last
as cordial as were our first affections.

*who neither fears the final day nor hopes for it

To John Adams, Monticello, March 14, 1820

Mine is the next turn, and I shall meet it with good
will, for after one's friends are all gone before them,
and our faculties leaving us, too, one by one, why
wish to linger in mere vegetation—as a solitary
trunk in a desolate field, from which all its former
companions have disappeared?

To Maria Cosway, Monticello, December 27, 1820

Your age of 84 and mine of 81 years ensure us a
speedy meeting. We may then communicate at
leisure, and more fully, on the good and evil which,
in the course of our long lives, we have both witnessed.

To John Cartwright, Monticello, June 5, 1824

Death of Daughter Polly

Others may lose of their abundance, but I, of my
want, have lost even the half of all I had. My evening prospects now hang on the slender thread of a
single life [his remaining daughter, Patsy].

To John Page, Washington, June 25, 1804

Dreams, Imagination, and Memories

Dreams

Do we dream more in age than in infancy? I suspect not. Dreams seem to be the consequence of some embarrassment in the animal system. A supper, or the undigested dregs of a dinner interrupt our sleep with dreams. But when all the functions of life are perfectly performed, sound sleep seems to be the consequence in every age.

To Benjamin Rush, Monticello, September 12, 1799

My theory has always been that if we are to dream, the flatteries of hope are as cheap, and pleasanter than the gloom of despair.

To François de Marbois, Monticello, June 14, 1817

Mine, after all, may be an Utopian dream; but being innocent, I have thought I might indulge in it till I go to the land of dreams, and sleep there with the dreamers of all past and future times.

To José Correa da Serra, Poplar Forest, November 25, 1817

The Future

I like the dreams of the future better than the history of the past. So good night! I will dream on.

To John Adams, Monticello, August 1, 1816

Hope

Hope is sweeter than despair.

To Maria Cosway, Paris, October 12, 1786

I had rather be deceived, than live without hope. It is so sweet! It makes us ride so smoothly over the roughnesses of life. When clambering a mountain, we always hope the hill we are on is the last. But it is the next, and the next, and still the next.

To Maria Cosway, Paris, December 24, 1786

I love to believe whatever I ardently wish.

To Alexander Donald, Monticello, May 30, 1795

Hope is so much more charming than disappointment and forebodings.

To Catherine Church, no date [1798]

Imagination

I am never happier than when I commit myself into dialogue with you, though it be but in imagination.

To Maria Cosway, Paris, November 29, 1786

Give my love to Mrs. Church & Mrs. Cosway. Tell them they will travel with me up the Rhine, one on each hand, & for this I shall be indebted, not to any goodness of theirs, but to my own imagination.

To John Trumbull, Amsterdam, March 27, 1788

We talk of you, we think of you, and try to enjoy your company by the force of imagination: and were the force of that sufficient, you would be with me every day.

To Angelica Schuyler Church, Paris, July 27, 1788

I remember that when under the hands of your Coëffeuse,* you used to amuse yourself with your pencil. Take then, some of these days, when fancy bites and the Coëffeuse is busy, a little visiting card, and crayon on it something for me. What shall it be? Cupid leading the lion by a thread? or Minerva clipping his wings? Or shall it be political? The father, for instance, giving the bunch of rods to his children to break, or Jupiter sending to the frogs a kite instead of the log for their king? Or shall it be something better than all this, a sketch of your own fancy? So that I have something from your hand, it will satisfy me; and it will be the better if of your own imagination. I will put a "Maria Cosway delint." at bottom, and stamp it on my visiting cards, that our names may be together if our persons cannot.

*hairdresser

To Maria Cosway, Paris, July 27, 1788

Memory (Good Thoughts)
My principal happiness is now in the retrospect of life.

To John Page, Paris, August 20, 1785

Heaven has submitted our being to some unkind laws. When those charming moments were present which I passed with you, they were clouded with the prospect that I was soon to lose you: and now, when I pass the same moments in review, I recollect nothing but the agreeable passages, and they fill me with regret. Thus, present joys are dumped by a consciousness that they are passing from us; and past ones are only the subjects of sorrow and regret.

To Maria Cosway, Paris, November 29, 1786

I remember old things better than new.

To Dabney Carr, Monticello, January 19, 1816

Reminiscing

The happy hours and days I have passed in your company are recollected with infinite sensibility. To talk them once again, would be to renew them.

To Elizabeth Blair Thompson, Paris, January 19, 1787

Duty, Honor, and Citizenship

Duty

I thought myself conscientiously called from those studies which were my delight by the political crisis of my country & by those events quorum pars magna fuisti.* In storms like those all hands must be aloft. But calm is now restored, & I leave the bark with joy to those who love the sea. I am but a landsman, forced from my element by accident, regaining it with transport, and wishing to recollect nothing of what I have seen, but my friendships.

*in which I was a major participant

To Horatio Gates, Monticello, February 3, 1794

It is to the partial & indulgent views of yourself and others of my fellow-citizens that I am indebted for such acknowledgements as you express, and not to any real service which would not have been rendered by others, had I not been employed. In taking my tour of duty, I have only done my duty; & acquired no merit.

To Ferdinando Fairfax, Monticello, April 25, 1794

There is a debt of service due from every man to his country, proportioned to the bounties which nature & fortune have measured to him.

To Edward Rutledge, Monticello, December 27, 1796

I never was more home-sick, or heart-sick. The life of this place is peculiarly hateful to me, and nothing but a sense of duty & respect to the public could keep me here a moment.

To John Wayles Eppes, Philadelphia, May 6, 1798

Some men are born for the public. Nature, by fitting them for the service of the human race on a broad scale, has stamped them with the evidences of her destination & their duty.

To James Monroe, Washington, January 13, 1803

I have been connected, as many fellow laborers were, with the great events which happened to mark the epoch of our lives. But these belong to no one in particular, all of us did our parts, & no one can claim the transactions to himself.

To Skelton Jones, Monticello,
July 28, 1809

The first of all our consolations is that of having faithfully fulfilled our duties; the next, the approbation & good will of those who have witnessed it.

To James Fishback, Monticello,
September 27, 1809

We have been thrown into times of a peculiar character, and to work our way through them has required services & sacrifices from our countrymen generally, and, to their great honor, these have been generally exhibited, by every one in his sphere, & according to the opportunities afforded. With them I have been a fellow laborer, endeavoring to do faithfully the part allotted to me, as they did theirs; & it is a subject of mutual congratulation that, in a state of things, such as the world had never before seen, we have gotten on so far well: and my confidence in our present high functionaries, as well as in my countrymen generally leaves me without much fear for the future.

To James Fishback, Monticello,
September 27, 1809

Honor

I know his* justice and honor so well that whatever he has demanded is right, & I would wish it to be paid of the first money possible.

*speaking of Doctor Walker

To Nicholas Lewis, Paris, July 11, 1788

Honor is a plant of such slow growth that where once it has been killed to the root new seeds must be sown & time allowed for their development. They will thrive too the worse as their bed is tainted.

To Thomas Pinckney, Philadelphia, May 29, 1797
[line crossed out by Jefferson]

Naturalization

I cannot omit recommending a revisal of the laws on the subject of naturalization. . . . Shall we refuse to the unhappy fugitives from distress, that hospitality which the savages of the wilderness extended to our fathers arriving in this land? Shall oppressed humanity find no asylum on this globe?

First Annual Message to Congress, December 8, 1801

Patriotism

However separated from my own country by space, all my affections and wishes are centered there.

To Henry Skipwith, Paris, May 6, 1786

I love my own country too much to stay from it long.

To Elizabeth Blair Thompson, Paris, January 19, 1787

That my country should be served is the first wish of my heart.

To the Mayor, Recorder, and Aldermen of Norfolk,
November 25, 1789

The man who loves his country on its own account, and not merely for its trappings of interest or power, can never be divorced from it; can never refuse to come forward when he finds that she is engaged in dangers which he has the means of warding off.

To Elbridge Gerry, Philadelphia, June 21, 1797

The first object of my heart is my own country. In that is embarked my family, my fortune, & my own existence. I have not one farthing of interest, nor one fibre of attachment out of it, nor a single motive of preference of any one nation to another, but in proportion as they are more or less friendly to us.

To Elbridge Gerry, Philadelphia, January 26, 1799

My affections were first for my own country, and then generally for all mankind.

To Thomas Law, Monticello, January 15, 1811

Promises

My word however being engaged with you it shall be religiously fulfilled.

To Alexander McCaul, Paris, July 12, 1788

Public Approbation

Amidst the direct falsehoods, the misrepresentations of truth, the calumnies & the insults resorted to by a faction to mislead the public mind, & to overwhelm those entrusted with its interests, our support is to be found in the approving voice of our conscience and country, in the testimony of our fellow citizens that their confidence is not shaken by these artifices. When to the plaudits of the honest multitude, the sober approbation of the sage in his closet is added, it becomes a gratification of an higher order. It is the sanction of wisdom superadded to the voice of affection.

To John Tyler, Washington, June 28, 1804

This approbation of my fellow citizens is the richest reward I can receive.

To Richard M. Johnson, Washington, March 10, 1808

The approbation of my political conduct by my republican countrymen generally, is a pillow of sweet repose to me, undisturbed by the noise of the enemies to our form of government.

To William Lambert, Monticello, July 16, 1810

If I have left in the breasts of my fellow citizens a sentiment of satisfaction with my conduct in the transaction of their business, it will soften the pillow of my repose thro' the residue of life.

To John B. Colvin, Monticello, September 20, 1810

I have ever found, in my progress thro' life, that, acting for the public, if we do always what is right, the approbation denied in the beginning will surely follow us in the end. It is from posterity we are to expect remuneration for the sacrifices we are making for their service, of time, quiet, and good will.

To Joseph C. Cabell, Monticello, January 11, 1825

Public Service

I may think public service & private misery inseparably linked together.

To James Monroe, Monticello, May 20, 1782

Honesty, knowledge & industry are the qualities which will lead you to the highest employments of your country, & to its highest esteem, and with these to that satisfaction which renders life pleasant, & death secure.

To Thomas Mann Randolph, Jr., Paris, November 25, 1785

To the sacrifice of time, labor, fortune, a public servant must count upon adding that of peace of mind and even reputation.

To James Currie, Paris, January 28, 1786

Laid up in port, for life, as I thought myself at one time, I am thrown out to sea, and an unknown one to me. By so slender a thread do all our plans of life hang!

To Eliza House Trist, Paris, December 15, 1786

A thorough disgust at these [party squabbles and reproaches] had withdrawn me from public life under an absolute determination to avoid whatever could disturb the tranquility of my mind. I have been recalled however by the only voice which I had not resolution to disregard. Whether their will or my own will first carry me back to the calm from which I have been extracted, is not yet very certain. A mutual consent is perhaps the most probable.

To Angelica Schuyler Church, Philadelphia, May 24, 1797

I have seen enough of political honors to know that they are but splendid torments: and however one might be disposed to render services on which any of their fellow citizens should set a value; yet when as many would deprecate them as a public calamity, one may well entertain a modest doubt of their real importance, and feel the impulse of duty to be very weak. The real difficulty is that being once delivered into the hands of others, whose feelings are friendly to the individual and warm to the public cause, how to withdraw from them without having a dissatisfaction in their mind and an impression of pusillanimity with the public.

To Martha Jefferson Randolph, Philadelphia, June 8, 1797

In the stormy ocean of public life the billows are more furious, the blasts more deadly, than those which assail the bark moored in a retired port, the world judges differently, and misjudges as is frequent.

Carlo Bellini, Monticello, April 24, 1799

If the good withhold their testimony, we shall be at the mercy of the bad.

To Benjamin Smith Barton, Washington,
February 14, 1801

It will be for ever seen that of bodies of men even elected by the people, there will always be a greater proportion aristocratic than among their constituents.

To Benjamin Hawkins, Washington, February 18, 1803

I will not say that public life is the line for making a fortune. But it furnishes a decent and honorable support, and places one's children on good grounds for public favor. The family of a beloved father will stand with the public on the most favorable ground of competition. Had Genl. Washington left children, what would have been denied to them?

To William Wirt, Washington, January 10, 1808

Nature intended me for the tranquil pursuits of science, by rendering them my supreme delight. But the enormities of the times in which I have lived, have forced me to take a part in resisting them, and to commit myself on the boisterous ocean of political passions.

To P. S. Dupont de Nemours, Washington, March 2, 1809

Reputation

I had rather be ruined in my fortune than in their [Congress's] esteem.

To James Monroe, Paris, June 17, 1785

A determination never to do what is wrong, prudence, and good humor, will go far towards securing to you the estimation of the world.

To Thomas Jefferson Randolph, Washington,
November 24, 1808

The good opinion of mankind, like the lever of Archimedes, with the given fulcrum, moves the world.

To José Correa da Serra, Monticello,
December 27, 1814

Responsibility
Responsibility weighs with its heaviest force on a single head.

To Samuel Kercheval, Monticello, July 12, 1816

Sacrifice
To save permanent rights, temporary sacrifices were necessary.

To William Eustis, Washington, January 14, 1809

Statesmanship
The man who is dishonest as a statesman would be a dishonest man in any station.

To George Logan, Monticello, November 12, 1816

Statues
A statue is not made, like a mountain, to be seen at a great distance. To perceive those minuter circumstances which constitute its beauty you must be near

it, and, in that case, it should be so little above the size of the life, as to appear actually of that size from your point of view.

To the Virginia delegates in Congress, Paris, July 12, 1785

The Economy

There is no man who has not some vice or folly the atoning of which would not pay his taxes.

To James Madison, Annapolis, May 8, 1784

It is a truth that if every nation will employ itself in what it is fittest to produce, a greater quantity will be raised of the things contributing to human happiness, than if every nation attempts to raise everything it wants within itself.

To Charles Philbert Lasteryrie-du Saillant, Washington, July 15, 1808

Bargains

You can combine quality & price, as, like the rest of the world, I like to have good things at a small price.

To John Trumbull, Paris, November 13, 1787

Commerce

It should be our endeavor to cultivate the peace and friendship of every nation. . . . Our interest will be to throw open the doors of commerce, and to knock off all its shackles, giving perfect freedom to all persons for the vent of whatever they may choose to bring into our ports, and asking the same in theirs.

Notes on the State of Virginia, 1782

All the world would gain by setting commerce at perfect liberty.

To John Adams, Paris, July 31, 1785

Nature too has conveniently assorted our wants & our superfluities to each other. Each nation has exactly to spare the articles which the other wants. . . . The governments have nothing to do but not to hinder their merchants from making the exchange.

To the Comte de Montmorin, Paris, July 23, 1787

I am sensible of the great interest which your state justly feels in the prosperity of commerce. It is of vital interest also to the states more agricultural, whose produce, without commerce, could not be exchanged. As the handmaid of agriculture therefore, Commerce will be cherished by me both from principle & duty.

To the General Assembly of Rhode Island, Washington, May 26, 1801

I trust the good sense of our country will see that its greatest prosperity depends on a due balance between agriculture, manufactures & commerce.

To Thomas Leiper, Washington, January 21, 1809

An equilibrium of agriculture, manufactures & commerce is certainly become essential to our independence. Manufactures sufficient for our own consumption of what we raise the raw material (and no more). Commerce sufficient to carry the surplus produce of agriculture, beyond our own consumption, to a market for exchanging it for articles we cannot raise (and no more). These are the true limits of manufactures & commerce. To go beyond them is to increase our dependence on foreign nations, and our liability to war. These three important branches of human industry will then grow together, & be really handmaids to each other.

To Governor James Jay, Monticello, April 7, 1809

The selfish spirit of commerce . . . knows no country, and feels no passion or principle but that of gain.

To Larkin Smith, Monticello, April 15, 1809

Money, & not morality, is the principle of commerce & commercial nations.

To Governor John Langdon, Monticello, March 5, 1810

Employment
Never fear the want of business. A man who qualifies himself well for his calling never fails of employment in it.

To Peter Carr, Philadelphia, June 22, 1792

Internal Improvements
The fondest wish of my heart ever was that the surplus portion of these taxes, destined for the payment

of that debt, should, when that object was accomplished, be continued, by annual or biennial re-enactments, and applied, in time of peace, to the improvement of our country by canals, roads and useful institutions, literary or others; and, in time of war, to the maintenance of the war.

To John Wayles Eppes, Poplar Forest, September 11, 1813

Manufactures

In general it is impossible that manufactures should succeed in America from the high price of labor. This is occasioned by the great demand of labor for agriculture.

To Thomas Digges, Paris, June 19, 1788

My idea is that we should encourage home manufactures to the extent of our own consumption of everything of which we raise the raw material.

To David Humphreys, Washington, January 20, 1809

I have not formerly been an advocate for great manufactories. I doubted whether our labor, employed in agriculture, and aided by the spontaneous energies of the earth, would not procure us more than we could make ourselves, of other necessaries. But other considerations entering into the question, have settled my doubts.

To John Melish, Monticello, January 13, 1813

We must place the manufacturer by the side of the agriculturist. . . . Experience has taught me that manufactures are now as necessary to our independence as to our comfort.

To Benjamin Austin, Monticello, January 9, 1816

Money

The want of money cramps every effort.

To George Washington, Richmond, June 11, 1780

Pillars of American Prosperity

Agriculture, manufactures, commerce, and navigation, the four pillars of our prosperity, are the most thriving when left most free to Individual enterprise.

First Annual Message to Congress, December 8, 1801

The Private Market

Having always observed that public works are much less advantageously managed than the same are by private hands, I have thought it better for the public to go to market for whatever it wants which is to be found there; for there competition brings it down to the minimum of value. I have no doubt we can buy brass cannon at market cheaper than we could make iron ones.

To William W. Bibb, Monticello, July 28, 1808

Public Credit

Tho' much an enemy to the system of borrowing, yet I feel strongly the necessity of preserving the power to borrow.

To the Commissioners of the Treasury, Paris,
February 7, 1788

It was easier to discover, than to remove, the causes which obstructed the progress of the loan.

To John Jay, Amsterdam, March 16, 1788

Tho' I am an enemy to the using our credit but under absolute necessity, yet the possessing a good credit I consider as indispensable.

To James Madison, Paris, May 3, 1788

The existence of a nation, having no credit, is always precarious.

To James Madison, Paris, May 3, 1788

Public Debt

I am for a government rigorously frugal & simple, applying all the possible savings of the public revenue to the discharge of the national debt.

To Elbridge Gerry, Philadelphia, January 26, 1799

I, however, place economy among the first and most important of republican virtues, and public debt as the greatest of the dangers to be feared.

To William Plumer, Monticello, July 21, 1816

The multiplication of public offices, increase of expense beyond income, growth and entailment of a public debt, are indications soliciting the employment of the pruning-knife.

To Spencer Roane, Monticello, March 9, 1821

Education and Knowledge

Academic Freedom

[Universities are] based on the illimitable freedom of the human mind. For here we are not afraid to follow truth wherever it may lead, nor to tolerate any error so long as reason is left free to combat it.

To William Roscoe, Monticello, December 27, 1820

Commonplace Books

I had, at an early period of life, read a good deal . . . & commonplaced what I read. This common-place has been my pillar.

To George Wythe, Philadelphia, February 28, 1800

He [Montesquieu] had been a great reader, and had commonplaced everything he read.

To William Duane, Monticello, August 12, 1810

Education

Experience hath shown, that even under the best forms [of government], those entrusted with power have, in time, and by slow operations, perverted it into tyranny; and it is believed that the most effectual means of preventing this would be, to illuminate, as far as practicable, the minds of the people at large, and more especially to give them knowledge of those facts, which history exhibiteth, that possessed thereby of the experience of other ages and countries, they may be enabled to know ambition under all its shapes, and prompt them to exert their natural powers to defeat its purposes.

A Bill for the More General Diffusion of Knowledge,
June 18, 1779

The bulk of mankind are school boys thro' life.

Notes on Coinage, Annapolis, March–May 1784

By far the most important bill in our whole code is that for the diffusion of knowledge among the people. No other sure foundation can be devised for the preservation of freedom, and happiness.

To George Wythe, Paris, August 13, 1786

Preach, my dear Sir, a crusade against ignorance; establish & improve the law for educating the common people. Let our countrymen know that the people alone can protect us against these evils, and that the tax which will be paid for this purpose is not more than the thousandth part of what will be paid to kings, priests, & nobles who will rise up among us if we leave the people in ignorance.

To George Wythe, Paris, August 13, 1786

I hope the education of the common people will be attended to; convinced that on their good sense we may rely with the most security for the preservation of a due degree of liberty.

To James Madison, Paris, December 20, 1787

Whenever the people are well informed, they can be trusted with their own government; that whenever things get so far wrong as to attract their notice, they may be relied on to set them to rights.

To Richard Price, Paris, January 8, 1789

Where are you, my dear Maria? How do you do? How are you occupied? Write me a letter by the first post, and answer me all these questions. Tell me whether you see the sun rise every day? How many pages a-day you read in Don Quixot? How far you are advanced in him? Whether you repeat a grammar lesson every day? What else you read? How many hours a-day you sew? Whether you have an opportunity of continuing your music? Whether you know how to make a pudding yet, to cut out a beefsteak, to sow spinach? or to set a hen?

To Mary Jefferson, New York, April 11, 1790

I join you therefore in branding as cowardly the idea that the human mind is incapable of further advances.

To William Green Munford, June 18, 1799

The boys of the rising generation are to be the men of the next, and the sole guardians of the principles we deliver over to them.

To Samuel Knox, Monticello, February 12, 1810

A part of my occupation, & by no means the least pleasing, is the direction of the studies of such young men as ask it. They place themselves in the neighboring village, and have the use of my library & counsel, & make a part of my society. In advising the course of their reading, I endeavor to keep their attention fixed on the main objects of all science, the freedom & happiness of man.

To Tadeusz Kosciusko, Monticello, February 26, 1810

Our post-revolutionary youths are born under happier stars than you and I were. They acquire all learning in their mothers' womb, and bring it into the world ready-made. The information of books is no longer necessary; and all knowledge which is not innate, is in contempt, or neglected at least. Every folly must run its round, and so, I suppose, must that of self-learning, & self-sufficiency; of rejecting the knowledge, acquired in past ages, and starting on the new ground of intuition. When sobered by experience I hope our successors will turn their attention to the advantages of education. I mean of education on the broad scale.

To John Adams, Monticello, July 5, 1814

Enlighten the people generally, and tyranny and oppressions of body & mind will vanish like evil spirits at the dawn of day.

To P. S. Dupont de Nemours, Poplar Forest, April 24, 1816

A system of general instruction, which shall reach every description of our citizens, from the richest to the poorest, as it was the earliest so will it be the

latest of all the public concerns in which I shall permit myself to take an interest.

To Joseph C. Cabell, January 14, 1818

If the condition of man is to be progressively ame-
liorated, as we fondly hope & believe, education is
to be the chief instrument in effecting it.

To Marc Antoine Jullien, Monticello, July 23, 1818

As well might it be urged that the wild and unculti-
vated tree, hitherto yielding sour and bitter fruit
only, can never be made to yield better; yet we know
that the grafting art implants a new tree on the sav-
age stock, producing what is most estimable both in
kind and degree. Education, in like manner, en-
grafts a new man on the native stock, and improves
what in his nature was vicious and perverse into
qualities of virtue and social worth.

Report of the Commissioners for the University of Virginia,
August 4, 1818

I accordingly prepared three bills for the Revisal,
proposing three distinct grades of education, reach-
ing all classes: 1. Elementary schools for all children
generally, rich and poor. 2. Colleges for a middle degree of instruction, calculated for the common purposes of life, and such as would be desirable for all
who are in easy circumstances. And 3. An ultimate
grade for teaching the sciences generally and in
their highest degree.

Autobiography, February 7, 1821

Nobody can doubt my zeal for the general instruction of the people. Who first started that idea? I may surely say myself.

To James Breckenridge, Monticello, February 15, 1821

That every man shall be made virtuous, by any process whatever, is indeed no more to be expected, than that every tree shall be made to bear fruit, and every plant nourishment. The briar and bramble can never become the vine and olive; but their asperities may be softened by culture, and their properties improved to usefulness in the order and economy of the world.

To Cornelius Camden Blatchly, Monticello, October 21, 1822

The article of discipline is the most difficult in American education. Premature ideas of independence, too little repressed by parents, beget a spirit of insubordination, which is the great obstacle to science with us, and a principal cause of its decay since the revolution.

To Thomas Cooper, Monticello, November 2, 1822

The insubordination of our youth is now the greatest obstacle to their education.

To George Ticknor, Monticello, July 16, 1823

Ignorance

Ignorance is preferable to error; and he is less remote from the truth who believes nothing, than he who believes what is wrong.

Notes on the State of Virginia, 1782

Ignorance of the law is a plea in no country & in no case.

To David Ramsay, Paris, August 8, 1787

Ignorance & bigotry, like other insanities, are incapable of self-government.

To the Marquis de Lafayette, Monticello, May 14, 1817

When I meet with a proposition beyond finite comprehension, I abandon it as I do a weight which human strength cannot lift: and I think ignorance, in these cases, is truly the softest pillow on which I can lay my head.

To John Adams, Monticello, March 14, 1820

Knowledge

Knowledge indeed is a desirable, a lovely possession.

To Thomas Mann Randolph, Jr., Paris,
August 27, 1786

The republic of letters is unaffected by the wars of geographical divisions of the earth.

To Robert Patterson, Monticello,
September 11, 1811

Mathematics

Having to conduct my grandson through his course of Mathematics, I have resumed that study with great avidity. It was ever my favorite one. We have no theories there, no uncertainties remain on the mind; all is demonstration & satisfaction. I have forgotten

much, and recover it with more difficulty than when
in the vigor of my mind, I originally acquired it.

To Benjamin Rush, Poplar Forest, August 17, 1811

Opinion

Subject opinion to coercion: whom will you make
your inquisitor? Fallible men; men governed by bad
passions, by private as well as public reasons. And
why subject it to coercion? To produce uniformity.
But is uniformity of opinion desirable? No more
than of face and stature.

Notes on the State of Virginia, 1782

The same facts impress us differently. This is
enough to make me suspect an error in my process of
reasoning tho' I am not able to detect it.

To John Adams, Paris, July 11, 1786

When a man whose life has been marked by its candor, has given a latter opinion contrary to a former
one, it is probably the result of further inquiry, reflection & conviction.

To Peregrine Fitzhugh, Monticello, April 9, 1797

Even if we differ in principle more than I believe we
do, you & I know too well the texture of the human
mind, & the slipperiness of human reason, to consider differences of opinion otherwise than differences of form or feature. Integrity of views more
than their soundness, is the basis of esteem.

To Elbridge Gerry, Philadelphia, January 26, 1799

Every difference of opinion is not a difference of principle—error of opinion may be tolerated where reason is left free to combat it.

First Inaugural Address, March 4, 1801

In every country where man is free to think & to speak, differences of opinion will arise from difference of perception, & the imperfection of reason. But these differences, when permitted, as in this happy country, to purify themselves by free discussion, are but as passing clouds overspreading our land transiently, & leaving our horizon more bright & serene.

To Benjamin Waring, Washington, March 23, 1801

Opinion, & the just maintenance of it, shall never be a crime in my view; nor bring injury on the individual.

To Samuel Adams, Washington, March 29, 1801

With the same honest views, the most honest men often form different conclusions.

To Robert R. Livingston, Monticello, September 9, 1801

I see too many proofs of the imperfection of human reason to entertain wonder or intolerance at any difference of opinion on any subject; and acquiesce in that difference as easily as on a difference of feature or form. Experience having long taught me the reasonableness of mutual sacrifices of opinion among those who are to act together for any common object,

and the expediency of doing what good we can;
when we cannot do all we would wish.

To John Randolph, Washington, December 1, 1803

I tolerate with the utmost latitude the right of others to differ from me in opinion without imputing to them criminality.

To Abigail Adams, Monticello, September 11, 1804

I may sometimes differ in opinion from some of my friends, from those whose views are as pure & sound as my own. I censure none, but do homage to every one's right of opinion.

To William Duane, Monticello, March 28, 1811

Our opinions are not voluntary.

To Benjamin Rush, Monticello, March 6, 1813

Difference of opinion leads to inquiry, and inquiry to truth; and that, I am sure, is the ultimate and sincere object of us both. We both value too much the freedom of opinion sanctioned by our constitution, not to cherish its exercise even where in opposition to ourselves.

To P. H. Wendover, Monticello, March 13, 1815

Opinion is power.

To John Adams, Monticello, January 11, 1816

The human mind will some day get back to the freedom it enjoyed 2000 years ago. This country, which has given to the world the example of physical liberty, owes to it that of moral emancipation also. For, as yet, it is but nominal with us. The inquisition of public opinion overwhelms in practice the freedom asserted by the laws in theory.

To John Adams, Monticello, January 22, 1821

As the Creator has made no two faces alike, so no two minds, and probably no two creeds.

To Timothy Pickering, Monticello, February 27, 1821

These cares however are no longer mine. I resign myself cheerfully to the managers of the ship, and the more contentedly as I am near the end of my voyage. I have learned to be less confident in the conclusions of human reason, and give more credit to the honesty of contrary opinions.

To Edward Livingston, Monticello, April 4, 1824

That form [i.e., the Declaration of Independence] which we have substituted restores the free right to the unbounded exercise of reason and freedom of opinion.

To Roger C. Weightman, Monticello, June 24, 1826

Reason

Reason and persuasion are the only practicable instruments. To make way for these, free inquiry must be indulged; and how can we wish others to indulge it while we refuse it ourselves.

Notes on the State of Virginia, 1782

Your own reason is the only oracle given you by heaven, and you are answerable not for the rightness but uprightness of the decision.

To Peter Carr, Paris, August 10, 1787

Reason, not rashness, is the only means of bringing our fellow citizens to their true minds.

To Nicholas Lewis, Philadelphia, January 30, 1799

Truth & reason are eternal. They have prevailed. And they will eternally prevail, however, in times & places, they may be overborne for a while by violence military, civil, or ecclesiastical.

To Samuel Knox, Monticello, February 12, 1810

Every man's own reason must be his oracle.

To Benjamin Rush, Monticello, March 6, 1813

Man, once surrendering his reason, has no remaining guard against absurdities the most monstrous, and like a ship without rudder, is the sport of every wind. With such persons, gullibility, which they call faith, takes the helm from the hand of reason and the mind becomes a wreck.

To James Smith, Monticello, December 8, 1822

Theories

The moment a person forms a theory, his imagination sees in every object only the tracts which favor that theory.

To Charles Thomson, Paris, September 20, 1787

In my mind, theories are more easily demolished than rebuilt.

To the Rev. James Madison, Paris, July 19, 1788

[M. de Saussure] is certainly one of the best philosophers of the present age. Cautious in not letting his assent run before his evidence, he possesses the wisdom which so few possess of preferring ignorance to error. The contrary disposition in those who call themselves philosophers in this country classes them in fact with the writers of romance.

To John Rutledge, Jr., Paris, September 9, 1788

All theory must yield to experience.

To James Maury, Monticello, June 16, 1815

Experience & frequent disappointment have taught me not to be over-confident in theories or calculations, until actual trial of the whole combination has stamped it with approbation.

To George Fleming, Monticello, December 29, 1815

Understanding

The more a subject is understood, the more briefly it may be explained.

To Joseph Milligan, Monticello, April 6, 1816

Universities

A university should not be a house but a village.

To Littleton Waller Tazewell, Washington, January 5, 1805

The University of Virginia. Engraving by Benjamin Tanner, published on the 1827 Böye map of Virginia. *Courtesy Manuscripts Department, University of Virginia Library*

The University of Virginia. Engraving by Benjamin Tanner, published on the 1827 Böye map of Virginia. (Courtesy Manuscripts Department, University of Virginia Library.)

I look to it as a germ from which a great tree may spread itself.

To Charles Yancey, Monticello, January 6, 1816

Wisdom

Wisdom, I know, is social. She seeks her fellows. But Beauty is jealous, and illy bears the presence of a rival.

To Abigail Adams, Paris, September 25, 1785

Wisdom and virtue were not hereditary.

To William Johnson, Monticello, June 12, 1823

Family

A lively and lasting sense of filial duty is more effectively impressed on the mind of a son or daughter by reading King Lear, than by all the dry volumes of ethics, and divinity that ever were written.

To Robert Skipwith, Monticello, August 3, 1771

You are going to be happy, whether you have something to do or nothing. You have a wife who will make you happy in spite of your teeth, even were you disposed to run restive against your own felicity. You will be having children too. Every day which will be making you happier & happier every day. Your sun of joy is climbing towards its zenith, whilst mine is descending from it.

To William Stephens Smith, Paris, December 31, 1787

I sincerely take part with you in your domestic felicity. There is no other in this world worth living for. The loss of it alone can make us know its full worth.

To James Monroe, Paris, August 9, 1788

Dear Brother: The very short period of my life which I have passed unconnected with public business suffices to convince me it is the happiest of all situations, and that no society is so precious as that of one's own family.

To Randolph Jefferson, Paris, January 11, 1789

The happiest moments of my life have been the few which I have past at home in the bosom of my family.

> To Francis Willis, Jr., New York, April 18, 1790

I am now in a tranquil situation which is my delight, with all my family living with me, and forming a delicious society.

> To Angelica Schuyler Church, Monticello,
> September 8, 1795

When I look to the ineffable pleasures of my family society, I become more and more disgusted with the jealousies, the hatred, and the rancorous and malignant passions of this scene, and lament my having ever again been drawn into public view. Tranquility is not my object.

> To Martha Jefferson Randolph, Philadelphia,
> June 8, 1797

[On hearing about the engagement of his daughter Mary] This event in completing the circle of our family has composed for us such a group of good sense, good humor, liberality, and prudent care of our affairs, & that without a single member of a contrary character, as families are rarely blessed with. It promises us long years of domestic concord & love, the best ingredient in human happiness, and I deem the composition of my family the most precious of all the kindnesses of fortune.

> To Mary Jefferson, Philadelphia, June 14, 1797

Without an object here which is not alien to me, &
barren of every delight, I turn to your situation with
pleasure, in the midst of a good family which loves
you, & merits all your love. Go on, my dear, in culti-
vating the invaluable possession of their affections.
The circle of our nearest connections is the only one
in which a faithful and lasting affection can be
found, one which will adhere to us under all changes
& chances. It is therefore the only soil on which it is
worth while to bestow much culture. Of this truth
you will become more convinced every day you advance into life.

> To Mary Jefferson Eppes, Philadelphia,
> January 1, 1799

I know no happiness but when we are all together.

> To Mary Jefferson Eppes, Philadelphia,
> February 12, 1800

I have here company enough, part of which is very
friendly, part well enough disposed, part secretly
hostile, and a constant succession of strangers. But
this only serves to get rid of life, not to enjoy it; it is
in the love of one's family only that heartfelt happiness is known. I feel it when we are all together,
and, when alone, beyond what can be imagined.

> To Mary Jefferson Eppes, Washington, October 26, 1801

I am held by the cords of love to my family & country.

> To Alexander von Humboldt, Washington,
> March 6, 1809

The happiness of the domestic fireside is the first boon of heaven; and it is well it is so, since it is that which is the lot of the mass of mankind.

To John Armstrong, Monticello, February 8, 1813

Children

Three sons, & hopeful ones too, are a rich treasure.

To John Tyler, Washington, June 28, 1804

A Child's Illness

Doctors always flatter, and parents always fear. It remains to see which is right.

To Martha Jefferson Randolph, Philadelphia, April 14, 1793

I am sorry to hear of Jefferson's* indisposition, but glad you do not physic him. This leaves nature free and unembarrassed in her own tendencies to repair what is wrong. I hope to hear or find that he is recovered.

*Thomas Jefferson Randolph, Jefferson's grandson

To Martha Jefferson Randolph, Philadelphia, May 31, 1798

Fatherhood

To be a good husband and a good father at this moment you must be also a good citizen.

To Elbridge Gerry, Philadelphia, June 21, 1797

Grandfathers

I receive with real pleasure your congratulations on my advancement to the venerable corps of grandfa-

thers, and can assure you with truth that I expect
from it more felicity than any other advancement
ever gave me.

To Elizabeth Wayles Eppes, Philadelphia,
May 15, 1791

Grandson

We are all well here. Jefferson particularly so. He is
become the finest boy possible. Always in good humor, always amusing himself, and very orderly.

To Martha Jefferson Randolph,
January 25, 1796

Home

And our own dear Monticello, where has Nature
spread so rich a mantle under the eye? mountains,
forests, rocks, rivers. With what majesty do we
there ride above the storms! How sublime to look
down into the workhouse of nature, to see her
clouds, hail, snow, rain, thunder, all fabricated at
our feet! And the glorious Sun, when rising as if out
of a distant water, just gilding the tops of the mountains, and giving life to all nature!

To Maria Cosway, Paris, October 12, 1786

I cannot fix the epoch of my return, tho I always
flatter myself it is not very distant. My habits are
formed to those of my own country. I am past the
time of changing them & am therefore less happy
anywhere else than there.

To James Currie, Paris, August 4, 1787

I had rather be shut up in a very modest cottage, with my books, my family, and a few old friends, dining on simple bacon, and letting the world roll on as it liked, than to occupy the most splendid post which any human power can give.

To Alexander Donald, Paris, February 7, 1788

I had rather be sick in bed there [at home], than in health here.

To George Gilmer, Philadelphia, May 11, 1792

I, like other people, am so much the dupe of the fondness for the natle solum* as to believe seriously there is no quarter of the globe so desirable as America, no state in America so desirable as Virginia, no county in Virginia equal to Albemarle, and no spot in Albemarle to compare to Monticello.

*native soil

To Alexander Donald, Monticello, May 30, 1795

My farm, my family, my books & my building give me much more pleasure than any public office would, and especially one which would keep me constantly from them.

To the Comte de Volney, Monticello, January 8, 1797

I envy those who stay at home, enjoying the society of their friendly neighbors, blessed with their firesides, and employed in doing something every day which looks usefully to futurity.

To Martha Jefferson Randolph, Philadelphia,
December 27, 1797

Marriage

[A Prayer for the Newly Married] May your nights and days be many and full of joy! May their fruit be such as to make you feel the sweet union of parent and lover, but not so many as that you may feel their weight! May they be handsome and good as their mother, wise and honest as their father, but more milky!

To William Stephens Smith, Paris, July 9, 1786

Your new condition will call for abundance of little sacrifices. But they will be greatly overpaid by the measure of affection they secure to you. The happiness of your life now depends on the continuing to please a single person. To this all other objects must be secondary.

To Martha Jefferson Randolph, New York, April 4, 1790

Your two last letters are those which have given me the greatest pleasure of any I ever received from you. The one announced that you were become a notable housewife; the other, a mother. The last is undoubtedly the key-stone of the arch of matrimonial happiness, as the first is its daily aliment.

To Martha Jefferson Randolph, Philadelphia,
February 9, 1791

Harmony in the married state is the very first object to be aimed at. Nothing can preserve affections uninterrupted but a firm resolution never to differ in will, and a determination in each to consider the love of the other as of more value than any object whatever on which a wish has been fixed. How light in fact is the sacrifice of any other wish, when weighed against the affections of one with whom we are to pass our whole life. And though opposition in a single instance will hardly of itself produce alienation; yet every one has their pouch into which all these little oppositions are put: while that is filling, the alienation is insensibly going on, & when filled, it is complete. It would puzzle either to say why; because no one difference of opinion has been marked enough to produce a serious effect by itself. But he finds his affections wearied out by a constant stream of little checks & obstacles. Other sources of discontent, very common indeed, are the little cross purposes of husband & wife in common conversation, a disposition in either to criticize & question whatever the other says, a desire always to demonstrate & make him feel himself in the wrong, & especially in company. Nothing is so goading. Much better therefore, if our companion views a thing in a light different from what we do, to leave him in quiet possession of his view. What is the use of rectifying him if the thing be unimportant; & if important let it pass for the present, & wait a softer moment, and more conciliatory occasion of revising the subject together. It is wonderful how many persons are rendered unhappy by inattention to these little rules of prudence.

To Mary Jefferson Eppes, Philadelphia, January 7, 1798

Parenting

Is it [parental love] not the strongest affection known? Is it not greater than even that of self-preservation?

A Bill for Proportioning Crime and Punishment,
November 1778

The post which a parent may take most advantageous for his child is that of his bosom friend.

To John Banister, Sr., Paris, February 7, 1787

My expectations from you are high; yet not higher than you may attain. Industry and resolution are all that are wanting. No body in this world can make me so happy, or so miserable as you.

To Martha Jefferson, Aix en Provence, March 28, 1787

The object most interesting to me for the residue of my life, will be to see you both developing daily those principles of virtue and goodness which will make you valuable to others and happy in yourselves, and acquiring those talents and that degree of science which will guard you at all times against ennui, the most dangerous poison of life.

To Martha Jefferson, Canal of Languedoc, May 21, 1787

Nature knows no laws between parent and child, but the will of the parent.

To Thomas Mann Randolph, Monticello,
October 22, 1790

Reuniting

I received . . . [a letter] from Mr. Eppes announcing to me that my dear Polly will come to us the ensuing summer. Tho' I am distressed when I think of this voyage, yet I know it is necessary for her happiness. She is better with you, my dear Madam, than she

Portrait of Jefferson's daughter Martha by Thomas Sully. (Monticello/Thomas Jefferson Foundation, Inc.)

could be any where else in this world, except with
those whom nature has allied still more closely to
her. It would be unfortunate thro' life both to her
and us, were those affections to be loosened which
ought to bind us together, and which should be the
principal source of our future happiness. Yet this
would be too probably the effect of absence at her
age. This is the only circumstance which has induced me to press her joining us.

To Elizabeth Wayles Eppes, Paris, December 14, 1786

Sisterly Advice

I have received letters which inform me that our dear
Polly will certainly come to us this summer. By the
time I return it will be time to expect her. When she
arrives, she will become a precious charge on your
hands. The difference of your age, and your common
loss of a mother, will put that office on you. Teach her
above all things to be good: because without that we
can neither be valued by others, nor set any value on
ourselves. Teach her to be always true. No vice is so
mean as the want of truth, & at the same time so useless. Teach her never to be angry. Anger only serves to
torment ourselves, to divert others, and alienate their
esteem. And teach her industry & application to useful
pursuits. I will venture to assure you that if you inculcate this in her mind you will make her a happy being
in herself, a most inestimable friend to you, and precious to all the world. In teaching her these dispositions of mind, you will be more fixed in them yourself,
and render yourself dear to all your acquaintances.

Practice them then, my dear, without ceasing. If ever you find yourself in difficulty and doubt how to extricate yourself, do what is right, & you will find it the easiest way of getting out of the difficulty. Do it for the additional incitement of increasing the happiness of him who loves you infinitely.

To Martha Jefferson, Toulon, April 7, 1787

Food and Drink

In the pleasures of the table they [i.e., the French] are far before us, because with good taste they unite temperance. They do not terminate the most sociable meals by transforming themselves into brutes. I have never yet seen a man drunk in France, even among the lowest of the people.

To Charles Bellini, Paris, September 30, 1785

I have lived temperately, eating little animal food, & that, not as an aliment so much as a condiment for the vegetables, which constitute my principal diet. I double however the doctor's glass and a half of wine, and even treble it with a friend; but halve its effect by drinking the weak wine only. The ardent wines I cannot drink, nor do I use ardent spirits in any form. Malt liquors & cider are my table drinks, and my breakfast, like that also of my friend, is of tea & coffee. I have been blessed with organs of digestion which accept and concoct without ever murmuring whatever the palate chooses to consign to them, and I have not yet lost a tooth by age.

To Vine Utley, Monticello, March 21, 1819

We never repent of having eaten too little.

To Thomas Jefferson Smith, Monticello, February 21, 1825

Beer

I wish to see this beverage become common instead of the whiskey which kills one third of our citizens and ruins their families.

To Charles Yancey, Monticello, January 6, 1816

Figs

I ever wish to have opportunities of enjoying your society. Knowing your fondness for figs, I have daily wished you could have partaken of ours this year. I never saw so great a crop, & they are still abundant. Of three kinds which I brought from France, there is one, of which I have a single bush, superior to any fig I ever tasted any where.

To George Wythe, Monticello, October 23, 1794

Olives

The Olive is a tree the least known in America, & yet the most worthy of being known. Of all the gifts of heaven to man, it is next to the most precious, if it be not the most precious. Perhaps it may claim a preference even to bread; because there is such an infinitude of vegetables which it renders a proper & comfortable nourishment.

To William Drayton, Paris, July 30, 1787

Tea

Having occasion for about 20 lb. of good tea annually, I think it best to rely for the choice of it on the good faith of some dealer in that article, both as to quality & price, and on no one do I rely more willingly than on yourself. I usually send to Philadelphia for my groceries once a quarter, and will on those occasions ask of you a quarter's supply of tea. At present I will beg the favor of you to pack for me in a cannister 5 lb. of good tea. Young hyson we prefer both for flavor & strength, but if you have none good, let it be hyson of the ancient kind. If, immediately on the receipt of this you will deliver it to Mr. Mussi, corner of 7th & Market streets, he will pay your bill, & pack the tea with some other articles he will be sending me. Not doubting to receive from you what will be good in quality & reasonable in price.

To John Barnes, Monticello, October 9, 1794

Tobacco

It is a culture productive of infinite wretchedness.

Notes on the State of Virginia, 1782

Whiskey

Whiskey claims to itself alone the exclusive office of sot-making.

To Samuel Smith, Monticello, May 3, 1823

Wine

[In talking about European crops that could grow in America] I do not speak of the vine, because it is the parent of misery. Those who cultivate it are always poor, and he who would employ himself with us in the culture of corn, cotton &c. can procure in exchange for that much more wine, & better than he could raise by its direct culture.

To George Wythe, Paris, September 16, 1787

When one calls in the taverns for the vin du pays they give you what is natural and unadulterated and cheap: when vin etrangere* is called for, it only gives a pretext for charging an extravagant price for an unwholesome stuff, very often of their own brewing.

*wine for foreigners

Travelling Notes for Mr. Rutledge and Mr. Shippen, Paris, June 3, 1788

We could, in the United States, make as great a variety of wines as are made in Europe, not exactly of the same kinds, but doubtless as good.

To Charles Philbert Lasteryrie-du Saillant, July 15, 1808

I rejoice, as a Moralist, at the prospect of a reduction of the duties on wine, by our national legislature. It is an error to view a tax on that liquor as merely a tax on the rich. It is a prohibition of its use to the middling class of our citizens, and a condemnation of them to the poison of whiskey, which is desolating their houses. No nation is drunken where wine is cheap; and none sober, where the dearness of wine substitutes ardent spirits as the common beverage. It is in truth the only antidote to the bane of whiskey.

Fix but the duty at the rate of other merchandise, and we can drink wine here as cheaply as we do grog; and who will not prefer it? Its extended use will carry health and comfort to a much enlarged circle. Every one in easy circumstances (as the bulk of our citizens are) will prefer it to the poison to which they are now driven by their government.

> To M. De Neuville, Monticello,
> December 13, 1818

Foreign Affairs

The politics of Europe render it indispensably necessary that with respect to every thing external we be one nation only, firmly looped together.

> To Rev. James Madison, Paris,
> February 8, 1786

The animosities of sovereigns are temporary & may be allayed; but those which seize the whole body of a people, and of a people too who dictate their own measures, produce calamities of long duration.

> To C.W.F. Dumas, Paris, May 6, 1786

It will procure us respect in Europe, and respect is a safe-guard to interest.

> To John Adams, Paris, July 11, 1786

Wretched indeed is the nation in whose affairs foreign powers are once permitted to intermeddle!

To Benjamin Vaughan, Paris, July 2, 1787

We certainly cannot deny to other nations that principle whereon our own government is founded, that every nation has a right to govern itself internally under what forms it pleases, and to change these forms at its own will: and externally to transact business with other nations thro' whatever organ it chooses, whether that be a king, convention, assembly, committee, president, or whatever it be. The only thing essential is the will of the nation.

To Thomas Pinckney, Philadelphia,
December 30, 1792

Their kicks & cuffs prove their contempt.

To Edward Rutledge, Philadelphia, June 24, 1797

As to everything except commerce, we ought to divorce ourselves from them all.

To Edward Rutledge, Philadelphia, June 24, 1797

We owe gratitude to France, justice to England, good will to all, and subservience to none.

To Arthur Campbell, Monticello,
September 1, 1797

Commerce with all nations, alliance with none should be our motto.

To Thomas Lomax, Monticello, March 12, 1799

Peace, commerce and honest friendship with all nations, entangling alliances with none.

First Inaugural Address, March 4, 1801

On the subject of treaties our system is to have none with any nation as far as can be avoided. The treaty with England has therefore not been renewed, and all overtures for treaty with other nations have been declined. We believe, that with nations as with individuals, dealings may be carried on as advantageously, perhaps more so, where their continuance depends on a voluntary good treatment, as if fixed by a contract which, when it becomes injurious to either is made by forced constructions to mean what suits you & becomes a cause of war instead of a bond of peace.

To Philip Mazzei, Washington, July 18, 1804

Unmeddling with the affairs of other nations, we presume not to prescribe or censure their course. Happy, could we be permitted to pursue our own in peace, and to employ all our means in improving the condition of our citizens.

To Madame de Stael de Holstein, Washington,
July 16, 1807

I hope that to preserve this weather-gauge of public opinion, & to counteract the slanders & falsehoods disseminated by the English papers, the government will make it a standing instruction to their ministers at foreign courts, to keep Europe truly informed of occurrences here, by publishing in their papers the naked truth always, whether favorable or unfavorable. For they will believe the good, if we candidly tell them the bad also.

To James Monroe, Monticello, January 1, 1815

Not in our day, but at no distant one, we may shake a rod over the heads of all, which may make the stoutest of them tremble. But I hope our wisdom will grow with our power, and teach us, that the less we use our power, the greater it will be.

To Thomas Leiper, Monticello, June 12, 1815

Nothing is so important as that America shall separate herself from the systems of Europe, & establish one of her own. Our circumstances, our pursuits, our interests, are distinct, the principles of our policy should be so also. All entanglements with that quarter of the globe should be avoided if we mean that peace & Justice shall be the polar stars of the American societies.

To José Correa da Serra, Monticello, October 24, 1820

The question presented by the letters you have sent me, is the most momentous which has ever been offered to my contemplation since that of Independence. That made us a nation, this sets our compass and points the course which we are to steer thro' the ocean of time opening on us. And never could we embark on it under circumstances more auspicious. Our first and fundamental maxim should be never to entangle ourselves in the broils of Europe. Our second never to suffer Europe to intermeddle with

Cis-Atlantic affairs. America, North and South, has a set of interests distinct from those of Europe, and peculiarly her own. She should therefore have a system of her own, separate and apart from that of Europe.

To President James Monroe, Monticello, October 24, 1823

Diplomacy

Circumstances sometimes require that rights the most unquestionable should be advanced with delicacy.

To William Short, Philadelphia, July 28, 1791

Foreign Visitors to America

It is the general interest of our country that strangers of distinction passing thro' it, should be made acquainted with its best citizens, and those most qualified to give favorable impressions of it.

To Jacob Hite, Monticello, June 29, 1796

Freedom and Liberty

Bill of Rights

A bill of rights is what the people are entitled to against every government on earth, general or particular, & what no just government should refuse or rest on inferences.

To James Madison, Paris, December 20, 1787

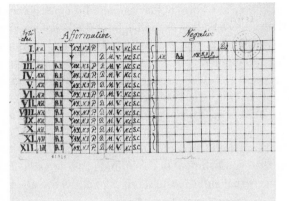

As Secretary of State, Jefferson was the official who certified
the adoption of amendments to the Constitution. This is his
tabulation of the actions taken on the first twelve amendments
sent to the states for their consideration on October 2, 1789.
The vertical columns are arranged from north to south.
Vermont adopted the Constitution in February 1789, and its
legislature then adopted all twelve of the proposed
amendments. Instead of redrawing his chart, Jefferson wrote
a "V" for Vermont on the line separating the Connecticut and
New York columns. (Jefferson Papers, Library of Congress.)

The Declaration of Independence

We hold these truths to be self-evident, that all
men are created equal; that they are endowed by
their Creator with certain unalienable Rights, that
among these are Life, Liberty and the pursuit of
Happiness.—That to secure these rights, Governments are instituted among Men, deriving their just
powers from the consent of the governed,—that

whenever any Form of Government becomes destructive of these ends, it is the Right of the People to alter or to abolish it; and to institute new government, laying its foundation on such principles and organizing its powers in such form, as to them shall seem most likely to effect their Safety and Happiness.

Declaration of Independence, July 1776

Nothing could so completely divest us of that liberty as the establishment of the opinion that the state has a perpetual right to the services of all its members.

To James Monroe, Monticello,
May 20, 1782

Freedom

The human mind will some day get back to the freedom it enjoyed 2000 years ago. This country, which has given to the world the example of physical liberty, owes to it that of moral emancipation also. For, as yet, it is but nominal with us. The inquisition of public opinion overwhelms in practice the freedom asserted by the laws in theory.

To John Adams, Monticello,
January 22, 1821

Habeas Corpus

The Habeas corpus secures every man here, alien or citizen, against every thing which is not law, whatever shape it may assume.

To Archibald Hamilton Rowan, Monticello,
September 26, 1798

Liberty

The God who gave us life gave us liberty at the same time; the hand of force may destroy, but cannot disjoin them.

A Summary View of the Rights of British America,
May 1774

The tree of liberty must be refreshed from time to time with the blood of patriots & tyrants. It is its natural manure.

To William Stephens Smith, Paris,
November 13, 1787

The natural progress of things is for liberty to yield, & government to gain ground.

To Edward Carrington, Paris, May 27, 1788

We have spent the prime of our lives in procuring them [youth] the precious blessing of liberty. Let them spend theirs in showing that it is the great parent of science & of virtue; and that a nation will be great in both, always in proportion as it is free.

To Joseph Willard, Paris, March 24, 1789

The ground of liberty is to be gained by inches, that we must be contented to secure what we can get from time to time, and eternally press forward for what is yet to get. It takes time to persuade men to do even what is for their own good.

To Charles Clay, Monticello,
January 27, 1790

We are not to expect to be translated from despotism to liberty in a feather bed.

To the Marquis de Lafayette, New York, April 2, 1790

I would rather be exposed to the inconveniencies attending too much liberty than those attending too small a degree of it.

To Archibald Stuart, Philadelphia, December 23, 1791

[Speaking of the French Revolution] In the struggle which was necessary, many guilty persons fell without the forms of trial, and with them some innocent. These I deplore as much as any body, & shall deplore some of them to the day of my death. But I deplore them as I should have done had they fallen in battle. It was necessary to use the arm of the people, a machine not quite so blind as balls and bombs, but blind to a certain degree. A few of their cordial friends met at their hands the fate of enemies. But time and truth will rescue & embalm their memories, while their posterity will be enjoying that very liberty for which they would never have hesitated to offer up their lives. The liberty of the whole earth was depending on the issue of the contest, and was ever such a prize won with so little innocent blood? My own affections have been deeply wounded by some of the martyrs to this cause, but rather than it should have failed, I would have seen half the earth desolated. Were there but an Adam & Eve left in every country, & left free, it would be better than as it is now.

To William Short, Philadelphia, January 3, 1793

Being myself a warm zealot for the attainment & enjoyment by all mankind of as much liberty as each may exercise without injury to the equal liberty of his fellow citizens.

To Jean Nicolas Démeunier, Monticello, April 29, 1795

This ball of liberty . . . is now so well in motion that it will roll round the globe. At least the enlightened part of it, for light & liberty go together. It is our glory that we first put it into motion, & our happiness that being foremost we had no bad examples to follow. What a tremendous obstacle to the future attempts at liberty will be the atrocities of Robespierre!

To Tench Coxe, Monticello, June 1, 1795

Timid men . . . prefer the calm of despotism to the boisterous sea of liberty.

To Philip Mazzei, Monticello, April 24, 1796

Our citizens generally are enjoying a very great degree of liberty and security in the most temperate manner. Every man being at his ease, feels an interest in the preservation of order, and comes forth to preserve it at the first call of the magistrate.

To Marc Auguste Pictet, Washington, February 5, 1803

Affectionate concern for the liberty & prosperity of my fellow citizens will cease but with life to animate my breast.

To the democratic citizens of Adams County, Pa.,
March 20, 1808

The true barriers [i.e., protections] of our liberty in this country are our State governments.

To Destutt de Tracy, Monticello, January 26, 1811

The last hope of human liberty in this world rests on us. We ought, for so dear a stake, to sacrifice every attachment & every enmity.

To William Duane, Monticello, March 28, 1811

The disease of liberty is catching.

To the Marquis de Lafayette, Monticello, December 26, 1820

The boisterous sea of liberty indeed is never without a wave.

To the Marquis de Lafayette, Monticello, December 26, 1820

Possessing ourselves the combined blessing of liberty and order, we wish the same to other countries, and to none more than yours [Greece], which, the first of civilized nations, presented examples of what man should be.

To Adamantios Coray, Monticello, October 31, 1823

Natural Rights

The idea is quite unfounded that on entering into society we give up any natural right.

To Francis W. Gilmer, Monticello, June 7, 1816

Nothing then is unchangeable but the inherent and unalienable rights of man.

To John Cartwright, Monticello, June 5, 1824

Friends and Enemies

Departing Friends

The departure of your family has left me in the dumps.

To John Adams, Paris, May 25, 1785

Having performed the last sad office of handing you into your carriage at the Pavillon de St. Denis, and seen the wheels get actually into motion, I turned on my heel and walked, more dead than alive. . . . I was carried home. Seated by my fireside, solitary and sad, the following dialogue took place between my head and my Heart.

To Maria Cosway, Paris, October 12, 1786

Heaven has submitted our being to some unkind laws. When those charming moments were present which I passed with you, they were clouded with the prospect that I was soon to lose you: and now, when I pass the same moments in review, I recollect nothing but the agreeable passages, and they fill me with regret. Thus, present joys are damped by a consciousness that they are passing from us; and past ones are only the subject of sorrow and regret.

To Maria Cosway, Paris, November 29, 1786

The morning you left us, all was wrong. Even the sun shine was provoking, with which I never quarreled

before. I took it into my head he shone only to throw
light on our loss: to present a cheerfulness not at all in
unison with my mind. I mounted my horse earlier
than common, and took by instinct the road you had
taken. Some spirit whispered this to me: but he whispered by halves only. . . . I think I have discovered a
method of preventing this dejection of mind on any
future parting. It is this. When you come again, I will
employ myself solely in finding or fancying that you
have some faults, and I will draw a veil over all your
good qualities, if I can find one large enough. I think I
shall succeed in this. For, trying myself to-day, by way
of exercise, I recollected immediately one fault in your
composition. It is that you give all your attention to
your friends, caring nothing about yourself. Now you
must agree that I christian this very mildly when I
call it a folly only. And I dare say I shall find many like
it when I examine you with more sang froid.*—I remember you told me, when we parted, you would
come to see me at Monticello. Now tho' I believe this
to be impossible, I have been planning what I would
show you: a flower here, a tree there; yonder a grove,
near it a fountain; on this side a hill, on that a river.
Indeed, madam, I know nothing so charming as our
own country.

*composure; determination

To Angelica Schuyler Church, Paris, February 17, 1788

I never blame heaven so much as for having clogged
the ethereal spirit of friendship with a body which

ties it to time and place. I am with you always in spirit; be with me sometimes.

To Angelica Schuyler Church, Paris, August 17, 1788

I am going to America, and you to Italy. The one or the other of us goes the wrong way, for the way will ever be wrong which leads us farther apart.

To Maria Cosway, Paris, September 26, 1788

Preserve for me always, my dear friend, the same sentiments of esteem you have been so good as to entertain for me hitherto. They will comfort me in going, and encourage me returning.

To Maria Cosway, Paris, September 11, 1789

I received, my dear friend, with great sensibility your favor of the 1st instant. It recalled to my mind many very dear scenes which passed while we had the happiness of possessing you here. Events have separated the actors & called them to other stages; but neither time, distance, nor events have weakened my affections for them.

To Carlo Bellini, Monticello, April 24, 1799

Enemies

An enemy generally says & believes what he wishes.

To C.W.F. Dumas, Paris, March 29, 1788

An injured friend is the bitterest of foes.

Opinion on the French Treaties, April 28, 1793

The vote of your opponents is the most honorable mark by which the soundness of your conduct could be stamped.

To Elbridge Gerry, Monticello, June 11, 1812

Friends

The way to make friends quarrel is to pit them in disputation under the public eye. An experience of near twenty years has taught me that few friendships stand this test, & that public assemblies where every one is free to act and speak are the most powerful looseners of the bands of private friendship.

To George Washington, Annapolis, April 16, 1784

Agreeable society is the first essential in constituting the happiness & of course the value of our existence: & it is a circumstance worthy great attention when we are making first our choice of a residence.

To James Madison, Paris, December 8, 1784

The society of our friends will sweeten all.

To Elizabeth Wayles Eppes, Paris, December 15, 1788

I shall be rendered very happy by the visit you promise me. The only thing wanting to make me completely so is the more frequent society of my friends.

To William Branch Giles, Monticello, April 27, 1795

Of those connected by blood the number does not depend on us. But friends we have if we have merited them. Those of our earliest years stand nearest in our affections. . . . Our college friends . . . are the dearest.

To John Page, Washington, June 25, 1804

Friends must enable us to hear every thing, & expect us to say nothing.

To William Duane, Washington, July 20, 1807

I consider it a great felicity, through a long and trying course of life, to have retained the esteem of my early friends unaltered. I find in old age that the impressions of youth are the deepest & most indelible.

To David Campbell, Monticello, January 28, 1810

I have never thought that a difference in political, any more than in religious opinions should disturb the friendly intercourse of society. There are so many other topics on which friends may converse & be happy, that it is wonderful they should select of preference the only one on which they cannot agree.

To David Campbell, Monticello, January 28, 1810

It seems as if, our ancient friends dying off, the whole mass of the affections of the heart survives undiminished to the few who remain.

To Elbridge Gerry, Monticello, June 11, 1812

Wherever I have been, it has been my good fortune to meet with or to make ardent and affectionate friends.

To Robert Taylor and Chapman Johnson, Monticello, May 16, 1820

It is right for old friends, now and then, to, ask each
other how they do? The question is short, and will
give little trouble either to ask, or answer. I ask it
therefore, observing in exchange that my own
health is tolerably good; but that I am too weak to
walk further than my garden without suffering, altho' I ride without fatigue 6 or 8 miles every day, and
sometimes 20. I salute you with constant and affectionate friendship & respect.

To Charles Willson Peale, Monticello, October 23, 1822

Friendship

Life is of no value but as it brings us gratifications.
Among the most valuable of these is rational society.
It informs the mind, sweetens the temper, cheers
our spirits, and promotes health.

To James Madison, Annapolis, February 20, 1784

The friendships of my youth are those which stick
closest to me, and in which I most confide.

To John Page, Paris, August 20, 1785

Head. Friendship is but another name for an alliance
with the follies & the misfortunes of others. Our own
share of miseries is sufficient: why enter then as volunteers into those of another? Is there so little gall
poured into our own cup that we must needs help to
drink that of our neighbor? A friend dies or leaves
us: we feel as if a limb was cut off. He is sick: he
must watch over him, & participate of his pains. His

fortune is shipwrecked; ours must be laid under contribution. He loses a child, a parent or a partner: we
must mourn the loss as if it was our own.

Heart. What more sublime delight than to
mingle tears with one whom the hand of heaven
hath smitten! To watch over the bed of sickness, &
to beguile its tedious & its painful moments! To
share our bread with one to whom misfortune has
left none! This world abounds indeed with misery;
to lighten its burden we must divide it with one another. . . . Friendship is precious, not only in the
shade but in the sunshine of life: & thanks to a
benevolent arrangement of things, the greater part
of life is sunshine.

To Maria Cosway, Paris, October 12, 1786

I am never happier than when I am performing
good offices for good people; and the most friendly
office one can perform is to make worthy characters acquainted with one another.

To Abigail Adams, Paris, November 1786

The happiest moments it [my heart] knows are
those in which it is pouring forth its affections to a
few esteemed characters.

To Eliza House Trist, Paris, December 15, 1786

The friendships contracted earliest in life, are those
which stand by us the longest.

To Elizabeth Blair Thompson, Paris, January 19, 1787

Your letter has kindled all the fond recollections of ancient times, recollections much dearer to me than any thing I have known since. There are minds which can be pleased by honors & preferments, but I see nothing in them but envy & enmity. It is only necessary to possess them to know how little they contribute to happiness, or rather how hostile they are to it. No attachments soothe the mind so much as those contracted in early life: nor do I recollect any societies which have given me more pleasure than those of which you have partaken with me. I had rather be shut up in a very modest cottage, with my books, my family and a few old friends, dining on simple bacon, and letting the world roll on as it liked, than to occupy the most splendid post which any human power can give. I shall be glad to hear from you often. Give me the small news as well as the great.

To Alexander Donald, Paris, February 7, 1788

Near friends falling out never reunite cordially.

To Alexander Donald, Paris, February 7, 1788

Every human being, my dear, must thus be viewed according to what it is good for, for none of us, no not one, is perfect; and were we to love none who had imperfections this world would be a desert for our love. All we can do is to make the best of our friends: love and cherish what is good in them, and keep out of the way of what is bad: but no more think of rejecting them for it than of throwing away a piece of music for a flat passage or two.

To Martha Jefferson Randolph, New York,
July 17, 1790

Trouble is a pleasure when it is to serve our friends living or dead.

To Elizabeth Wayles Eppes, Philadelphia,
May 15, 1791

I find friendship to be like wine, raw when new, ripened with age, the true old man's milk & restorative cordial.

To Benjamin Rush, Monticello, August 17, 1811

You will find me in habitual good health, great contentedness, enfeebled in body, impaired in memory, but without decay in my friendships.

To Cæsar Rodney, Monticello, March 16, 1815

Indifference

With those who wish to think amiss of me, I have learnt to be perfectly indifferent.

To Abigail Adams, Monticello, September 11, 1804

Government

The whole art of government consists in the art of being honest.

A Summary View of the Rights of British America,
May 1774

The legitimate powers of government extend to such acts only as are not injurious to others.

Notes on the State of Virginia, 1782

I love energy in government dearly.

To Abigail Adams, Paris, July 7, 1785

I do not flatter myself with the immortality of our governments.

To George Washington, Paris,
November 14, 1786

Societies exist under three forms sufficiently distinguishable. 1. Without government, as among our Indians. 2. Under governments wherein the will of every one has a just influence, as is the case in England in a slight degree, and in our states in a great one. 3. Under governments of force: as is the case in all other monarchies & in most of the other republics.

To James Madison, Paris,
January 30, 1787

We are now vibrating between too much & too little government, & the pendulum will rest finally in the middle.

To William Stephens Smith, Paris, February 2, 1788

The care of human life & happiness, & not their destruction, is the first & only legitimate object of good government.

To the republican citizens of Washington County, Md., Monticello, March 31, 1809

The happiness & prosperity of our citizens . . . is the only legitimate object of government.

To Tadeusz Kosciusko, Monticello, April 16, 1811

The only orthodox object of the institution of government is to secure the greatest degree of happiness possible to the general mass of those associated under it.

To Francis A. Van Der Kemp, Monticello, March 22, 1812

Freedom of religion, freedom of the press, trial by jury, Habeas corpus and a representative legislature. These I consider as the essentials constituting free government, and that the organization of the Executive is interesting, as it may ensure wisdom and integrity in the first place, but next as it may favor or endanger the preservation of these fundamentals.

To P. S. Dupont de Nemours, Monticello, February 28, 1815

A government of reason is better than one of force.

To Richard Rush, Monticello, October 20, 1820

The equal rights of man, and the happiness of every individual are now acknowledged to be the only legitimate objects of government.

To Adamantios Coray, Monticello, October 31, 1823

Abuse of Government

What institution is insusceptible of abuse in wicked hands?

To Louis H. Girardin, Monticello, March 12, 1815

Alien and Sedition Acts of 1798

For my own part I consider these laws as merely an experiment on the American mind to see how far it will bear an avowed violation of the constitution.

To Stevens Thomson Mason, Monticello,
October 11, 1798

I discharged every person under punishment or prosecution under the Sedition law, because I considered & now consider that law to be a nullity as absolute and as palpable as if Congress had ordered us to fall down and worship a golden image; and that it was as much my duty to arrest its execution in every stage, as it would have been to have rescued from the fiery furnace those who should have been cast into it for refusing to worship their image.

To Abigail Adams, Washington, July 22, 1804

Aristocracy

To know the mass of evil which flows from this fatal
source, a person must be in France, he must see the
finest soil, the finest climate, the most compact state,
the most benevolent character of people, and every
earthly advantage combined, insufficient to prevent
this scourge from rendering existence a curse to 24
out of 25 parts of the inhabitants of this country.

To George Washington, Paris, November 14, 1786

Cabinet (Presidential)

It is certain that those of the cabinet council of the
President should be of his bosom-confidence.

To Samuel Dexter, Washington, February 20, 1801

Our government, altho' in theory subject to be directed by the unadvised will of the President, is,
and from its origin has been, a very different thing
in practice. The minor business in each department
is done by the head of the department, on consulta-
tion with the President alone. But all matters of importance or difficulty are submitted to all the heads
of departments composing the cabinet; sometimes
by the President's consulting them separately &
successively, as they happen to call on him; but in
the greatest cases, by calling them together, dis-
cussing the subject maturely, and finally taking the
vote, on which the President counts himself but as
one. So that in all important cases the Executive is,
in fact, a Directory, which certainly the President

might control, but of this there was never an example, either in the first or the present administration. I have heard, indeed, that my predecessor sometimes decided things against his council by dashing & trampling his wig on the floor.

To William Short, Washington, June 12, 1807

Changing Governments

It is very important to unlearn the lessons we have learnt under our former government, to discard the maxims which were the bulwark of that, but would be the ruin of the one we have erected.

To Edmund Randolph, Baltimore, February 15, 1783

It is better that improvements should be late when thereby all voices can be united in making them.

To C.W.F. Dumas, Paris, September 22, 1786

Coercive Power

What has been the effect of coercion? To make one half the world fools, and the other half hypocrites.

Notes on the State of Virginia, 1782

It has been said too that our governments both federal and particular [i.e., states] want energy; that it is difficult to restrain both individuals & states from committing wrongs. This is true, & it is an inconvenience on the other hand that energy which absolute governments derive from an armed force, which is the effect of the bayonet constantly held at the breast of every citizen, and which resembles very much the stillness of the grave, must be admitted also to have its inconveniences. We weigh the two together, and like best to submit to the former. Compare the number of wrongs committed with impunity by citizens among us, with those committed by the sovereign in other countries, and the last will be found most numerous, most oppressive on the mind, and most degrading of the dignity of man.

To Jean Nicolas Démeunier, Paris, January 24, 1786

God send that our country may never have a government, which it can feel [a government of energy]. This is the perfection of human society.

To Francis Hopkinson, Paris, May 8, 1788

Congress
Congress . . . is the great commanding theatre of this nation.

To William Wirt, Washington, January 10, 1808

If there be any thing amiss therefore, in the present state of our affairs, as the formidable deficit lately unfolded to us indicates, I ascribe it to the inattention of Congress to its duties, to their unwise dissipation & waste of the public contributions. They seemed, some little while ago to be at a loss for objects whereon to throw away the supposed fathomless funds of the treasury.

To Thomas Ritchie, Monticello, December 25, 1820

Constitutional Conventions

The ultimate Arbiter is the people of the Union, assembled by their deputies in Convention, at the call of Congress, or of two-thirds of the states. Let them decide to which they mean to give an authority claimed by two of their organs. And it has been the peculiar wisdom and felicity of our constitution, to have provided this peaceable appeal, where that of other nations is at once to force.

To William Johnson, Monticello, June 12, 1823

Democracy

Every government degenerates when trusted to the rulers of the people alone. The people themselves therefore are its only safe depositories.

Notes on the State of Virginia, 1782

The happiness of governments like ours, wherein the people are truly the mainspring, is that they are never to be despaired of. When an evil becomes so glaring as to strike them generally, they arouse themselves, and it is redressed. He only is then the popular man and can get into office who shows the best dispositions to reform the evil.

To Richard Price, Paris, February 1, 1785

It is an axiom in my mind that our liberty can never be safe but in the hands of the people themselves, & that too of the people with a certain degree of instruction.

To George Washington, Paris, January 4, 1786

Sometimes it is said that man cannot be trusted with the government of himself. Can he, then, be trusted with the government of others? Or have we found angels in the forms of kings to govern him? Let history answer this question.

First Inaugural Address, March 4, 1801

The government which can wield the arm of the people must be the strongest possible.

To Isaac Weaver, Jr., Washington, June 7, 1807

Where the Law of the majority ceases to be acknowledged, there government ends, the Law of the strongest takes its place, & life & property are his who can take them.

To John Gassway, Washington,
February 17, 1809

What a germ have we planted, and how faithfully should we cherish the parent tree at home!

To Benjamin Austin, Monticello, January 9, 1816

We of the United States, you know are constitutionally & conscientiously Democrats.

To P. S. Dupont de Nemours, Poplar Forest,
April 24, 1816

I am not among those who fear the people. They, and not the rich, are our dependence for continued freedom.

To Samuel Kercheval, Monticello, July 12, 1816

I know no safe depository of the ultimate powers of the society but the people themselves: and if we think them not enlightened enough to exercise their control with a wholesome discretion, the remedy is not to take it from them, but to inform their discretion by education. This is the true corrective of abuses of constitutional power.

To William Charles Jarvis, Monticello,
September 28, 1820

The general spread of the light of science has already laid open to every view the palpable truth that the mass of mankind has not been born, with saddles on their backs, nor a favored few booted and spurred, ready to ride them legitimately, by the grace of god.

To Roger C. Weightman, Monticello, June 24, 1826

Despotism

Ignorance and despotism seem made for each other.

To Robert Pleasants, August 27, 1796

Division of Power

To make us one nation as to foreign concerns, & keep us distinct in Domestic ones, gives the outline of the proper division of powers between the general & particular governments.

To James Madison, Paris, December 16, 1786

The system of the General government is to seize all doubtful ground. We must join in the scramble, or get nothing. Where first occupancy is to give right, he who lies still loses all.

To James Monroe, Monticello,
September 7, 1797

I have always thought that where the line of demarcation between the powers of the general & the state governments was doubtfully or indistinctly drawn, it would be prudent and praise-worthy in both parties never to approach it but under the most urgent necessity.

To Joseph C. Cabell, Monticello,
January 31, 1814

The way to have good and safe government, is not trust it all to one; but to divide it among the many, distributing to every one exactly the functions he is competent to. Let the National government be entrusted with the defense of the nation, and its foreign & federal relations; the State governments with the civil rights, laws, police, & administration of what concerns the State generally; the Counties with the local concerns of the counties, and each Ward direct the interests within itself. It is by dividing and subdividing these republics from the great National one down thro' all its subordinations, until it ends in the administration of every man's farm and affairs by himself; by placing under every one what his own eye may superintend, that all will be done for the best. What has destroyed liberty and the rights of man in every government which has ever existed under the sun? The generalizing & concentrating all cares and powers into one body, no matter whether of the Autocrats of Russia or France, or of the Aristocrats of a Venetian Senate. And I do believe that if the Almighty has not decreed that Man shall never be free (and it is a blasphemy to believe it) that the secret will be found to be in the making himself the depository of the powers respecting himself, so far as he is competent to them, and delegating only what is beyond his competence by a synthetical process, to higher & higher orders of functionaries, so as to trust fewer and fewer powers in proportion as the trustees become more and more oligarchical.

To Joseph C. Cabell, Monticello, February 2, 1816

Executive Privilege

Reserving the necessary right of the President of the U.S. to decide, independently of all other authority, what papers, coming to him as President, the public interests permit to be communicated, & to whom, I assure you of my readiness, under that restriction, voluntarily to furnish on all occasions whatever the purposes of justice may require.

To George W. Hay, Washington, June 12, 1807

Faith In Government

The times have been awful, but they have proved an useful truth, that the good citizen must never despair of the commonwealth.

To Nathaniel Niles, Washington, March 22, 1801

Federalism

My idea is that we should be made one nation in every case concerning foreign affairs, & separate ones in whatever is merely domestic.

To John Blair, Paris, August 13, 1787

It is of immense consequence that the States retain as complete authority as possible over their own citizens.

To James Monroe, Monticello, September 7, 1797

It is a singular phenomenon, that while our state governments are the very best in the world without exception or comparison, our general government has, in the rapid course of 9 or 10 years, become more arbitrary, and has swallowed more of the public liberty than even that of England.

To John Taylor, Monticello, November 26, 1798

The true theory of our constitution is surely the wisest & best, that the states are independent as to every thing within themselves, & united as to everything respecting foreign nations. Let the general government be reduced to foreign concerns only, and let our affairs be disentangled from those of all other nations, except as to commerce, which the merchants will manage the better, the more they are left free to manage for themselves, and our general government may be reduced to a very simple organization, & a very unexpensive one; a few plain duties to be performed by a few servants.

To Gideon Granger, Monticello, August 13, 1800

When we consider that this government is charged with the external & mutual relations only of these states; that the states themselves have principal care of our persons, our property, & our reputation, constituting the great field of human concerns, we may well doubt whether our organization is not too complicated, too expensive; whether offices & officers have not been multiplied unnecessarily & sometimes injuriously to the service they were meant to promote.

First Annual Message to Congress, Washington, December 8, 1801

When all government, domestic and foreign, in little as in great things, shall be drawn to Washington as the center of all power, it will render powerless the checks provided of one government on another, and will become as venal and oppressive as the government from which we separated.

To Charles Hammond, Monticello, August 18, 1821

I see as you do, and with the deepest affliction, the rapid strides with which the federal branch of our government is advancing towards the usurpation of all the rights reserved to the states, and the consolidation in itself of all powers foreign and domestic; and that too by constructions which, if legitimate, leave no limits to their power. Take together the decisions of the federal court, the doctrines of the President, and the misconstructions of the constitutional compact, acted on by the legislature of the federal branch, and it is but too evident that the three ruling branches of that department are in combination to strip their Colleagues, the State authorities, of the powers reserved by them, and to exercise themselves all functions foreign and domestic. Under the power to regulate Commerce, they assume indefinitely that also over agriculture and manufactures, and call it regulation to take the earnings of one of these branches of industry, and that too the most depressed, and put them into the pockets of the other, the most flourishing of all. Under the authority to establish post roads, they claim that of cutting down mountains for the construction of roads, of digging canals, and, aided by a little sophistry on the words "general welfare," a right to do, not only the acts to effect that, which are specifically enumerated and permitted, but whatsoever they shall think, or pretend will be for the general welfare. And what is our resource for the preservation of the constitution? Reason and argument? You might as well reason and argue with the marble columns encircling them. The representatives chosen by ourselves? They are joined in the combination, some from incorrect views of government, some from corrupt ones, sufficient voting together to out-number the sound parts; and, with majorities of only 1, 2, or 3 bold enough to go forward in defiance.

To William Branch Giles, Monticello, December 26, 1825

Gaining Unanimity

It is better that improvements should be late when thereby all voices can be united in making them.

To C.W.F. Dumas, Paris, September 22, 1786

Governing

I have no ambition to govern men, no passion which would lead me to delight to ride in a storm. Flumina amo, sylvasque, inglorius.*

*May I love the rivers and the woods, though fame be lost (Virgil, *Georgics* 2:486).

To Edward Rutledge, Monticello, December 27, 1796

I love to see honest men & honorable men at the helm, men who will not bend their politics to their purses, nor pursue measures by which they may profit, & then profit by their measures. Au diable les Bougres!*

*To the devil with fools, hicks, etc.

To Edward Rutledge, Monticello, December 27, 1796

I leave to others the sublime delights of riding in the storm, better pleased with sound sleep & a warmer birth below it encircled, with the society of neighbors, friends & fellow laborers of the earth rather than with spies & sycophants. . . . I have no ambition to govern men. It is a painful and thankless office.

To John Adams, Monticello, December 28, 1796

Neither the splendor, nor the power, nor the difficulties, nor the fame, or defamation as may happen, attached to the first magistracy have any attractions for me. The helm of a free government is always arduous, and never was ours more so.

To James Sullivan, Monticello,
February 9, 1797

I have never been so well pleased, as when I could shift power from my own, on the shoulders of others; nor have I ever been able to conceive how any rational being could propose happiness to himself from the exercise of power over others.

To Destutt de Tracy, Monticello,
January 26, 1811

An honest man can feel no pleasure in the exercise of power over his fellow citizens. . . . There has never been a moment of my life in which I should have relinquished for it the enjoyments of my family, my farm, my friends & books.

To John Melish, Monticello,
January 13, 1813

Institutions

Laws and institutions must go hand in hand with the progress of the human mind. As that becomes more developed, more enlightened, as new discoveries are made, new truths disclosed, and manners and opinions change with the change of circumstances, institutions must advance also, and keep pace with the times.

To Samuel Kercheval, Monticello, July 12, 1816

The Law

The system of law in most of the United States, in imitation of that of England, is divided into two departments, the Common law & the Chancery.

The Common law is a written law the text of which is preserved from the beginning of the 13th century downwards, but what preceded that is lost. Its substance however has been retained in the memory of the people & committed to writing from time to time in the decisions of the judges and treatises of the jurists, insomuch that it is still considered as a lex scripta,* the letter of which is sufficiently known to guide the decisions of the courts. In this department the courts restrain themselves to the letter of the law. Anciently indeed, before the improvement or perhaps the existence of the court of Chancery, they allowed themselves greater latitude, extending the provisions of every law not only to the cases within its letter but to those also which came within the spirit and reason of it. This was called the equity of the law. . . . The power of that court [of Chancery], as acknowledged at this day, is to relieve

1. where the Common law gives no remedy.
2. where its remedy is imperfect.
3. where it would do injustice by comprehending within its letter cases not within its reason, nor intended to have been comprehended.

*the written law

To Philip Mazzei, Paris, November 1785

Laws

Laws made by common Consent must not be trampled on by Individuals.

To Garret Van Meter, Richmond,
April 27, 1781

We lay it down as a fundamental, that laws, to be just, must give a reciprocation of right; that, without this, they are mere arbitrary rules of conduct, founded in force, and not in conscience.

Notes on the State of Virginia, 1782

The execution of the laws is more important than the making them.

To L'Abbé Arnoux, Paris, July 19, 1789

That love of order and obedience to the laws, which so remarkably characterize the citizens of the United States, are sure pledges of internal tranquility.

To Benjamin Waring and others, Washington,
March 23, 1801

In the construction of a law, . . . where the opposite parties have a right & counter-right in the very words of the law, the judge considers the intention of the law-giver as his true guide, and gives to all the parts & expressions of the law, that meaning which will effect, instead of defeating, its intention.

To Governor William H. Cabell, Monticello,
August 11, 1807

Whenever the words of a law will bear two meanings, one of which will give effect to the law, & the other will defeat it, the former must be supposed to have been intended by the legislature, because they could not intend that meaning which would defeat their intention, in passing the law; and in a statute, as in a Will, the intention of the party is to be sought after.

To Albert Gallatin, Monticello, July 29, 1808

Laws are made for men of ordinary understanding, and should therefore be construed by the ordinary rules of common sense. Their meaning is not to be sought for in metaphysical subtleties, which may make any thing mean every thing or nothing, at pleasure.

To William Johnson, Monticello, June 12, 1823

Legislative Delay

There is a snail-paced gate for the advance of new ideas on the general mind, under which we must acquiesce. A forty years' experience of popular assemblies has taught me, that you must give them time for every step you take. If too hard pushed, they balk, & the machine retrogrades.

To Joel Barlow, Washington,
December 10, 1807

Procrastination is unavoidable. How can expedition be expected from a body which we have saddled with an hundred lawyers, whose trade is talking?

To Thomas Leiper, Monticello, June 12, 1815

Loyal Minority

Our majority in the H. of Representatives has been about 2 to 1; in the Senate, 18 to 15. After another election it will be 2 to 1 in the Senate, and it would not be for the public good to have it greater. A respectable minority is useful as Censors.

To Joel Barlow, Washington, May 3, 1802

Majority Rule

It is my principle that the will of the Majority should always prevail.

To James Madison, Paris, December 20, 1787

A great revolution has taken place at Paris. The people of that country, having never been in the habit of self government, are not yet in the habit of acknowledging that fundamental law of nature, by which alone self government can be exercised by a society, I mean the lex majoris partis.* Of the sacredness of this law, our countrymen are impressed from their cradle, so that with them it is almost innate. This single circumstance may possibly decide the fate of the two nations. . . . And whatever may be the fate of republicanism there, we are able to preserve it inviolate here: we are sensible of the duty and expediency of submitting our opinions to the will of the majority, and can wait with patience till they get right, if they happen to be at any time wrong. Our vessel is moored at such a distance, that should theirs blow up, ours is still safe, if we will but think so.

*the law of majority

To John Breckinridge, Philadelphia, January 29, 1800

No mortal can foresee in favor of which party the election will go. There is one supreme consolation. That our people have so innate a spirit of order & obedience to the law, so religious an acquiescence in the will of the majority, and deep conviction of the fundamental importance of the principle that the will of the majority ought to be submitted to by the minority, that a majority of a single vote, as at the last election, produces as absolute & quiet a submission as an unanimous vote.

To William Short, Philadelphia, March 26, 1800

Monarchy

A court has no affections. But those of the people whom they govern influence their decisions even in the most arbitrary governments.

To James Monroe, Paris, June 17, 1785

I am astonished at some people's considering a kingly government as a refuge. Advise such to read the fable of the frogs who solicited Jupiter for a king. If that does not put them to rights, send them to Europe to see something of the trappings of monarchy, and I will undertake that every man shall go back thoroughly cured. If all the evils which can arise among us from the republican form of our government from this day to the day of judgment could be put into a scale against what this country suffers from its monarchical form in a week, or England in a month, the latter would preponderate.

To Benjamin Hawkins, Paris, August 4, 1787

I am sensible that there are defects in our federal government: yet they are so much lighter than those of monarchies that I view them with much indulgence. I rely too on the good sense of the people for remedy, whereas the evils of monarchical government are beyond remedy. If any of our countrymen wish for a king, give them Aesop's fable of the frogs who asked a king; if this does not cure them, send them to Europe: they will go back good republicans.

To David Ramsay, Paris, August 4, 1787

I was much an enemy to monarchy before I came to Europe. I am ten thousand times more so since I have seen what they are. There is scarcely an evil known in these countries which may not be traced to their king as its source, nor a good which is not derived from the small fibres of republicanism existing among them.

To George Washington, Paris, May 2, 1788

Natural Aristocracy
I agree with you that there is a natural aristocracy among men. The grounds of this are virtue & talents.

To John Adams, Monticello, October 28, 1813

Oppression

For what oppression may not a precedent be found in this world.

Notes on the State of Virginia, 1782

Perfectibility

It suffices for a man to be a philosopher, and to believe that human affairs are susceptible of improvement, & to look forward, rather than back to the Gothic ages, for perfection, to mark him as an anarchist, disorganizer, atheist & enemy of the government.

To Thomas Mann Randolph, Philadelphia, May 3, 1798

The Gothic idea that we are to look backwards instead of forwards for the improvement of the human mind, and to recur to the annals of our ancestors for what is most perfect in government, in religion & in learning, is worthy of those bigots in religion & government, by whom it has been recommended, & whose purposes it would answer. But it is not an idea which this country will endure; and the moment of their showing it is fast ripening.

To Joseph Priestley, Philadelphia, January 27, 1800

Petitions

The right of our fellow citizens to represent to the public functionaries their opinion on proceedings interesting to them, is unquestionably a constitutional right, often useful, sometimes necessary, and will always be respectfully acknowledged by me.

To New Haven merchants, Washington, July 12, 1801

The Presidency

No man will ever bring out of that office the reputation which carries him into it.

To William Cocke, Monticello, October 21, 1796, and to
Edward Rutledge, Monticello, December 27, 1796

The second office of this government is honorable &
easy, the first is but a splendid misery.

To Elbridge Gerry, Philadelphia, May 13, 1797

If some period be not fixed, either by the constitution or by practice, to the services of the first magistrate, his office, tho' nominally elective, will, in fact, be for life; & that will soon degenerate into an inheritance.

To Isaac Weaver, Jr., Washington, June 7, 1807

[Speaking about presidential appointments] How greatly we were deceived in this character, as is generally the case in appointments not on our own knowledge.

To James Madison, Monticello, February 8, 1813

Protocol

I am sorry that your first impressions have been disturbed by matters of etiquette, where surely they should least have been expected to occur. These disputes are the most insusceptible of determination, because they have no foundation in reason. Arbitrary & senseless in their nature, they are arbitrarily decided by every nation for itself. These decisions are meant to prevent disputes, but they produce ten where they prevent one. It would have been better therefore in a new country to have excluded etiquette altogether; or, if it must be admitted in some form or other, to have made it depend on some circumstance founded in nature, such as the age or stature of the parties.

To the Comte de Moustier, Paris, May 17, 1788

Public Accounts

The accounts of the U.S. ought to be, and may be made as simple as those of a common farmer, and capable of being understood by common farmers.

To James Madison, Monticello, March 6, 1796

Public Confidence

It would be a dangerous delusion were a confidence in the man of our choice to silence our fears for the safety of our rights: that confidence is everywhere the parent of despotism—free government is founded in jealousy, and not in confidence; it is jealousy and not confidence which prescribes limited constitutions, to bind down those whom we are obliged to trust with power. . . . In questions of power, then, let no more be heard of confidence in man, but bind him down from mischief by the chains of the Constitution.

Kentucky Resolutions, October 1798

It is not wisdom alone, but public confidence in that wisdom, which can support an administration.

To President James Monroe, Monticello, July 18, 1824

Reform

What is good is often spoiled by trying to make it better.

To William Buchanan and James Hay, Paris,
January 26, 1786

The hole & the patch should be commensurate.

To James Madison, Paris, June 20, 1787

I am sensible how far I should fall short of effecting all the reformation which reason would suggest and experience approve, were I free to do whatever I thought best. But when we reflect how difficult it is to move or inflect the great machine of society, how impossible to advance the notions of a whole people suddenly to ideal right, we see the wisdom of Solon's remark, that no more good must be attempted than the nation can bear.

To Walter Jones, Washington, March 31, 1801

I am a friend to the reformation generally of whatever can be made better.

To John Wilson, Monticello, August 17, 1813

Republican Form of Government

But with all the defects of our constitutions, whether general or particular, the comparison of our governments with those of Europe are like a comparison of heaven & hell. England, like the earth, may be allowed to take the intermediate station. And yet I hear there are people among you who think the

experience of our governments has already proved
that republican governments will not answer. Send
those gentry here to count the blessings of monarchy.

To Joseph Jones, Paris, August 14, 1787

I received with great pleasure the present of your
pamphlets, as well for the thing itself as that it was a
testimony of your recollection. Would you believe it
possible that in this country there should be high and
important characters who need your lessons in republicanism and who do not heed them? It is but too true
that we have a sect preaching up and pouting after an
English constitution of kings, lords, and commons,
and whose heads are itching for crowns, coronets, and
mitres. But our people, my good friend, are firm and
unanimous in their principles of republicanism and
there is no better proof of it than they love what you
write and read it with delight. . . . Go on then in doing with your pen what in other times was done with
the sword; show that reformation is more practicable
by operating on the mind than on the body of man.

To Thomas Paine, June 19, 1792

How much superior is the glory of establishing a
republic to that of wearing a crown.

To Thomas Mann Randolph, Philadelphia,
February 4, 1800

A nation ceases to be republican only when the will
of the majority ceases to be the law.

To the democratic citizens of Adams County, Pa.,
March 20, 1808

The true principle is ever that of republicanism.

To William Duane, Monticello, August 12, 1810

[France] will end ... in a representative government, in a government in which the will of the people will be an effective ingredient. This important
element has taken root in the European mind, and
will have its growth; their despots, sensible of this,
are already offering this modification of their governments, as if of their own accord.

To Benjamin Austin, Monticello, January 9, 1816

Action by the citizens in person, in affairs within
their reach and competence and in all others by
representatives, chosen immediately, & removable
by themselves, constitutes the essence of a republic; that all governments are more or less republican in proportion as this principle enters more or
less their composition; and that a government
by representation is capable of extension over a
greater surface of country than one of any other
form.

To P. S. Dupont de Nemours, Poplar Forest, April 24, 1816

Governments are more or less republican, as they
have more or less of the element of popular election
and control in their composition; and believing, as I
do, that the mass of the citizens is the safest depository of their own rights, and especially, that the evils
flowing from the duperies of the people, are less injurious than those from the egoism of their agents, I am

a friend to that constitution of government which has in it the most of their ingredient.

To John Taylor, Monticello, May 28, 1816

The true foundation of republican government is the equal right of every citizen in his person & property, & in their management.

To Samuel Kercheval, Monticello, July 12, 1816

In truth, the abuses of monarchy had so much filled all the space of political contemplation, that we imagined everything republican which was not monarchy. We had not yet penetrated to the mother principle, that "governments are republican only in proportion as they embody the will of their people, and execute it." Hence, our first constitutions had really no leading principles in them. But experience & reflection have but more & more confirmed me in the particular importance of the equal representation then proposed.

To Samuel Kercheval, Monticello, July 12, 1816

[In the age of Aristotle] They had just ideas of the value of personal liberty; but none at all of the structure of government best calculated to preserve it. They knew no medium between a democracy (the only pure republic, but impracticable beyond the limits of a town) and an abandonment of themselves to an aristocracy, or a tyranny, independent of the people. It seems not to have occurred that where the citizens cannot meet to transact their business in person, they alone have the right to choose the agents who shall transact it; and that, in this way a republican, or popular government, of the 2d grade of purity, may be exercised over any extent of country. The full experiment of a government democratical, but representative, was and is still reserved for us. The idea (taken indeed from the little specimen formerly existing in the English constitution, but now lost) has been carried by us, more or less, into all our legislative and Executive departments; but it has not yet, by any of us, been pushed into all the ramifications of the system, so far as to leave no authority existing not responsible to the people: whose rights however to the exercise & fruits of their own industry, can never be protected against the selfishness of rulers not subject to their control at short periods. The introduction of this new principle of representative democracy has rendered useless almost every thing written before on the structure of government.

To Isaac H. Tiffany, Monticello, August 26, 1816

All Europe, Russia excepted, has caught the spirit; and all will attain representative government, more or less perfect. This is now well understood to be a necessary check on kings, whom they will probably think it more prudent to chain and tame, than to exterminate. To attain all this however rivers of blood must yet flow, & years of desolation pass over, yet the object is worth rivers of blood, and years of desolation. For what inheritance, so valuable, can man leave to his posterity?

To John Adams, Monticello, September 4, 1823

Modern times have the signal advantage too of having discovered the only device by which these rights can be secured, to wit, government by the people, acting, not in person, but by representatives chosen by themselves, that is to say, by every man of ripe years, and sane mind, who either contributes by his purse or person to the support of his country.

To Adamantios Coray, Monticello, October 31, 1823

In a republican nation, whose citizens are to be led by reason and persuasion, and not by force, the art of reasoning becomes of first importance.

To David Harding, Monticello, April 20, 1824

Road Building

Have you considered all the consequences of your proposition respecting post roads? I view it as a source of boundless patronage to the executive, jobbing to members of Congress & their friends, and a bottomless abyss of public money. You will begin by only appropriating the surplus of the post-office revenues; but the other revenues will soon be called into their aid, and it will be a source of eternal scramble among the members, who can get the most money wasted in their state; and they will always get most who are meanest. We have thought hitherto that the roads of a state could not be so well administered even by the state legislature as by the magistracy of the county, on the spot. What will it be when a member of N. H. is to mark out a road for Georgia? Does the power to establish post roads, given you by the Constitution, mean that you shall make the roads, or only select from those already made, those on which there shall be a post? If the term be equivocal (& I really do not think it so) which is the safest construction? That which permits a majority of Congress to go to cutting down mountains & bridging of rivers, or the other which if too restricted may be referred to the states for amendment, securing still due measures & proportion among us, and providing some means of information to the members of Congress tantamount to that ocular inspection which even in our county determinations, the magistrate finds cannot be supplied by any other evidence? The fortification of harbors was liable to great objection. But national circumstances furnished some color. In this case there is none. The roads of America are the best in the world except those of France and England. But does the state of our population, the extent of our internal commerce, the want of sea & river navigation, call for such expense on roads here, or are our means adequate to it? Think of all this and a great deal more which your good judgment will suggest, and pardon my freedom.

To James Madison, Monticello, March 6, 1796

Searching for the Right Government
We have chanced to live in an age which will probably be distinguished in history, for its experiments in government on a larger scale than has yet taken place. But we shall not live to see the result. The

grosser absurdities, such as hereditary magistracies, we shall see exploded in our day, long experience having already pronounced condemnation against them. But what is to be the substitute? This our children or grandchildren will answer. We may be satisfied with the certain knowledge that none can ever be tried so stupid, so unrighteous, so oppressive, so destructive of every end for which honest men enter into government, as that which their forefathers had established, & their fathers alone venture to tumble headlong from the stations they have so long abused. It is unfortunate that the efforts of mankind to recover the freedom of which they have been so long deprived, will be accompanied with violence, with errors & even with crimes. But while we weep over the means, we must pray for the end.

To François D'Ivernois, Monticello, February 6, 1795

Self-Preservation
Self-preservation is paramount to all law. . . . Should we have ever gained our revolution, if we had bound our hands by manacles of the law, not only in the beginning, but in any part of the revolutionary conflict? There are extreme cases where the laws become inadequate even to their own preservation, and where the universal resource is a dictator, or martial law.

To James Brown, Washington, October 27, 1808

The question you propose, Whether circumstances do not sometimes occur which make it a duty in

officers of high trust to assume authorities beyond
the law, is easy of solution in principle, but sometimes embarrassing in practice. A strict observance of
the written laws is doubtless one of the high duties of
a good citizen, but it is not the highest. The laws of
necessity, of self-preservation, of saving our country
when in danger, are of higher obligation. To lose our
country by a scrupulous adherence to written law,
would be to lose the law itself, with life, liberty, property & all those who are enjoying them with us; thus
absurdly sacrificing the end to the means. . . . The
unwritten laws of necessity, of self-preservation, & of
the public safety control the written laws of meum &
tuum.* . . .

The officer who is called to act on this superior
ground, does indeed risk himself on the justice of
the controlling powers of the constitution, and his
station makes it his duty to incur that risk. But
those controlling powers, and his fellow citizens
generally, are bound to judge according to the circumstances under which he acted. They are not to
transfer the information of this place or moment to
the time & place of his action; but to put themselves
into his situation. . . .

From these examples & principles you may see
what I think on the question proposed. They do not
go to the case of persons charged with petty duties,
where consequences are trifling, and time allowed for
a legal course, nor to authorize them to take such cases out of the written law. In these, the example of
overleaping the law is of greater evil than a strict

adherence to its imperfect provisions. It is incumbent on those only who accept of great charges, to risk themselves on great occasions, when the safety of the nation, or some of its very high interests are at stake. An officer is bound to obey orders; yet he would be a bad one who should do it in cases for which they were not intended, and which involved the most important consequences. The line of discrimination between cases may be difficult; but the good officer is bound to draw it at his own peril, & throw himself on the justice of his country and the rectitude of his motives.

*the distinction between what is mine or one's own and what is yours or another's

John B. Colvin, Monticello, September 20, 1810

Separation of Powers

The constitution intended that the three great branches of the government should be co-ordinate, & independent of each other. As to acts, therefore, which are to be done by either, it has given no control to another branch.

To George W. Hay, Washington, June 2, 1807

The leading principle of our constitution is the independence of the Legislative, Executive and Judiciary of each other.

To George W. Hay, Washington, June 20, 1807

State Constitutions

For tho' we may say with confidence that the worst of the American constitutions is better than the best

which ever existed before in any other country, &
that they are wonderfully perfect for a first essay, yet
every human essay must have defects. It will remain
therefore to those now coming on the stage of public
affairs to perfect what has been so well begun by
those going off it.

To Thomas Mann Randolph, Jr., Paris, July 6, 1787

I have stated that the constitutions of our several
states vary more or less in some particulars. But
there are certain principles in which all agree, and
which all cherish as vitally essential to the protection of the life, liberty, property, and safety of the
citizen.

1. Freedom of religion, restricted only from acts
of trespass on that of others.

2. Freedom of person, securing every one from imprisonment, or other bodily restraint, but by the
laws of the land. This is effected by the well-
known law of Habeas Corpus.

3. Trial by jury, the best of safeguards for the
person, the property and the fame of every individual.

4. The Exclusive right of legislation and taxation
in the representatives of the people.

5. Freedom of the press, subject only to liability
for personal injuries. This formidable Censor of
the public functionaries, by arraigning them at the
tribunal of public opinion, produces reform peaceably, which must otherwise be done by revolution.
It is also the best instrument for enlightening the

mind of man, and improving him as a rational, moral, and social being.

To Adamantios Coray, Monticello, October 31, 1823

Taxation

No experience has shown that a gift of perpetual revenue secures a perpetual return of duty or of kind disposition.

Resolutions of Congress on Lord North's Conciliatory Proposal, February 20, 1775

There never will be money in the treasury till the confederacy shows its teeth. The states must see the rod; perhaps it must be felt by some one of them. I am persuaded all of them would rejoice to see every one obliged to furnish its contributions. It is not the difficulty of furnishing them which beggars the treasury, but the fear that others will not furnish as much.

To James Monroe, Paris, August 11, 1786

Every circumstance we hear induces us to believe that it is the want of will, rather than of ability, to furnish contributions which keeps the public treasury so poor.

To David Humphreys, Paris, August 14, 1786

If we can prevent the government from wasting the labors of the people, under the pretense of taking care of them, they must become happy.

To Thomas Cooper, Washington, January 29, 1802

It is a wise rule, and should be fundamental in a government disposed to cherish its credit, and at the same time to restrain the use of it within the limits of its faculties, "never to borrow a dollar without laying a tax in the same instant for paying the interest annually, and the principal within a given term; and to consider that tax as pledged to the creditors on the public faith." On such a pledge as this, sacredly observed, a government may always command, on a reasonable interest, all the lendable money of their citizens, while the necessity of an equivalent tax is a salutary warning to them & their constituents against oppressions, bankruptcy, & its inevitable consequence, Revolution.

To John Wayles Eppes, Monticello, June 24, 1813

Taxation is in fact the most difficult function of government, and that against which their citizens are most apt to be refractory. The general aim is therefore to adopt the mode most consonant with the circumstances and sentiments of the country.

To Joseph Milligan, Monticello, April 6, 1816

The frequent recurrence of this chastening operation can alone restrain the propensity of governments to enlarge expense beyond income.

To Albert Gallatin, Monticello, December 26, 1820

Taxes on consumption like those on Capital or Income, to be just, must be uniform.

To Samuel Smith, Monticello, May 3, 1823

Two-Term President

I am sensible of the kindness of your rebuke on my determination to retire from office at a time when our country is laboring under difficulties truly great. But if the principle of rotation be a sound one, as I conscientiously believe it to be with respect to this office, no pretext should ever be permitted to dispense with it, because there never will be a time when real difficulties will not exist, & furnish a plausible pretext for dispensation.

To Henry Guest, Washington, January 4, 1809

Tyranny

The time to guard against corruption and tyranny, is before they shall have gotten hold of us. It is better to keep the wolf out of the fold, than to trust to drawing his teeth and talons after he shall have entered.

Notes on the State of Virginia, 1782

I have sworn upon the altar of god eternal hostility against every form of tyranny over the mind of man.

To Benjamin Rush, Monticello, September 23, 1800

The Union

I consider the Union of these states as the first of blessings, and as the first of duties the preservation of that constitution which secures it.

Address to the U.S. Senate, Philadelphia, March 4, 1797

We shall never give up our Union, the last anchor of our hope, & that alone which is to prevent this

heavenly country from becoming an arena of gladi-
ators.

To Elbridge Gerry, Philadelphia, May 13, 1797

Who can say what would be the evils of a scisson
and when & where they would end? Better keep
together as we are, hawl off from Europe as soon
as we can & from all attachments to any portions of
it, and if we feel their power just sufficiently to
hoop us together, it will be the happiest situation
in which we can exist.

To John Taylor, Philadelphia, June 4, 1798

It is a momentous truth, & happily of universal impression on the public mind that our safety rests on
the preservation of our union. Our citizens have wisely formed themselves into one nation as to others, and
several states as among themselves.

To the General Assembly of Rhode Island, Washington,
May 26, 1801

The cement of this Union is in the heart blood of
every American.

To the Marquis de Lafayette, Monticello, February 14, 1815

A nation united can never be conquered.

To John Adams, Monticello, January 11, 1816

Should time not be given [for both political parties
to cool], and the schism be pushed to separation, it
will be for a short term only. Two or three years trial

will bring them back, like quarrelling lovers, to renewed embraces, and increased affection. The experiment of separation would soon prove to both that they had mutually miscalculated their best interests. And even were the parties in Congress to secede in a passion, the soberer people would call a Convention and cement again the severance attempted by the insanity of their functionaries.

To Richard Rush, Monticello,
October 20, 1820

Vice President

The second is the only office in the world about which I cannot decide in my own mind whether I had rather have it or not have it. Pride does not enter into the estimate. For I think with the Romans of old, that the General of today should be a common soldier tomorrow if necessary. But as to Mr. Adams particularly, I could have no feelings which would revolt at being placed in a secondary station to him. I am his junior in life, I was his junior in Congress, his junior in the diplomatic line, and lately his junior in our civil government.

To James Madison, Monticello,
January 1, 1796

Health, Medicine, and Exercise

Alcoholism

Mr. B's habitual intoxication will destroy himself, his fortune & family. Of all calamities this is the greatest.

To Mary Jefferson Eppes, Philadelphia,
January 7, 1798

The prostration of body and mind which the cheapness of this liquor [i.e., whiskey] is spreading thro' the mass of our citizens, now calls the attention of the legislator on a very different principle. One of his important duties is as guardian of those who from causes susceptible of precise definition, cannot take care of themselves. Such are infants, maniacs, gamblers, drunkards. The last, as much as the maniac, requires restrictive measures to save him from the fatal infatuation under which he is destroying his health, his morals, his family and his usefulness to society.

To Samuel Smith, Monticello, May 3, 1823

Anatomy

Of all machines ours is the most complicated and inexplicable.

To James Madison, Monticello,
August 31, 1783

No knowledge can be more satisfactory to a man than that of his own frame, its parts, their function & actions.

To Thomas Cooper, Monticello,
October 7, 1814

Cold-Water Bathing

Your practice of the cold bath thrice a week during the winter, and at the age of 70, is a bold one, which I should not, à priori,* have pronounced salutary. But all theory must yield to experience, and every constitution has its own laws. I have for 50 years bathed my feet in cold water every morning (as you mention) and having been remarkably exempted from colds (not having had one in every 7 years of my life on an average) I have supposed it might be ascribed to that practice. When we see two facts accompanying one another for a long time, we are apt to suppose them related as cause and effect.

*deductively

To James Maury, Monticello,
June 16, 1815

So free from catarrhs that I have not had one, (in the breast, I mean) on an average of 8 or 10 years thro' life. I ascribe this exemption partly to the habit of bathing my feet in cold water every morning, for 60 years past.

To Vine Utley, Monticello,
March 21, 1819

Cures

Where the disease is most deeply seated, there it will be slowest in eradication.

To David Barrow, Monticello,
May 1, 1815

Euthanasia

The most elegant thing of that kind known is a preparation of the Jamestown weed, Datura-Stramonium, invented by the French in the time of Robespierre. Every man of firmness carried it constantly in his pocket to anticipate the Guillotine. It brings on the sleep of death as quietly as fatigue does the ordinary sleep, without the least struggle or motion. Condorcet, who had recourse to it, was found lifeless on his bed a few minutes after his landlady had left him there, and even the slipper which she had observed half suspended on his foot, was not shaken off. It seems far preferable to the Venesection of the Romans, the Hemlock of the Greeks, and the Opium of the Turks. I have never been able to learn what the preparation is, other than a strong concentration of its lethiferous principle. Could such a medicament be restrained to self-administration, it ought not to be kept secret. There are ills in life as desperate as intolerable, to which it would be the rational relief, e.g. the inveterate cancer.

To Samuel Brown, Monticello,
July 14, 1813

Exercise

If the body be feeble, the mind will not be strong. The sovereign invigorator of the body is exercise, and of all the exercises walking is best.

> To Thomas Mann Randolph, Jr., Paris,
> August 27, 1786

Exercise and application produce order in our affairs, health of body, cheerfulness of mind, and these make us precious to our friends.

> To Martha Jefferson, Aix en Provence,
> March 28, 1787

You are not . . . to consider yourself as unemployed while taking exercise. That is necessary for your health, and health is the first of all objects.

> To Martha Jefferson, Aix en Provence,
> March 28, 1787

I give more time to exercise of the body than of the mind, believing it wholesome to both.

> To David Howell, Monticello, December 15, 1810

The loss of the power of taking exercise would be a sore affliction to me.

> To Benjamin Rush, Poplar Forest, August 17, 1811

Health

Health must not be sacrificed to learning. A strong body makes the mind strong.

> To Peter Carr, Paris, August 19, 1785

Health is the first object.

To Thomas Mann Randolph, Jr., Paris, November 25, 1785

Knowledge indeed is desirable, a lovely possession, but I do not scruple to say that health is more so. It is of little consequence to store the mind with science if the body be permitted to become debilitated. If the body be feeble, the mind will not be strong.

To Thomas Mann Randolph, Jr., Paris, August 27, 1786

Experience learns us to be always anxious about the health of those whom we love.

To Martha Jefferson, Toulon, April 7, 1787

Health, without which there is no happiness. An attention to health then should take place [over] every other object. The time necessary to secure this by active exercises, should be devoted to it in preference to every other pursuit. I know the difficulty with which a studious man tears himself from his studies at any given moment of the day. But his happiness & that of his family depends on it. The most uninformed mind with a healthy body, is happier than the wisest valetudinarian.

To Thomas Mann Randolph, Jr., Paris, July 6, 1787

Health is the first requisite after morality.

To Peter Carr, Paris, August 10, 1787

My florid health is calculated to keep my friends as well as foes quiet as they should be.

To Benjamin Rush, Washington, December 20, 1801

I was sorry . . . to learn the ill state of your health, and I sincerely wish that this may find you better. Young, temperate & prudent as you are, great confidence may be reposed in the provision nature has made for restoration of order in our system when it has become deranged; she effects her object by strengthening the whole system, towards which medicine is generally mischievous. Nor are the sedentary habits of office friendly to it.

To Gideon Granger, Monticello, January 24, 1810

Hunger

Our machine, unsupported by food, is no longer under the control of reason.

To George Gilmer, Philadelphia, June 28, 1793

Illness

Written accounts can hardly give one an exact idea of the situation of a sick person.

To Mary Jefferson Eppes, Philadelphia, April 6, 1800

Medicine and Medical Practices

I am sorry to hear of Jefferson's* indisposition, but glad you do not physic him. This leaves nature free and unembarrassed in her own tendencies to repair what is wrong. I hope to hear or to find that he is recovered.

> *Jefferson's grandson, Thomas Jefferson Randolph

To Martha Jefferson Randolph, Philadelphia, May 31, 1798

The state of medicine is worse than that of total ignorance. Could we divest ourselves of every thing we
suppose we know in it, we should start from a higher
ground & with fairer prospects. From Hippocrates to
Brown we have had nothing but a succession of hy-
pothetical systems each having its day of vogue, like
the fashions & fancies of caps & gowns, & yielding in
turn to the next caprice. Yet the human frame, which
is to be the subject of suffering & torture under these
learned modes, does not change. We have a few medicines, as the bark, opium, mercury, which in a few
well defined diseases are of unquestionable virtue:
but the residuary list of the materia medica,* long as
it is, contains but the charlataneries of the art; and of
the diseases of doubtful form, physicians have ever
had a false knowledge, worse than ignorance, yet
surely the list of unequivocal diseases & remedies is
capable of enlargement.

> *the remedial substances used in the practice of
> medicine

To William Green Munford, June 18, 1799

The only sure foundations of medicine are in intimate knowledge of the human body and observation
on the effects of medicinal substances on that.

To Caspar Wistar, Washington, June 21, 1807

Altho' much of a skeptic in the practice of medicine,
I read with pleasure its ingenious theories.

To Benjamin Rush, Monticello, January 16, 1811

I acknowledge facts in medicine as far as they go, distrusting only their extension by theory.

To Benjamin Rush, Poplar Forest,
August 17, 1811

[For] some forms of disease, well known and well defined, [medicine] has found substances which will restore order to the human system, & it is to be hoped that observation & experience will add to their number. But a great mass of diseases remains undistinguished, & unknown, exposed to the random shot of the theory of the day.

To John Crawford, Monticello, January 2, 1812

Having little confidence in the theories of that art [i.e., medicine], which change in their fashion with the ladies' caps and gowns, he has much in the facts it has established by observation. The experience of physicians has proved that in certain forms of disease, certain substances will restore order to the human system; and he doubts not that continued observation will enlarge the catalogue, and give relief to our posterity in cases wherein we are without it.

To Ezra Sargeant, Monticello, February 3, 1812

Sports

Games played with the ball & others of the nature, are too violent for the body & stamp no character on the mind.

To Peter Carr, Paris, August 19, 1785

Walking

The object of walking is to relax the mind. You should therefore not permit yourself even to think while you walk. But direct your attention by the objects surrounding you. Walking is the best possible exercise. Habituate yourself to walk very far.

To Peter Carr, Paris, August 19, 1785

Of all exercises walking is best. . . . No one knows, till he tries, how easily a habit of walking is acquired. A person who never walked three miles will in the course of a month become able to walk 15 or 20 without fatigue. I have known some great walkers & had particular accounts of many more; and I never knew or heard of one who was not healthy & long lived. This species of exercise therefore is much to be advised.

To Thomas Mann Randolph, Jr., Paris, August 27, 1786

History

History, by apprizing them of the past, will enable them to judge of the future; it will avail them of the experience of other times and other nations; it will qualify them as judges of the actions and designs of men; it will enable them to know ambition under every disguise it may assume; and knowing it, to defeat its views.

Notes on the State of Virginia, 1782

I learn with great satisfaction that you are about committing to the press the valuable historical and state-papers you have been so long collecting. Time & accident are committing daily havoc on the originals deposited in our public offices. The late war has done the work of centuries in this business. The lost cannot be recovered; but let us save what remains: not by vaults and locks which fence them from the public eye and use, in consigning them to the waste of time, but by such a multiplication of copies, as shall place them beyond the reach of accident.

To Ebenezer Hazard, Philadelphia, February 18, 1791

Wars & contentions indeed fill the pages of history with more matter. But more blest is that nation whose silent course of happiness furnishes nothing for history to say. This is what I ambition for my own country.

To the Comte Diodati, Washington, March 29, 1807

History in general only informs us what bad government is.

To John Norvell, Washington, June 11, 1807

We are certainly indebted to those who think our revolution worthy of their pen, and who will do justice to our actions and motives.

To Charles G. G. Botta, Monticello, July 15, 1810

Wisdom & duty dictate an humble resignation to the verdict of our future peers.

To John Adams, Monticello, June 27, 1813

It is truly unfortunate that those engaged in public affairs so rarely make notes of transactions passing within their knowledge. Hence history becomes fable instead of fact. The great outlines may be true, but the incidents and coloring are according to the faith or fancy of the writer.

To William Wirt, Monticello,
August 14, 1814

The only exact testimony of a man is his actions, leaving the reader to pronounce on them his own judgment.

To Louis H. Girardin, Monticello, March 27, 1815

Prophecy is one thing, history another.

To Abigail Adams, Monticello, January 11, 1817

You say I must go to writing history. While in public life, I had not time: and now that I am retired, I am past the time. To write history requires a whole life of observation, of enquiry, of labor and correction. Its materials are not to be found among the ruins of a decayed memory.

To Josephus B. Stuart, Monticello, May 10, 1817

[In sending Adams a pamphlet Jefferson asks that it be returned.] I will ask its return, because I value it as a morsel of genuine history, a thing so rare as to be always valuable.

To John Adams, Poplar Forest, September 8, 1817

I feel a much greater interest in knowing what passed two or three thousand years ago, than in what is now passing.

To Nathaniel Macon, Monticello, January 12, 1819

Multiplied testimony, multiplied views will be necessary to give solid establishment to truth. Much is known to one which is not known to another, and no one knows everything. It is the sum of individual knowledge which is to make up the whole truth, and to give its correct current thro' future time.

To William Johnson, Monticello, March 4, 1823

History may distort truth, and will distort it for a time, by the superior efforts at justification of those who are conscious of needing it most. Nor will the opening scenes of our present government be seen in their true aspect until the letters of the day, now held in private hoards, shall be broken up and laid open to public view.

To William Johnson, Monticello, June 12, 1823

It is the duty of every good citizen to use all the opportunities which occur to him, for preserving documents relating to the history of our country.

To Hugh P. Taylor, Monticello, October 4, 1823

Historical facts . . . belong to the present, as well as future times.

To William Branch Giles, Monticello,
December 26, 1825

Jefferson's Papers

The letters I have written while in public office are in fact memorials of the transactions with which I have been associated, and may at a future day furnish something to the historian.

To William Short, Monticello, May 5, 1816

Altho' I had not time to prepare anything express, my letters (all preserved) will furnish the daily occurrences and views from my return from Europe in 1790, till I retired finally from office. These will command more conviction than anything I could have written after my retirement; no day having ever passed during that period without a letter to somebody, written too in the moment, and in the warmth and freshness of fact and feeling they will carry internal evidence that what they breathe is genuine. Selections from these after my death, may come out successively as the maturity of circumstances may render their appearance seasonable.

To William Johnson, Monticello, March 4, 1823

Human Action and Interaction

Acquiescence

An instance too of acquiescence, on our part, under a wrong, rather than disturb our friendship by altercations, may have its value in some future case.

To John Jay, Paris, August 11, 1786

[In writing from his deathbed] Acquiescence is a duty, under circumstances not placed among those we are permitted to control.

To Roger C. Weightman, Monticello, June 24, 1826

Anger

Anger only serves to torment ourselves, to divert others, and alienate their esteem.

To Martha Jefferson, Toulon, April 7, 1787

Be good, my dear, as I have always found you, never be angry with any body nor speak harm of them, try to let every body's faults be forgotten as you would wish your's to be.

To Mary Jefferson, New York, April 11, 1790

When angry, count ten before you speak; if very angry, an hundred.

To Thomas Jefferson Smith,
February 21, 1825

Argumentativeness

An association of men who will not quarrel with one another is a thing which never yet existed.

To John Taylor, Philadelphia, June 4, 1798

In stating prudential rules for our government in society, I must not omit the important one of never entering into dispute or argument with another. I never yet saw an instance of one of two disputants convincing the other, by argument. I have seen many, of them getting warm, becoming rude, & shooting one another. Conviction is the effect of our own dispassionate reasoning, either in solitude, or weighing within ourselves, dispassionately what we hear from others standing uncommitted in argument ourselves. It was one of the rules which above all others made Doctor Franklin the most amiable of men in society, "never to contradict any body." If he was urged to announce an opinion, he did it rather by asking questions, as if for information, or by suggesting doubts. When I hear another express an opinion, which is not mine, I say to myself, he has a right to his opinion, as I to mine; why should I question it? His error does me no injury, and shall I become a Don Quixote to bring all men by force of argument to one opinion? If a fact be misstated, it is probable he is gratified by a belief of it, & I have no right to deprive him of the gratification. If he wants information he will ask for it, & then I will give it in measured terms; but if he still believes his own story, & shows a desire to dispute the fact with me, I hear him & say nothing. It is his affair not mine, if he prefers error. There are two classes of disputants most frequently to be met with among us. The first is of young students just entered the threshold of science, with a first view of its outlines, not yet filled up with the details & modifications which a further progress would bring to their knowledge. The other consists of the ill-tempered & rude men in society who have taken up a passion for politics. (Good humor & politeness never introduce into mixed society, a question on which they foresee there would be a difference of opinion.) From both of those classes of disputants, my dear Jefferson, keep aloof, as you would from the infected subjects of yellow fever or pestilence. Consider yourself, when with them, as among the patients of Bedlam, needing medical more than moral counsel. Be a listener only, keep within yourself, and endeavor to establish with yourself the habit of silence, especially in politics. In the fevered state of our country, no good can ever result from any attempt to set one of these fiery zealots to rights, either in fact or principle. They are determined as to the facts. They will believe, and the opinions on which they will act. Get by them, therefore, as you would by an angry bull; it is not for a man of sense to dispute the road with such an animal.

To Thomas Jefferson Randolph, Washington,
November 24, 1808

In little disputes with your companions, give way rather than insist on trifles, for their love and the approbation of others will be worth more to you than the trifle in dispute.

To Francis Eppes, Monticello, May 21, 1816

Bearing Arms

None but an armed nation can dispense with a standing army; to keep ours armed and disciplined, is therefore at all times important, but especially so at a moment when rights the most essential to our welfare have been violated, and an infraction of treaty committed without color or pretext.

To Unknown, Washington, February 25, 1803

The representation of the Committee of the county of Jefferson, in New York, of which you are chairman, stating their want of arms, and asking a supply, has been duly received and considered. I learn with great concern that a portion of our frontier so interesting, so important, and so exposed, should be so entirely unprovided with common fire-arms. I did not suppose any part of the U.S. so destitute of what is considered as among the first necessaries of a farm-house. This circumstance gives me the more concern as the laws of the U.S. do not permit their arms to be delivered from the magazines but to troops actually taking the field; and, indeed, were the inhabitants on the whole of our frontier, of so many thousands of miles, to be furnished from our magazines, little would be left in them for actual war. For the ordinary safety of the citizens of the several states, whether against dangers from within or without, reliance has been placed either on the domestic means of the individuals, or on those provided by the respective states. What those means are in the state of New York, I am not informed; but I have transmitted your representation to Governor Tompkins, with an earnest recommendation of it to his attention; and I have no doubt that his solicitude for the welfare & safety of a portion so imminently exposed of those under his immediate care, will ensure to you whatever his authority and his means will permit.

To Jacob J. Brown, Washington, January 27, 1808

Business Associates

A friendly intercourse between individuals who do business together produces a mutual spirit of accommodation useful to both parties.

To James Monroe, Paris, June 17, 1785

Candor

I always suppose that the most honest way of acting for another is to give a true state of things without disguise.

To Thomas Barclay, Paris, July 4, 1787

I fear this opinion may appear to you officious. But having been consulted confidentially I cannot speak by halves. I feel myself bound to express the whole of my opinion if I express any part of it, and for this the parties have called on me.

To Robert Pigott, Paris, June 3, 1788

My own dispositions are as much against writing mysteries, innuendos & half confidences.

To John Taylor, November 26, 1798

When I sat down to answer your letter, but two courses presented themselves. Either to say nothing or every thing; for half-confidences are not in my character.

To Elbridge Gerry, Philadelphia, January 26, 1799

Opportunities of candid explanation are so seldom afforded me, that I must not lose them when they occur.

To Barnabas Bidwell, Washington, July 5, 1806

I prefer candid and open expression.

To George Logan, Monticello, May 19, 1816

I cannot say things by halves.

To Samuel Kercheval, Monticello, July 12, 1816

Causation

It is impossible, where one sees like courses of events commence, not to ascribe them to like causes.

To Governor William Plumer, Monticello, January 31, 1815

When we see two facts accompanying one another for a long time, we are apt to suppose them related as cause and effect.

To James Maury, Monticello, June 16, 1815

Ceremony

I expect we shall rise in May. I shall go through the Eastern shore, by Norfolk & up the S. side of James river to Petersburg to Eppington, because the whole route will be through a country I have never yet seen. I say nothing of it to any body because I do not wish to beget ceremony anywhere; or have any thing to do with it. For the same reason I shall not call on you in Richmond, but go from Eppington the direct road home. Besides my hatred of ceremony, I believe it better to avoid every occasion of the expression of sentiments which might drag me into the newspapers. I know that sometimes it is useful to furnish occasions for the flame of public opinion to break out from time to time; & that that opinion strengthens & rallies numbers in that way. The federal party have made powerful use of this. Yet I doubt whether we ought not to rest solely on the slow but sure progress of good sense & attachment to republicanism, & build our fabric on a basis which can never give way. This is most consonant to my own opinion, & especially to my dislike of being the Mannequin of a ceremony. I shall therefore avoid Richmond.

To James Monroe, Philadelphia, March 26, 1800

I never doubted the impropriety of our adopting as a system that of pomp & fulsome attentions by our citizens to their functionaries. I am decidedly against it as degrading the citizen in his own eye, exalting his functionary, & creating a distance between the

two which does not tend to aid the morals of either.
I think it a practice which we ought to destroy &
must destroy, & therefore must not adopt as a general thing, even for a short time.

> To James Monroe, Philadelphia, April 13, 1800

Changing People's Opinions

Don Quixote undertook to redress the bodily
wrongs of the world, but the redressment of mental
vagaries would be an enterprise more than Quixotic.

> To Benjamin Waterhouse, Monticello,
> July 19, 1822

Communications

Nothing but good can result from an exchange of
information and opinions between those whose circumstances and morals admit no doubt of the integrity of their views.

> To Elbridge Gerry, Philadelphia, May 13, 1797

Compromise

A government held together by the bands of reason
only, requires much compromise of opinion; that
things, even salutary, should not be crammed down
the throats of dissenting brethren, especially when
they may be put into a form to be willingly swallowed, and that a great deal of indulgence is necessary to strengthen habits of harmony and fraternity.

> To Edward Livingston, Monticello,
> April 4, 1824

Conversation

An hour of conversation would be worth a volume of letters.

To John Adams, Monticello, April 8, 1816

Correcting Deception

[Referring to the newspaper essayist Decius] His facts are far from truth and should be corrected.

To William A. Burwell, Monticello, September 17, 1806

Correspondence

Nothing can equal the dearth of American intelligence in which we live here. I had formed no conception of it. We might as well be in the moon. . . . Our friends think that facts known to every body there, cannot be unknown here. And all thinking so, no one writes them.

To Francis Hopkinson, Paris, January 13, 1785

But why has no body else written to me? Is it that one is forgotten as soon as their back is turned? I have a better opinion of men. It must be either that they think that the details known to themselves are known to every body and so come to us thro' a thousand channels, or that we should set no value on them. Nothing can be more erroneous than both those opinions. We value those details, little and great, public and private, in proportion to our distance from our own country: and so far are they from getting to us through a thousand channels, that we hear no more of them or of our country here than if we were among the dead.

To James Monroe, Paris, April 15, 1785

Unable to converse with my friends in person, I am happy when I do it in black and white.

To Elizabeth House Trist, Paris, December 15, 1786

Letters of business claiming their rights before those of affection, we often write seldomest to those whom we love most.

To Mary Jefferson Bolling, Paris, July 23, 1787

If you knew how agreeable to me are the details of the small news of my neighborhood, your charity would induce you to write frequently.

To George Gilmer, Paris, August 12, 1787

Young poets complain often that life is fleeting & transient. We find in it seasons & situations however which move heavily enough. It will lighten them to me if you will continue to honor me with your correspondence.

To Abigail Adams, Paris, February 2, 1788

In matters of correspondence as well as of money, you must never be in debt.

To Mary Jefferson, New York, June 13, 1790

I return to farming with an ardor which I scarcely knew in my youth, and which has got the better entirely of my love of study. Instead of writing 10 or 12 letters a day, which I have been in the habit of doing as a thing in course, I put off answering my letters now, farmer-like, till a rainy day, & then find them sometimes postponed by other necessary occupations.

To John Adams, Monticello, April 25, 1794

I have long owed you a letter, for which my conscience would not have let me rest in quiet but on the consideration that the payment would not be worth your acceptance. The debt is not merely for a letter the common traffic of a day, but for valuable ideas, which instructed me, which I have adopted, & am acting on them.

To John Taylor, Monticello, December 29, 1794

A right of free correspondence between citizen & citizen, on their joint interests, whether public or private, & under whatsoever laws these interests arise (to wit, of the state, of Congress, of France, Spain, or Turkey) is a natural right; it is not the gift of any municipal law either of England, of Virginia, or of Congress, but in common with all our other natural rights, is one of the objects for the protection of which society is formed and municipal laws established.

To James Monroe, Monticello, September 7, 1797

Truth requires me to add also that after being so long chained to the writing table, I go to it with reluctance, and listen with partiality to every call from any other quarter.

To William Lambert, Monticello, May 28, 1809

We must continue while here to exchange occasionally our mutual good wishes.

To Benjamin Rush, Poplar Forest, August 17, 1811

Sundays and rainy days are always days of writing for the farmer.

To Charles Willson Peale, Poplar Forest, August 20, 1811

I cannot relinquish the right of correspondence with those I have learnt to esteem.

To Levi Lincoln, Monticello, August 25, 1811

[Referring to his decade-long estrangement from John and Abigail Adams] There is an awkwardness which hangs over the resuming a correspondence so long discontinued.

To Benjamin Rush, Poplar Forest, December 5, 1811

Time, which withers the fancy, as the other faculties of the mind and body, presses on me with a heavy hand, and distance intercepts all personal intercourse.

To Thomas Sully, Monticello, January 8, 1812

The drudgery of letter-writing often denies the leisure of reading a single page in a week.

To Ezra Stiles, Monticello, June 25, 1819

A line from my good old friends is like balm to my soul.

To Nathaniel Macon, Monticello, November 23, 1821

Debt

Be assured that it gives much more pain to the mind to be in debt, than to do without any article whatever which we may seem to want.

To Martha Jefferson, Paris, June 14, 1787

The maxim of buying nothing without money in our pocket to pay for it, would make of our country one of the happiest upon earth.

To Alexander Donald, Paris, July 28, 1787

The torment of mind I endure till the moment shall arrive when I shall not owe a shilling on earth is such really as to render life of little value.

To Nicholas Lewis, Paris, July 29, 1787

The accumulation of debts is a most fearful evil.

To William Carmichael, Paris, September 25, 1787

I made a point of paying my workmen in preference to all other claimants. I never parted with one without settling with him, and giving him either his money or my note. Every person that ever worked from me can attest this, and that I always paid their notes pretty soon. I am sure there did not exist one of these notes unpaid when I left Virginia.

To Nicholas Lewis, Paris, July 11, 1788

It is our principle to pay to a moment whatever we have engaged, and never to engage what we cannot, and mean not faithfully to pay.

To P. S. DuPont de Nemours, Washington,
February 1, 1803

Defamation

Defamation is becoming a necessary of life; insomuch that a dish of tea, in the morning or evening, cannot be digested without this stimulant. Even those who do not believe these abominations, still read them with complacence to their auditors, and instead of the abhorrence & indignation which should fill a virtuous mind, betray a secret pleasure in the possibility that some may believe them, tho they do not themselves. It seems to escape them that it is not he who prints, but he who pays for printing a slander, who is its real author.

To John Norvell, Washington, June 11, 1807

Delegation of Authority

There is no delegating a trust by halves.

To Alexander Donald, Philadelphia,
November 25, 1790

Dependence

Dependence begets subservience and venality, suffocates the germ of virtue, and prepares fit tools for the designs of ambition.

Notes on the State of Virginia, 1782

Details

By analyzing too minutely we often reduce our subject to atoms of which the mind loses its hold.

To Edward Everett, Monticello, February 24, 1823

Duplicity

I disdain everything like duplicity.

To James Madison, Monticello, August 3, 1797

Errors

Error is the stuff of which the web of life is woven: and he who lives longest and wisest is only able to weave out the more of it.

To the Marquis de Chastellux, Paris, October 1786

It is always better to have no ideas than false ones and to believe nothing, than to believe what is wrong. In my mind, theories are more easily demolished than rebuilt.

To Rev. James Madison, Paris, July 19, 1788

The errors and misfortunes of others should be a school for our own instruction.

To Mary Jefferson Eppes, Philadelphia, January 7, 1798

I may have erred at times, no doubt I have erred. This is the law of human nature. For honest errors however indulgence may be hoped.

Speech to the U.S. Senate, February 28, 1801

Time and truth will at length correct error.

To the Comte de Volney, Washington, February 8, 1805

Exceptions

There is no rule without exceptions: but it is false reasoning which converts exceptions into the general rule.

To Thomas Law, Poplar Forest, June 13, 1814

Experience

I have ever found it dangerous to quit the road of experience. New essays generally fail.

To John Trumbull, Paris, July 17, 1788

The ground I have already passed over enables me to see my way into that which is before me.

To George Washington, Chesterfield, December 15, 1789

A little experience is worth a great deal of reading.

To Mary Jefferson Eppes, Washington, October 26, 1801

Experience alone brings skill.

To William H. Crawford, February 11, 1815

What has passed may be a lesson.

To James Maury, Monticello, June 15, 1815

But all theory must yield to experience, and every constitution has its own laws.

To James Maury, Monticello, June 16, 1815

Yet experience & frequent disappointment have taught me not to be overconfident in theories or calculations, until actual trial of the whole combination has stamped it with approbation.

To George Fleming, Monticello, December 29, 1815

Forty years of experience in government is worth a century of book-reading.

To Samuel Kercheval, Monticello, July 12, 1816

Explanations

Explanations between reasonable men can never but do good.

To James Monroe, Washington, March 10, 1808

False Hopes

To give you false hopes, would be to injure & not to serve you.

To Jean Baptiste Duler, Paris, January 17, 1787

Favors

Those who have had, and who may yet have occasion to ask favors, should never ask small ones.

To the Marquis de Lafayette, Paris, June 15, 1786

Favors are doubly precious which, promoting the present purposes of interest and of friendship, enlarge the foundations for their continuance and increase.

To Charles Alexandre de Calonne, Paris, November 2, 1786

I am never happier than when I am performing good offices for good people.

To Abigail Adams, Paris, November 1786

Firmness

When we see ourselves in a situation which must be endured & gone through, it is best to make up our minds to it, meet it with firmness, & accommodate every thing to it in the best way practicable. This lessens the evil, while fretting & fuming only serves to increase our own torment.

> To Mary Jefferson Eppes, Philadelphia,
> January 7, 1798

Firmness on our part, but a passive firmness is the true course.

> To James Madison, Philadelphia,
> January 30, 1799

The patriot, like the Christian, must learn that to bear revilings & persecutions is a part of his duty; and in proportion as the trial is severe, firmness under it becomes more requisite & praiseworthy.

> To James Sullivan, Washington, May 21, 1805

First Impressions

The only thing to be feared is that the first impressions will produce measures, which reflection & an analysis of the whole transactions will be too late to remedy.

> To John Taylor, Philadelphia, April 6, 1798

Folly

Every folly must run its round.

> To John Adams, Monticello, July 5, 1814

Force

With every barbarous people . . . force is law.

Notes on the State of Virginia, 1782

Force without conduct is easily baffled.

To Theodorus Bailey, Monticello,
February 6, 1813

Force cannot change right.

To John Cartwright, Monticello, June 5, 1824

Formalities

It would be ridiculous in the present case to talk about forms. There are situations when form must be dispensed with. A man attacked by assassins will call for help to those nearest him, & will not think himself bound to silence till a magistrate may come to his aid.

To William Short, Philadelphia, November 24, 1791

Fortunes

It is a quick multiplication of small profits which makes the surest fortune in the end.

To J.P.P. Derieux, Paris, July 25, 1788

Future Conduct

You have justly resorted to the only proper ground, that of estimating my future by my past conduct.

To William Jackson, Washington,
February 18, 1801

Gambling

Gambling . . . corrupts our dispositions, and teaches us a habit of hostility against all mankind.

To Martha Jefferson, Canal of Languedoc, May 21, 1787

Gentlemen, I received, some time ago your letter of Feb. 28, covering a printed scheme of a lottery for the benefit of the East Tennessee college, & proposing to send tickets to me to be disposed of. It would be impossible for them to come to a more inefficient hand. I rarely go from home, & consequently see but a few neighbors & friends, who occasionally call on me. And having myself made it a rule never to engage in a lottery or any other adventure of mere chance, I can, with the less candor or effect, urge it on others, however laudable & desirable its object may be.

To the trustees for the lottery of East Tennessee College, Monticello, May 6, 1810

General Agreement

You & I may differ occasionally in details of minor consequence, as no two minds, more than two faces are the same in every feature. But our general objects are the same.

To William Johnson, Monticello, June 12, 1823

Good People

Good people naturally grow together.

To Maria Cosway, Paris, November 19, 1786

Good Wishes

Good wishes are all an old man has to offer to his country or friends.

To Thomas Law, Monticello, January 15, 1811

Prayers . . . are the only weapons of an old man.

To Edward Coles, Monticello, August 25, 1814

Gradualness

We must be contented to travel on towards perfection, step by step.

To the Comte de Moustier, Paris, May 17, 1788

If we cannot do everything at once, let us do one thing at a time.

To John Breckenridge, Monticello, February 15, 1821

Guidelines

We find that both law and expediency draw a line for our guide.

To Samuel Smith, Washington, July 30, 1807

Halfway Measures

Things which are just or handsome should never be done by halves.

To Benjamin Harrison, Paris, January 12, 1785

Hospitality

You shall find with me a room, bed, & plate with a hearty welcome.

To James Monroe, Paris, December 10, 1784

Such is the hospitality in that country [America], & their disposition to assist strangers, that he may boldly go to any good house he sees, and make the enquiry he needs. He will be sure to be kindly received, honestly informed, and accommodated in a hospitable way, without any other introduction than an information who he is, & what are his views.

To Thomas Digges, Paris, June 19, 1788

When we have long expected the visit of a dear friend, he is welcome when he comes, and all who come with him.

To Angelica Schuyler Church, Paris, July 27, 1788

Call on me in your turn, whenever you come to town: and if it should be about the hour of three, I shall rejoice the more. You will find a bad dinner, a good glass of wine, and a host thankful for your favor, and desirous of encouraging repetitions of it without number, form or ceremony.

To Richard Peters, Philadelphia, June 30, 1791

Should you return to the U.S., perhaps your curiosity may lead you to visit the hermit of Monticello. He will receive you with affection & delight.

To P. S. Dupont de Nemours, Washington,
March 2, 1809

Come as you will, or as you can, it will always be joy enough to me.

To Caesar A. Rodney, Monticello, March 16, 1815

You know our practice of placing our guests at their ease, by showing them we are so ourselves & that we follow our necessary vocations, instead of fatiguing them by hanging unremittingly on their shoulders.

To Francis W. Gilmer, Monticello, June 7, 1816

Idealism

Men come into business at first with visionary principles. It is practice alone which can correct & conform them to the actual current of affairs.

To James Madison, Paris, May 25, 1788

Immigration

I am of opinion that American tenants for Western lands could not be procured, & if they could, they would be very unsure. The best as far as I have been able to judge are foreigners who do not speak the language. Unable to communicate with the people of the country they confine themselves to their farms & their families, compare their present state to what it was in Europe, & find great reason to be contented. Of all foreigners I should prefer Germans. They are the easiest got, the best for their landlord, & do best for themselves.

To Richard Claiborne, Paris, August 8, 1787

If ever there was a case where a law could impose no other obligation than the risk of the arbitrary penalty it is that which makes the country in which a man happens to be born his perpetual prison,

obliging him to starve in that rather than seek another where he can find the means of subsistence.

To Alexander McRae, Monticello, August 27, 1809

I lament the misfortune of the persons who have been
driven from Cuba to seek Asylum with you [in New
Orleans]. This it is impossible to refuse them, or to
withhold any relief they can need. We should be mon-
sters to shut the door against such sufferers. True, it is
not a population we can desire, at that place, because
it retards the desired epoch of its becoming entirely
American in spirit. No people on earth retain their national adherence longer or more warmly than the
French. But such considerations are not to prevent us
from taking up human beings from a wreck at sea.
Gratitude will doubtless secure their fidelity to the
country which has received them into its bosom.

To William C. C. Claiborne, Monticello,
September 10, 1809

Incredulity

On account of the multitude of falsehoods always
current here, under specious appearances, I am
obliged to be slow of belief.

To John Jay, Paris, February 5, 1788

Indiscretions

It is sometimes difficult to decide whether indiscre-
tions . . . had better be treated with silence, or due
notice.

To George Washington, Philadelphia, February 16, 1793

Indulgence

I may have erred at times—no doubt I have erred; this is the law of human nature. For honest errors, however, indulgence may be hoped.

Speech to the U.S. Senate, February 28, 1801

Information

I value no act of friendship so highly as the communicating facts to me which I am not in the way of knowing otherwise, and could not therefore otherwise guard against.

To Wilson Cary Nicholas, Washington, March 20, 1808

I always consider it as the most friendly office which can be rendered me, to be informed of any thing which is going amiss, and which I can remedy.

To Wilson Cary Nicholas, Washington,
December 22, 1808

Insufficient Clues

You have puzzled me with your scrap about a something which has turned up of which you say you spoke to me in November &c. &c. I cannot find this out. You should remember that tho' a word is enough to the wise, it is not to the foolish. I shall hope therefore a further detail.

To William Stephens Smith, Paris, May 4, 1786

Insult

An insult unpunished is the parent of many others.

To John Jay, the secretary for foreign affairs, Paris,
August 23, 1785

It should ever be held in mind that insult & war are the consequences of a want of respectability in the national character.

To James Madison, Paris, February 8, 1786

One insult pocketed soon produces another.

To President George Washington, New York,
August 28, 1790

Acquiescence under insult is not the way to escape war.

To Henry Tazwell, Monticello, September 13, 1795

Interest

Interest is not the strongest passion in the human breast.

To David Ross, Paris, May 8, 1786

Intrigue

Nothing is so mistaken as the supposition that a person is to extricate himself from a difficulty, by intrigue, by chicanery, by dissimulation, by trimming, by an untruth, by an injustice. This increases the difficulties tenfold, & those who pursue these methods, get themselves so involved at length that they can turn no way but their infamy becomes more exposed.

To Peter Carr, Paris, August 19, 1785

Introductions

The most friendly office one can perform is to make worthy characters acquainted with one another.

To Abigail Adams, Paris, November 1786

It is rendering mutual service to men of virtue & understanding to make them acquainted with one another.

To Richard Price, Paris, July 11, 1788

Joy

Present joys are damped by a consciousness that they are passing from us; and past ones are the subject of sorrow and regret.

To Maria Cosway, Paris, November 24, 1786

Kindness

Above all things lose no occasion of exercising your dispositions to be grateful, to be generous, to be charitable, to be humane, to be true, just, firm, orderly, courageous, &c. Consider every act of this kind as an exercise which will strengthen your moral faculties & increase your worth.

To Peter Carr, Paris, August 10, 1787

The Lesser of Two Evils

It is a melancholy law of human societies to be compelled sometimes to choose a great evil in order to ward off a greater.

To William Short, Monticello, November 28, 1814

Lies

It is of great importance to set a resolution, not to be shaken, never to tell an untruth. There is no vice so mean, so pitiful, so contemptible & he who permits himself to tell a lie once, finds it much easier to do it a second & third time, till at length it becomes habitual, he tells lies without attending to it, & truths without the world's believing him. This falsehood of the tongue leads to that of the heart, & in time depraves all its good dispositions.

To Peter Carr, Paris, August 19, 1785

Teach her to be always true. No vice is so mean as the want of truth, and at the same time so useless.

To Martha Jefferson, Toulon, April 7, 1787

Wonderful is the effect of impudent & persevering lying.

To William Stephens Smith, Paris,
November 13, 1787

By often repeating an untruth men come to believe it themselves.

To John Melish, Monticello, January 13, 1813

Listening

Be a listener only, keep within yourself, and endeavor to establish with yourself the habit of silence, especially in politics.

To Thomas Jefferson Randolph, Washington,
November 24, 1808

Living within Our Means

To conform to our circumstances is true honor: and the only shame is to live beyond them.

To J.P.P. Derieux, Paris, July 25, 1788

Long-Windedness

Speeches measured by the hour, die with the hour.

To David Harding, Monticello, April 20, 1824

Manners

The imitation of European manners which you will find in our towns will I fear be little pleasing.

To Madame de Bréhan, Paris, October 9, 1787

The manners of every nation are the standard of orthodoxy within itself. But these standards being arbitrary, reasonable people in all allow free toleration for the manners, as for the religion of others.

To Jean Baptiste Say, Monticello, March 2, 1815

Mischief

Mischief may be done negatively as well as positively.

To John Adams, Monticello, October 28, 1813

Motivation

Every honest man will suppose honest acts to flow from honest principles [not from a desire for popularity].

To Benjamin Rush, Washington,
December 20, 1801

Naysayers

There is nothing against which human ingenuity will not be able to find something to say.

To Gideon Granger, Washington, May 3, 1801

Neighbors

Without society, and a society to our taste, humans are never contented.

To James Monroe, Paris, December 18, 1786

I am happy to find you are on good terms with your neighbors. It is almost the most important circumstance in life, since nothing is so corroding as frequently to meet persons with whom one has any difference. The ill-will of a single neighbor is an immense drawback on the happiness of life, and therefore their good will cannot be bought too dear.

To Martha Jefferson Randolph, Philadelphia, May 8, 1791

The Next Generation

These recollections prove, my friend, that we are no longer young. Those whom we knew [as] children have now their children and are pressing us towards a door out of which they must follow us.

To Samuel Henley, Paris, November 27, 1785

That the earth belongs in usufruct to the living: that the dead have neither powers nor rights over it. The portion occupied by any individual ceases to be his when [he] himself ceases to be, & reverts to the society.

To James Madison, Paris, September 6, 1789

I console myself with the reflection that those who will come after us will be as wise as we are, & as able to take care of themselves as we have been.

To P. S. Dupont de Nemours, Monticello, April 15, 1811

Nothing is more incumbent on the old, than to know when they should get out of the way, and relinquish to younger successors the honors they can no longer earn, and the duties they can no longer perform.

To John Vaughan, Monticello, February 5, 1815

The boys of this age are to be the men of the next; . . . they should be prepared to receive the holy charge which we are cherishing to deliver over to them.

To James Breckenridge, Monticello, February 15, 1821

It is a law of nature that the generations of men should give way, one to another, and I hope that the one now on the stage will preserve for their sons the political blessings delivered into their hands by their fathers. Time indeed changes manners and notions, and so far we must expect institutions to bend to them. But time produces also corruption of principles, and against this it is the duty of good citizens to be ever on the watch, and if the gangrene is to prevail at last, let the day be kept off as long as possible.

To Spencer Roane, Monticello, March 9, 1821

Opportunity

You live in a country where talents, learning, and honesty are so much called for that every man who possesses these may be what he pleases. Can there be a higher inducement to acquire them at every possible expense of time and labor?

To John Garland Jefferson, Monticello, October 11, 1791

Nature will not give you a second life wherein to atone for the omissions of this.

To Joseph C. Cabell, Monticello, January 31, 1821

Patience

Patience will bring all to rights.

To Horatio Gates, Philadelphia, May 30, 1797

Persuasiveness

I have no supernatural power to impress truth on the mind of another.

To Elbridge Gerry, Philadelphia, May 13, 1797

Persuasion, perseverance, and patience are the best advocates on questions depending on the will of others.

To James Heaton, Monticello, May 20, 1826

Politeness

With respect to what are termed political manners, without sacrificing too much the sincerity of language, I would wish my countrymen to adopt just so much of European politeness as to be ready to make all those little sacrifices of self which really render European manners amiable, and relieve society from the disagreeable scenes to which rudeness often exposes it. Here it seems that a man might pass a life without encountering a single rudeness.

To Charles Bellini, Paris, September 30, 1785

In truth, politeness is artificial good humor, it covers the natural want of it, & ends by rendering habitual a substitute nearly equivalent to the real virtue. It is the practice of sacrificing to those whom we meet in society all the little conveniences & preferences which will gratify them, & deprive us of nothing worth a moment's consideration; it is the giving a pleasing & flattering turn to our expressions which will conciliate others, and make them pleased with us as well as themselves. How cheap a price for the good will of another!

To Thomas Jefferson Randolph, Washington, November 24, 1808

Praise

Go on deserving applause, and you will be sure to meet with it: and the way to deserve it is, to be good, & to be industrious.

To John Wayles Eppes, Paris, July 28, 1787

Approbation of my fellow citizens is the richest reward I can receive.

To Richard M. Johnson, Washington, March 10, 1808

To be praised by those who themselves deserve all praise, is a gratification of high order. Their approbation who, having been high in office themselves, have information & talents to guide their judgment, is a consolation deeply felt.

To Larkin Smith, Monticello, April 15, 1809

The approbation of the good is always consoling.

To Count Pahlen of Russia, Monticello, July 13, 1810

Precedents

A departure from principle in one instance becomes a precedent for a 2d., that 2d. for a 3d. and so on, till the bulk of the society is reduced to be mere automatons of misery, to have no sensibilities left but for sinning and suffering.

To Samuel Kercheval, Monticello, July 12, 1816

Privacy

If we are made in some degree for others, yet in a greater are we made for ourselves.

To James Monroe, Monticello, May 20, 1782

A room to myself, if it be but a barrack, is indispensable.

To James Madison, Monticello, August 31, 1783

Private Meetings

I have always seen business done more easily and more amicably, where the parties have met in a friendly way and at a private house where they would have the leisure and the dispositions to explain and approximate their opinions, than in a public place, confined to a particular hour, and pressed and interrupted by other business.

To Benjamin Carter Waller, Monticello, October 9, 1794

Procrastination

[Jefferson's not responding to letters has] been delayed by a blamable spirit of procrastination for ever suggesting to our indolence that we need not do to-day what may be done tomorrow.

To Thomas Pinckney, Philadelphia, May 29, 1797

Instead of acting on the good old maxim of not putting off to tomorrow what we can do to-day, we are too apt to reverse it, & not to do today what we can put off tomorrow.

To James Maury, Monticello, April 25, 1812

Progress

Truth advances, & error recedes step by step only; and to do to our fellow-men the most good in our power, we must lead where we can, follow where we cannot, and still go with them, watching always the favorable moment for helping them to another step.

To Thomas Cooper, Monticello, October 7, 1814

Proof

Proof is the duty of the affirmative side. A negative cannot be positively proved.

To Martin Van Buren, Monticello, June 29, 1824

Reclusion

Nobody will care for him who cares for nobody.

To Maria Cosway, Paris, October 12, 1786

Recovery

It is better to turn from the contemplation of our misfortunes to the resources we possess for extricating ourselves.

To James Currie, Paris, August 4, 1787

Repentence

When sins are dear to us we are but too prone to slide into them again. The act of repentance itself is often sweetened with the thought that it clears our account for a repetition of the same sin.

To Maria Cosway, Paris, November 19, 1786

Resolution

We are always equal to what we undertake with resolution. . . . Industry and resolution are all that are wanting. . . . Be industrious then, my dear child. Think nothing insurmountable by resolution and application, you will be all that I wish you to be.

To Martha Jefferson, Aix en Provence, March 28, 1787

Ridicule

Ridicule was also resorted to, the ordinary substitute for reason, when that fails.

To Lewis M. Wiss, Monticello, November 27, 1825

Rules

Learn yourself the habit of adhering vigorously to the rules you lay down for yourself.

To Martha Jefferson, Paris, June 14, 1787

The forming a general rule requires great caution.

To George Washington, Philadelphia, no date
[September 1793]

Second Best

We cannot always do what is absolutely best.

To Thomas Cooper, Monticello, October 7, 1814

Secrecy

I have news from America as late as July 19. Nothing had then transpired from the Federal convention. I am sorry they began their deliberations by so abominable a precedent as that of tying up the tongues of their members. Nothing can justify this example but the innocence of their intentions, & ignorance of the value of public discussions. I have no doubt that all their other measures will be good & wise. It is really an assembly of demigods.

To John Adams, Paris, August 30, 1787

I have not been in the habit of mysterious reserve on any subject, nor of buttoning up my opinions within my own doublet.

To Samuel Kercheval, Monticello, July 12, 1816

Sensibility

Sensibility of mind is indeed the parent of every virtue: but it is the parent of much misery too.

To Lucy Paradise Barziza, Paris, July 8, 1788

Series of Events

Good things, as well as evil, go in a train.

To John Taylor, Monticello, December 29, 1794

Silence

Silence speaks I think plain enough.

To Peregrine Fitzhugh, Philadelphia,
February 23, 1798

Remember that we often repent of what we have said, but never of that which we have not.

To Gideon Granger, Monticello, March 9, 1814

Sincerity
It is a proof of sincerity, which I value above all things; as, between those who practice it, falsehood & malice work their efforts in vain.

To William Duane, Washington, March 22, 1806

Slander
There is not a truth on earth which I fear or would disguise. But secret slanders cannot be disarmed because they are secret.

To William Duane, Washington, March 22, 1806

Let us not then, my dear friend, embark our happiness and our affections on the ocean of slander, of falsehood and of malice, on which our credulous friends are floating.

To James Monroe, Washington, March 10, 1808

Solitude
The bloom of Monticello is chilled by my solitude.

To Martha Jefferson Randolph, Monticello,
March 27, 1797

Speculation
The wealth acquired by speculation & plunder is fugacious in its nature and fills society with the spirit of gambling.

To George Washington, Paris, August 14, 1787

It is vain for common sense to urge that nothing can produce but nothing: that it is an idle dream to believe in a philosopher's stone which is to turn every thing into gold, and to redeem man from the original sentence of his maker, "in the sweat of his brow shall he eat his bread."

To Charles Yancey, Monticello, January 6, 1816

Surprises
I suspect, by the account you give me of your garden, that you mean a surprise, as good singers always preface their performances by complaints of cold, hoarseness, etc.

To Martha Jefferson Randolph, Philadelphia,
June 22, 1792

Suspicions
I should not be willing to substitute suspicion for proof.

To James Jackson, Washington, February 16, 1803

It is so easy to excite suspicions, that none are to be wondered at.

To Benjamin Hawkins, Washington, February 18, 1803

Sympathy
When languishing then under disease, how grateful is the solace of our friends! How are we penetrated with their assiduities & attentions! How much are we supported by their encouragements & kind offices! When Heaven has taken from us some object

of our love, how sweet is it to have a bosom whereon to recline our heads, & into which we may pour the torrents of our tears! Grief, with such a comfort, is almost a luxury!

To Maria Cosway, Paris, October 12, 1786

Tranquility

Tranquility is the old man's milk.

To Edward Rutledge, Philadelphia, June 24, 1797

Tranquility is the summum bonum* of a Septage-naire.

*the supreme good

To John Melish, January 13, 1813

I had hoped, when I retired from the business of the world, that I should have been permitted to pass the evening of life in tranquility, undisturbed by the peltings and passions of which the public papers are the vehicles.

To Thomas Leiper, Monticello, January 1, 1814

Tranquility, at my age, is the balm of life.

To P. H. Wendover, Monticello, March 13, 1815

Tranquility is the softest pillow for the head of old age.

To William Short, Monticello, May 5, 1816

To procure tranquility of mind we must avoid desire & fear, the two principal diseases of the mind.

To William Short, Monticello, October 31, 1819

Truth

It is error alone which needs the support of government. Truth can stand by itself.

Notes on the State of Virginia, 1782

Truth, between candid minds, can never do harm.

To John Adams, Philadelphia, July 17, 1791

There is not a truth on earth which I fear or would disguise.

To William Duane, Washington, March 22, 1806

I feel no falsehood, and fear no truth.

To Isaac Hillard, Monticello, October 9, 1810

About facts you and I cannot differ; because truth is our mutual guide.

To John Adams, Monticello, June 15, 1813

Truth advances, & error recedes step by step only.

To Thomas Cooper, Monticello, October 7, 1814

The man who fears no truths has nothing to fear from lies.

To George Logan, Monticello, June 20, 1816

Truth being as cheap as error, it is as well to rectify it for our own satisfaction.

To John Adams, Monticello, September 4, 1823

Time, will in the end, produce the truth.

To William Short, Monticello, January 8, 1825

All should be laid open to you without reserve, for there is not a truth existing which I fear, or would wish unknown to the whole world.

To Henry Lee, Monticello, May 15, 1826

Human Nature

Mankind soon learn to make interested uses of every right and power which they possess, or may assume.

Notes on the State of Virginia, 1782

Human nature is the same on every side of the Atlantic, and will be alike influenced by the same cause.

Notes on the State of Virginia, 1782

The reflections into which it leads us are not very flattering to the human species. In the whole Animal kingdom I recollect no family but Man, steadily & systematically employed in the destruction of itself. Nor does what is called civilization produce any other effect than to teach him to pursue the principle of the bellum omnium in omnia* on a greater scale, & instead of the little contest between tribe and tribe, to comprehend all the quarters of the earth in the same work of destruction. If to this we add that as to other animals, the lions & tigers are mere lambs compared with Man as a destroyer, we must conclude that Nature has been able to find in Man alone a sufficient barrier against the too great multiplication of other animals and of Man himself, an equilibrating power against the fecundity of generation.

*the war of all against all

To James Madison, Monticello, January 1, 1796

I am among those who think well of the human character generally. I consider man as formed for society, and endowed by nature with those dispositions which fit him for society.

To William Green Munford, June 18, 1799

Morality, compassion, generosity are innate elements of the human constitution.

To P. S. Dupont de Nemours, Poplar Forest, April 24, 1816

Ambition

The little spice of ambition which I had in my younger days has long since evaporated, and I set still less store by a posthumous than present name.

To James Madison, Monticello, April 27, 1795

Ambition is long since dead in my mind.

To Thomas Mann Randolph, Monticello, November 28, 1796

Bigotry

All bigotries hang to one another.

To John Adams, Monticello, January 24, 1814

Bigotry is the disease of ignorance, of morbid minds; enthusiasm of the free and buoyant. Education & free discussion are the antidotes of both.

To John Adams, Monticello, August 1, 1816

Ignorance & bigotry, like other insanities, are incapable of self-government.

To the Marquis de Lafayette, Monticello,
May 14, 1817

Common Sense

I can never fear that things will go far wrong where common sense has fair play.

To John Adams, Paris, December 20, 1786

Let common sense & common honesty have fair play & they will soon set things to rights.

To Ezra Stiles, Paris, December 24, 1786

There are no mysteries in it. Difficulties indeed sometimes arise; but common sense and honest intentions will generally steer thro' them.

To Josephus B. Stuart, Monticello,
May 10, 1817

Confidence

We confide in our own strength, without boasting of it; we respect that of others, without fearing it.

To William Carmichael and William Short, Philadelphia,
June 30, 1793

Conviction

A conviction that we are right accomplishes half the difficulty of correcting wrong.

To Archibald Thweat, Monticello, January 19, 1821

Curiosity

Man . . . is in all his shapes a curious animal.

To the Comte de Volney, Monticello, January 8, 1797

Cynicism

There is no act, however virtuous, for which ingenuity may not find some bad motive.

To Edward Dowse, Washington, April 19, 1803

Doubt

In cases of doubt it is better to say too little than too much.

To President George Washington, Philadelphia,
July 30, 1791

Ennui

Ennui, the most dangerous poison of life. . . . In a world which furnishes so many employments which are useful, and so many which are amusing, it is our own fault if we ever know what ennui is.

To Martha Jefferson, Canal of Languedoc,
May 21, 1787

Envy

Envy & malice will never be quiet.

To Abigail Adams, Paris, September 25, 1785

Evil

It is a happy circumstance in human affairs that evils which are not cured in one way, will cure themselves in some other.

To Sir John Sinclair, Philadelphia,
August 24, 1791

When great evils happen, I am in the habit of looking out for what good may arise from them as consolations to us; and Providence has in fact so established the order of things as that most evils are the means of producing some good.

To Benjamin Rush, Monticello,
September 23, 1800

It is the melancholy law of human societies to be compelled sometimes to choose a great evil in order to ward off a greater.

To William Short, Monticello, November 28, 1814

Expedience

The mind of man is full of expedients.

To the Comte de Moustier, Paris, May 20, 1789

Fallibility

I do not pretend . . . to be infallible.

To Nicholas Lewis, Paris, July 11, 1788

I have no right to assume infallibility.

To Caesar A. Rodney, Monticello,
September 25, 1810

Favoritism

To unequal privileges among members of the same society the spirit of our nation is, with one accord adverse.

To Hugh White, Washington, May 2, 1801

Fortitude

Fortitude . . . teaches us to meet and surmount difficulties; not to fly from them, like cowards, and to fly too in vain, for they will meet and arrest us at every turn of our road.

To William Short, Monticello,
October 31, 1819

Frugality

Would a missionary appear who would make frugality the basis of his religious system, and go thro the land preaching it up as the only road to salvation, I would join his school.

To John Page, Paris, May 4, 1786

Generosity

True generosity . . . will induce you to give me opportunities of returning your obligations.

To Abigail Adams, Paris, November 20, 1785

Take more pleasure in giving what is best to another than in having it yourself, and then all the world will love you, and I more than all the world.

To Mary Jefferson, New York, April 11, 1790

Good Faith

Good faith is every man's surest guide.

Proclamation announcing Paris Peace Treaty of 1783,
January 14, 1784

Good Humor

We had all rather associate with a good humored,
light-principled man than with an ill tempered rigorist in morality.

To Benjamin Rush, Washington, January 3, 1808

Above all things, and at all times, practice yourself
in good humor; this of all human qualities is the
most amiable and endearing to society.

To Francis Eppes, Monticello, May 21, 1816

Good Qualities

Good qualities are sometimes misfortunes.

To Francis Hopkinson, Paris, January 3, 1786

Good Sense

The good sense of the people will be found the best
army.

To William Stephens Smith, Paris,
December 20, 1786

The good sense of the people will soon lead them
back, if they have erred in a moment of surprise.

To Abigail Adams, Paris,
December 21, 1786

I am satisfied the good sense of the people is the strongest army our government can ever have, & that it will not fail them.

To William Carmichael, Paris, December 26, 1786

Habits

I am past the age for changing habits.

To Eliza House Trist, Paris, December 15, 1786

To introduce the habit we have only to let the merchants alone.

To the Comte de Montmorin, Paris, July 23, 1787

I find as I advance in life I become less capable of acquiring new affections & therefore I love to hang by my old ones.

To Alexander Donald, Philadelphia, May 13, 1791

It is very difficult to persuade the great body of mankind to give up what they have once learned, & are now masters of, for something to be learnt anew. Time alone insensibly wears down old habits, and produces small changes at long intervals, and to this process we must all accommodate ourselves, and be content to follow those who will not follow us.

To John Wilson, Monticello, August 17, 1813

Habit alone confounds what is civil practice with natural right.

To Thomas Earle, Monticello,
September 24, 1823

Happiness

Our greatest happiness . . . is always the result of a good conscience, good health, occupation, and freedom in all just pursuits.

Notes on the State of Virginia, 1782

My principal happiness is now in the retrospect of life.

To John Page, Paris, August 20, 1785

He is happiest of whom the world says least, good or bad.

To John Adams, Paris, August 27, 1786

You have seen enough of the different conditions of life to know that it is neither wealth nor splendor, but tranquility and occupation that give happiness. This truth I can confirm to you from longer observation and a greater scope of experience.

To Anna Jefferson Marks, Paris, July 12, 1788

Be assiduous in learning, take much exercise for your health & practice much virtue. Health, learning & virtue will ensure your happiness; they will give you a quiet conscience, private esteem & public honor. Beyond these we want nothing but physical necessaries; and they are easily obtained.

To Peter Carr, Paris, August 6, 1788

Your own happiness will be the greater as you perceive that you promote that of others.

To Martha Jefferson Randolph, New York, July 17, 1790

There has been a time when . . . perhaps the esteem of the world was of higher value in my eye than every thing in it. But age, experience, & reflection, preserving to that only its due value, have set a higher on tranquility. The motion of my blood no longer keeps time with the tumult of the world. It leads me to seek for happiness in the lap and love of my family, in the society of my neighbors & my books, in the wholesome occupations of my farm & my affairs, in an interest or affection in every bud that opens, in every breath that blows around me, in an entire freedom of rest or motion, of thought or incogitancy, owing account to myself alone of my hours & actions.

To James Madison, Philadelphia, June 9, 1793

Honesty

A wise man, if nature has not formed him honest, will yet act as if he were honest: because he will find it the most advantageous & wise part in the long run.

To James Monroe, Paris, March 18, 1785

An honest heart being the first blessing, a knowing head is the second.

To Peter Carr, Paris, August 19, 1785

Next to the fulfilling your wishes, the most grateful thing I can do is to give a faithful answer.

To Tadeusz Kosciusko, Washington, April 2, 1802

I cannot act as if all men were unfaithful because some are so; nor believe that all will betray me, because

some do. I had rather be the victim of occasional infi-
delities, than relinquish my general confidence in the
honesty of man.

To Thomas Lieper, Monticello, January 1, 1814

Honesty is the 1st chapter in the book of wisdom.

To Nathaniel Macon, Monticello, January 12, 1819

Idleness

If at any moment, my dear, you catch yourself in
idleness, start from it as you would from the
precipice of a gulf.

To Martha Jefferson, Aix en Provence, March 28, 1787

Determine never to be idle. No person will have occasion to complain of the want of time who never
loses any. It is wonderful how much may be done if
we are always doing.

To Martha Jefferson, Marseilles, May 5, 1787

A mind always employed is always happy. This is
the true secret, the grand recipe, for felicity. The
idle are the only wretched.

To Martha Jefferson, Toulouse, May 21, 1787

Indolence

Of all the cankers of human happiness none cor-
rodes with so silent, yet so baneful an influence, as
indolence. Body and mind both unemployed, our
being becomes a burden, and every object about us
loathsome, even the dearest. Idleness begets ennui,

ennui the hypochondria, and that a diseased body. No laborious person was ever yet hysterical. Exercise and application produce order in our affairs, health of body, cheerfulness of mind, and these make us precious to our friends.

To Martha Jefferson, Aix en Provence, March 28, 1787

Innovation

Great innovations should not be forced on slender majorities.

To Tadeusz Kosciusko, Washington, May 2, 1808

Intolerance

I never will, by any word or act, bow to the shrine of intolerance.

To Edward Dowse, Washington, April 19, 1803

Jealousy

Doubts or jealousy . . . often beget the facts they fear.

To Albert Gallatin, Washington, October 12, 1806

Moderation

We never repent of having eaten too little.

To Thomas Jefferson Smith, Monticello, February 21, 1825

Modesty

There is a modesty often which does itself injury. Our countrymen possess this. They do not know their own superiority.

To John Rutledge, Jr., Paris, February 2, 1788

Optimism

Search in every object only what it contains of good.

To Madame de Bréhan, Paris, May 9, 1788

I steer my bark with Hope in the head, leaving Fear astern. My hopes indeed sometimes fail; but not oftener than the forebodings of the gloomy.

To John Adams, Monticello, April 8, 1816

Passions

The passions of men will take their course, that they are not to be controlled but by despotism, & that this melancholy truth is the pretext for despotism.

To George Logan, Washington, May 11, 1805

All men who have attended to the workings of the human mind, who have seen the false colors under which passion sometimes dresses the actions & motives of others, have seen also these passions subsiding with time and reflection, dissipating, like mists before the rising sun, and restoring to us the sight of all things in their true shape and colors.

To John Adams, Monticello, October 12, 1823

Perseverance

An indifferent measure carried through with perseverance is better than a good one taken up only at intervals.

To Timothy Pickering, Richmond,
September 6, 1780

Pessimism

There are indeed (who might say Nay) gloomy & hypochondriac minds, inhabitants of diseased bodies, disgusted with the present, & despairing of the future; always counting that the worst will happen, because it may happen. To these I say How much pain have cost us the evils which have never happened?

To John Adams, Monticello, April 8, 1816

Pragmatism

I have ever thought that forms should yield to whatever should facilitate business.

To James Monroe, Washington, July 11, 1801

Prejudice

The hope . . . that prejudices would at length give way to facts has never been entirely extinguished.

To Walter Franklin, Washington, June 22, 1808

Pride

Pride costs us more than hunger, thirst and cold.

To Thomas Jefferson Smith, Monticello, February 21, 1825

Qualities of the Mind

In the ensuing autumn, I shall be sending on to Philadelphia, a grandson of about 15 years of age, to whom I shall ask your friendly attentions. Without that bright fancy which captivates, I am in hopes he possesses sound judgment and much observation;

and, what I value more than all things, good humor. For thus I estimate the qualities of the mind; 1. good humor. 2. integrity. 3. industry. 4. science. The preference of the 1st to the 2d quality may not at first be acquiesced in, but certainly we had all rather associate with a good humored, light-principled man, than with an ill tempered rigorist in morality.

To Benjamin Rush, Washington, January 3, 1808

Skepticism

The natural course of the human mind is certainly from credulity to skepticism.

To Caspar Wistar, Washington, June 21, 1807

Steadfastness

Our part then is to pursue with steadiness what is right, turning neither to right nor left for the intrigues or popular delusions of the day, assured that the public approbation will in the end be with us.

To John Breckinridge, Monticello, April 9, 1822

Thrift

We must make our election between economy & liberty, or profusion and servitude.

To Samuel Kercheval, Monticello, July 12, 1816

Never spend your money before you have it.

To Thomas Jefferson Smith, Monticello, February 21, 1825

Indians

The two principles on which our conduct towards the Indians should be founded are justice & fear. After the injuries we have done them, they cannot love us, which leaves us no alternative but that of fear to keep them from attacking us. But justice is what we should never lose sight of, & in time it may recover their esteem.

To Benjamin Hawkins, Paris, August 13, 1786

It has become questionable whether the condition of our aboriginal neighbors, who live without laws or magistrates, be not preferable to that of the great mass of the nations of the earth who feel their laws & magistrates but in the weight of their burdens.

Petition to the Virginia Assembly, November [2 or 3], 1798

In keeping agents among the Indians, two objects are principally kept in view: 1. The preservation of peace; 2. The obtaining lands. Towards effecting the latter object we consider the leading the Indians to agriculture as the principal means from which we can expect much effect in future. When they shall cultivate small spots of earth, & see how useless their extensive forests are, they will sell from time to time to help out their personal labor in stocking their farms, & procuring clothes & comforts from our trading houses. Towards the attainment of our

two objects of peace & lands, it is essential that our
agent acquire that sort of influence over the Indians
which rests on confidence.

To James Jackson, Washington, February 16, 1803

I am myself alive to the obtaining lands from the Indians by all honest & peaceable means, and I believe
that the honest and peaceable means adopted by
us will obtain them as fast as the expansion of our
settlements with due regard to compactness will require.

To James Jackson, Washington, February 16, 1803

The promotion of agriculture therefore and household manufacture are essential in their preservation,
and I am disposed to aid and encourage it liberally.
This will enable them to live on much smaller portions of land, and indeed will render their vast
forests useless but for the range of cattle.

To Benjamin Hawkins, Washington, February 18, 1803

In truth, the ultimate point of rest & happiness for
them is to let our settlements and theirs meet and
blend together, to intermix and become one people,
incorporating themselves with us as citizens of the
U.S. This is what the natural progress of things will
of course bring on, and it will be better to promote
than to retard it. Surely it will be better for them to
be identified with us, and preserved in the occupation of their lands, than be exposed to the many

casualties which may endanger them while a separate people.

To Benjamin Hawkins, Washington, February 18, 1803

The best conduct we can pursue to countervail these movements among the Indians is to confirm our friends by redoubled acts of justice & favor, & to endeavor to draw over the individuals indisposed towards us.

To Henry Dearborn, Monticello, August 12, 1807

Commerce is the great engine by which we are to coerce them, & not war.

To Meriwether Lewis, Monticello, August 21, 1808

The plan of civilizing the Indians is undoubtedly a great improvement on the ancient & totally ineffectual one of beginning with religious missionaries. Our experience has shown that this must be the last step of the process. The following is what has been successful. 1. To raise cattle etc. & thereby acquire a knowledge of the value of property. 2. Arithmetic to calculate that value. 3. Writing, to keep accounts and here they begin to enclose farms, & the men to labor, the women to spin & weave. 4. To read. Aesop's fables & Robinson Crusoe are their first delight. The Creeks & Cherokees are advanced thus far, & the Cherokees are now instituting a regular government.

To James Jay, Monticello, April 7, 1809

There is an error into which most of the speculators on government have fallen, and which the well-known state of society of our Indians ought before now to have corrected. In their hypothesis of the origin of government, they suppose it to have commenced in the patriarchal, or monarchical form. Our Indians are evidently in that state of nature which has passed the association of a single family; & not yet submitted to the authority of positive laws, or of any acknowledged magistrate. Every man, with them, is perfectly free to follow his own inclinations. But if in doing this, he violates the rights of another, if the case be slight, he is punished by the disesteem of his society, or, as we say, by public opinion; if serious, he is tomahawked as a dangerous enemy. Their leaders conduct them by the influence of their character only; and they follow, or not, as they please, him of whose character for wisdom or war they have the highest opinion. Hence the origin of the parties among them adhering to different leaders, and governed by their advice, not by their command.

To Francis W. Gilmer, Monticello,
June 7, 1816

Inventions and Ideas

❦

Balloons

What think you of these balloons? They really begin to assume a serious face. The Chevalier Luzerne communicated to me a letter received from his brother who mentions one which he had seen himself. The persons who ascended in it regulated its height at about 3000 feet, and passed with the wind about 6 miles in 20 minutes when they chose to let themselves down, tho' they could have traveled triple the distance. This discovery seems to threaten the prostration of fortified works unless they can be closed above, the destruction of fleets and what not. The French may now run over their laces, wines, &c. to England duty free. The whole system of British statutes made on the supposition of goods being brought into some port must be revised. Inland countries may now become maritime states unless you choose rather to call them aerial ones as their commerce is in future to be carried on through that element.

To Francis Hopkinson, Annapolis, February 18, 1784

We were entertained here lately with the ascent of Mr. Blanchard in a balloon. The security of the thing appeared so great that every body is wishing for a balloon to travel in. I wish for one sincerely, as, instead of ten days, I should be within five hours of home.

To Martha Jefferson Randolph, Philadelphia,
January 14, 1793

Copying Machines

Have you a copying press? If you have not, you should get one. Mine (exclusive of paper which costs a guinea a ream) has cost me about 14 guineas. I would give ten times that sum that I had had it from the date of the stamp act.

To James Madison, Paris, September 1, 1785

Jefferson saw a portable press copy machine such as this while visiting in England in 1786. He took the dimensions and had a French artisan make three such machines. He kept one for himself and sent the others to James Madison in America and William Carmichael, the United States chargé d'affaires in Madrid. (Monticello/Thomas Jefferson Foundation, Inc.)

The polygraph was invented by Mr. Hawkins of Frankfort, Pa., and built for Jefferson by Charles Willson Peale around 1811. (University of Virginia; photo courtesy of Monticello/Thomas Jefferson Foundation, Inc.)

Having a great desire to have a portable copying machine, & being satisfied from some experiments that the principle of the large machine might be applied in a small one, I planned one when in England & had it made. It answers perfectly. I have since set a workman to making them here, & they are in such demand that he has his hands full. Being assured that you will be pleased to have one, when you shall have tried its convenience, I send you one by Colo. Franks. The machine costs 96 livres, the appendages 24 livres, and I send you paper & ink for 12 livres, in all 132 livres. There is a printed paper of directions: but you must expect to make many essays before you succeed perfectly. A soft brush, like a shaving brush, is more convenient than the sponge. You can get as much ink & paper as you please from London. The paper costs a guinea a ream.

To James Madison, Paris, January 30, 1787

I believe that when you left America the invention of the Polygraph had not yet reached Boston. It is for copying with one pen while you write with the other & without the least additional embarrassment or exertion to the writer. I think it the finest invention of the present age, and so much superior to the copying machine that the latter will never be continued a day by any one who tries the Polygraph. It was invented by a Mr. Hawkins of Frankford near Philadelphia, who is now in England turning it to good account. Knowing that you are in the habit of writing much, I have flattered myself that I could add acceptably to your daily convenience by presenting you with one of these delightful machines. I have accordingly had one made, & to be certain of its perfection I have used it myself some weeks, & have the satisfaction to find it the best one I have ever tried; and in the course of two years' daily use of them, I have had opportunities of trying several. As a Secretary which copies for us what we write without the power of revealing it, I find it a most precious possession to a man in public business.

To James Bowdoin, Washington, July 10, 1806

I could never be a day without thinking of you, were it only for my daily labors at the Polygraph for which

I am indebted to you. It is indeed an excellent one, and after 12 or 14 years hard service it has failed in nothing except the spiral springs of silver wire which suspend the pen-frame. These are all but disabled, and my fingers are too clumsy to venture to rectify them, were they susceptible of it. I am tempted to ask you if you have ever thought of trying a cord of elastic gum. If this would answer, its simplicity would admit any bungler to prepare & apply it.

To Charles Willson Peale, Monticello, October 23, 1822

Ideas

He who receives an idea from me, receives instruction himself, without lessening mine; as he who lights his taper at mine, receives light without darkening me.

To Isaac McPherson, Monticello, August 13, 1813

Inventions

Every discovery which multiplies the subsistence of men, must be a matter of joy to every friend to humanity.

To Jeudy de l'Hommande, Paris, August 9, 1787

The machines which perform the labors of man are peculiarly valuable in a country where there is more to do than men to do it.

To Richard Claiborne, Monticello, February 21, 1795

I am not afraid of new inventions or improvements, nor bigoted to the practices of our forefathers. It is that bigotry which keeps the Indians in a state of barbarism in the midst of the arts, would have kept us in the same state even now. . . . Where a new invention is supported by well known principles, & promises to be useful, it ought to be tried.

To Robert Fulton, Monticello, March 17, 1810

The fact is that one new idea leads to another, that to a 3d, and so on thro' a course of time, until some one, with whom no one of these ideas was original, combines all together, and produces what is justly called a new invention.

To Benjamin Waterhouse, Monticello, March 3, 1818

Patents

It is not the policy of the government in that country [America] to give any aid to works of any kind. They let things take their natural course, without help or impediment, which is generally the best policy.

To Thomas Digges, Paris, June 19, 1788

Certainly an inventor ought to be allowed a right to the benefit of his invention for some certain time. It is equally certain it ought not to be perpetual; for to embarrass society with monopolies for every utensil existing, & in all the details of life, would be more injurious to them than had the supposed inventors never existed. . . . Nobody wishes more than I do that ingenuity should receive a liberal encouragement.

To Oliver Evans, Monticello, May 2, 1807

Steam Power

I could write you volumes on the improvements which I find made & making here in the arts. One deserves particular notice, because it is simple, great, and likely to have extensive consequences. It is the application of steam as an agent for working grist mills.

To Charles Thomson, London, April 22, 1786

Jefferson's Presidency

We are endeavoring too to reduce the government to the practice of a rigorous economy, to avoid burdening the people, and arming the magistrate with a patronage of money and offices, which might be used to corrupt & undermine the principles of our government.

To Marc Auguste Pictet, Washington,
February 5, 1803

Our administration now drawing towards a close, I have a sublime pleasure in believing it will be distinguished as much by having placed itself above all the passions which could disturb its harmony, as by the great operations by which it will have advanced the well-being of the nation.

To Albert Gallatin, Washington, October 12, 1806

I had hoped to keep the expenses of my office within the limits of its salary, so as to apply my private income entirely to the improvement & enlargement of my estate; but I have not been able to do it.

To Charles Clay, Washington, January 11, 1807

I have tired you my friend, with a long letter. But your tedium will end in a few lines more. Mine has yet two years to endure. I am tired of an office where I can do no more good than many others who would be glad to be employed in it.

To John Dickinson, Washington, January 13, 1807

I have the consolation too of having added nothing to my private fortune, during my public service, and of retiring with hands as clean, as they are empty.

To the Comte Diodati, Washington, March 29, 1807

That I should lay down my charge at a proper season is as much a duty as to have borne it faithfully.

To Isaac Weaver, Jr., Washington, June 7, 1807

Something now occurs almost every day on which it is desirable to have the opinions of the heads of departments, yet to have a formal meeting every day would consume so much of their time as seriously to obstruct their regular business. I have proposed to them as most convenient for them, & wasting less of their time, to call on me at any moment of the day which suits their separate convenience, when, besides any other business they may have to do, I can learn their opinions separately on any matter which has occurred, & also communicate the information received daily. Perhaps you could find it more convenient, sometimes to make your call at the hour of dinner, instead of going so much further to dine alone. You will always find a plate & a sincere welcome.

To Albert Gallatin, Washington, July 10, 1807

I have thought it right to take no part myself in proposing measures the execution of which will devolve on my successor. I am therefore chiefly an unmeddling listener to what others say. On the same ground I shall make no new appointments which can be deferred till the 4th of March, thinking it fair to leave to my successor to select the agents for his own administration.

To George Logan, Washington, December 27, 1808

A conscientious devotion to republican government, like charity in religion, has obtained for me much indulgence from my fellow citizens, and the aid of able counsellors has guided me through many difficulties which have occurred.

To Larkin Smith, Monticello, April 15, 1809

Permit me first to explain the principles which I had laid down for my own observance. In a government like ours it is the duty of the Chief Magistrate, in order to enable himself to do all the good which his station requires, to endeavor, by all honorable means, to unite in himself the confidence of the whole people.

This alone, in any case where the energy of the nation is required, can produce an union of the powers of the whole, and point them in a single direction, as if all constituted but one body & one mind, and this alone can render a weaker nation unconquerable by a stronger one. Towards acquiring the confidence of the people the very first measure is to satisfy them of his disinterestedness, & that he is directing their affairs with a single eye to their good, & not to build up fortunes for himself & family: & especially that the officers appointed to transact their business, are appointed because they are the fittest men, not because they are his relations. So prone are they to suspicion that where a President appoints a relation of his own, however worthy, they will believe that favor & not merit, was the motive. I therefore laid it down as a law of conduct for myself never to give an appointment to a relation.

To John Garland Jefferson, Monticello, January 25, 1810

I have thought it among the most fortunate circumstances of my late administration that during its eight years continuance, it was conducted with a cordiality and harmony among all the members which never were ruffled on any, the greatest or smallest occasions. I left my brethren with sentiments of sincere affection & friendship, so rooted in the uniform tenor of a long & intimate intercourse, that the evidence of my own senses alone ought to be permitted to shake them.

To William Duane, Monticello, August 12, 1810

My affections were first for my own country, and then generally for all mankind.

To Thomas Law, Monticello, January 15, 1811

While in public service especially, I have thought the public entitled to frankness, and intimately to know whom they employed.

To Samuel Kercheval, Monticello, July 12, 1816

Answering Addresses

Averse to receive addresses, yet unable to prevent them, I have generally endeavored to turn them to some account, by making them the occasion, by way of answer, of sowing useful truths & principles among the people, which might germinate and become rooted among their political tenets.

To Levi Lincoln, Washington, January 1, 1802

Appointments

There is nothing I am so anxious about as good nominations, conscious that the merit as well as reputation of an administration depends as much on that as on its measures.

To Archibald Stuart, Monticello, April 8, 1801

[After receiving three letters from Vice President Burr on offices] These letters all relating to office, fall within the general rule which even the very first week of my being engaged in the administration obliged me to establish, to wit, that of not answering letters on office specifically, but leaving the answer to be found in what is done or not done on them. You will readily conceive into what scrapes one would get by saying no, either with or without reasons, by using a softer language which might excite false hopes or by saying yes prematurely. And to take away all offense from this silent answer, it is necessary to adhere to it in every case rigidly, as well with bosom friends as strangers.

To Aaron Burr, Washington, November 18, 1801

I did not answer your letter applying for office, but if you will reflect a moment you may judge whether this ought to be expected. To the successful applicant for an office the commission is the answer. To the unsuccessful multitude, am I to go with every one into the reasons for not appointing him? Besides that this correspondence would literally engross my whole time, into what controversies would it lead me? Sensible of this dilemma, from the moment of coming into office, I laid it down as a rule to leave the applicants to collect their answer from the fact. To entitle myself to the benefit of the rule in any case it must be observed in every one, and I never have departed from it in a single case, not even for my bosom friends.

To Larkin Smith, Washington, November 26, 1804

My usage is to make the best appointment my information & judgment enable me to do, & then fold myself up in the mantle of conscience & abide unmoved the peltings of the storm. And oh! for the day when I shall be withdrawn from it; when I shall have leisure to enjoy my family, my friends, my farm & books!

To Benjamin Rush, Washington, January 3, 1808

I dare say you have found that the solicitations for office are the most painful incidents to which an Executive magistrate is exposed. The ordinary affairs of a nation offer little difficulty to a person of any experience; but the gift of office is the dreadful burden which oppresses him. A person who wishes to make it an engine of self-elevation, may do wonders with it; but to one who wishes to use it conscientiously for the public good, without regard to the ties of blood or friendship, it creates enmities without number, many open, but more secret, and saps the happiness and peace of his life.

To Governor James Sullivan, Washington, March 3, 1808

The Judiciary and Justice

Judicial Appointments

[Federalists] have got their judiciary bill forwarded to commitment. I dread this above all the measures meditated, because appointments in the nature of freehold render it difficult to undo what is done.

To James Madison, Washington, December 26, 1800

Judicial Review

In Virginia, where a great proportion of the legislature consider the constitution but as other acts of
legislation, laws have been frequently passed which
controlled its effect. I have not heard that in the other states they have ever infringed their constitutions;
& I suppose they have not done it; as the judges
would consider any law as void, which was contrary
to the constitution.

To Jean Nicolas Démeunier, January 24, 1786

The opinion which gives to the judges the right to
decide what laws are constitutional, and what not,
not only for themselves in their own sphere of action, but for the legislature & executive also in their
spheres, would make the judiciary a despotic branch.

To Abigail Adams, Monticello, September 11, 1804

The Judiciary

We find the judiciary on every occasion, still driving
us into consolidation. . . . The constitution . . . is a
mere thing of wax in the hands of the judiciary,
which they may twist and shape into any form they
please. It should be remembered as an axiom of
eternal truth in politics that whatever power in any
government is independent, is absolute.

To Spencer Roane, Poplar Forest, September 6, 1819

But it is not from this branch of government [i.e.,
Congress] we have most to fear. Taxes & short elections will keep them right. The Judiciary of the U.S.

is the subtle corps of sappers & miners constantly working under ground to undermine the foundations of our confederated fabric. They are construing our constitution from a coordination of a general and special governments to a general & supreme one alone. This will lay all things at their feet, and they are too well versed in English law to forget the maxim, "boni judicis est ampliare jurisdictionem."*

. . . Having found from experience that impeachment is an impracticable thing, a mere scarecrow, they consider themselves secure for life; they skulk from responsibility to public opinion, the only remaining hold on them, under a practice first introduced into England by Lord Mansfield. An opinion is huddled up in Conclave, perhaps by a majority of one, delivered by a crafty Chief Justice as if unanimous, and, with the silent acquiescence of lazy or timid associates. He sophisticates the law to his mind by the turn of his own reasoning. A judiciary law was once reported by the Attorney Genl. to Congress, requiring each judge to deliver his opinion seriatim & openly, and then to give it in writing to the clerk to be entered in the record. A judiciary independent of a king or executive alone, is a good thing; but independence of the will of the nation is a solecism, at least in a republican government.

*Good judges expand their jurisdiction.

To Thomas Ritchie, Monticello, December 25, 1820

The legislative and executive branches may sometimes err, but elections and dependence will bring

them to rights. The judiciary branch is the instrument which working, like gravity, without intermis-
sion, is to press us at last into one consolidated mass.

To Archibald Thweat, Monticello, January 19, 1821

The great object of my fear is the federal judiciary.
That body, like Gravity, ever acting, with noiseless
foot, & unalarming advance, gaining ground step by
step, and holding what it gains, is ingulphing insid-
iously the special [i.e., state] governments into the
jaws of that which feeds them.

To Spencer Roane, Monticello, March 9, 1821

It has long however been my opinion, and I have
never shrunk from its expression . . . that the germ
of dissolution of our federal government is in the
constitution of the federal judiciary; an irresponsible
body, (for impeachment is scarcely a scare-crow,)
working like gravity by night and by day, gaining a
little to-day & a little to-morrow, and advancing its
noiseless step like a thief, over the field of jurisdiction, until all shall be usurped from the states, & the
government of all be consolidated into one.

To Charles Hammond, Monticello, August 18, 1821

I must comfort myself with the hope that the judges
will see the importance and the duty of giving their
country the only evidence they can give of fidelity to
its constitution, and integrity in the administration
of its laws, that is to say, by every one's giving his
opinion seriatim and publicly on the cases he decides.

Let him prove by his reasoning that he has read the papers, that he has considered the case, that in the application of the law to it, he uses his own judgment independently and unbiased by party views, and personal favor or disfavor.

To William Johnson, Monticello, March 4, 1823

At the establishment of our constitutions, the judiciary bodies were supposed to be the most helpless and harmless members of the government. Experience however soon showed in what way they were to become the most dangerous; that the insufficiency of the means provided for their removal gave them a freehold and irresponsibility in office, that their decisions, seeming to concern individual suitors only, pass silent and unheeded by the public at large, that these decisions nevertheless became law by precedent, sapping by little and little the foundations of the Constitution, and working its change by construction, before any one has perceived that this invisible and helpless worm has been busily employed in consuming its substance. In truth, man is not made to be trusted for life, if secured against all liability to account.

To Adamantios Coray, Monticello, October 31, 1823

One single object, if your provision attains it, will entitle you to the endless gratitude of society; that of restraining judges from usurping legislation. And with no body of men is this restraint more wanting than with the judges of what is commonly called our General government, but what I call our Foreign department. They are practicing on the Constitution by inferences, analogies and sophisms, as they would on an ordinary law. They do not seem aware that it is not even a Constitution, formed by a single authority, and subject to a single superintendence and control: but that it is a Compact of many independent powers, every single one of which claims an equal right to understand it, and to require its observance. However strong the cord of compact may be, there is a point of tension at which it will break.

. . . This member of the government was at first considered as the most harmless and helpless of all its organs. But it has proved that the power of declaring what the law is, ad libitum,* by sapping and mining, slyly, and without alarm, the foundations of the constitution, can do what open force would not dare to attempt.

*as one wishes

To Edward Livingston, Monticello, March 25, 1825

Justice

What the laws of Virginia are, or may be, will in no wise influence my conduct. Substantial justice is my object, as decided by reason, & not by authority or compulsion.

To Alexander McCaul, Paris, January 4, 1787

All the tranquility, the happiness & security of mankind rest on justice, on the obligation to respect the rights of others.

Opinion on the French Treaties, April 28, 1793

Equal and exact justice to all men, of whatever state or persuasion, religious or political.

First Inaugural Address, March 4, 1801

It is necessary that all important testimony should be brought to one center, in order that the guilty may be convicted, & the innocent left untroubled.

To James Wilkinson, Washington,
January 3, 1807

The most sacred of the duties of a government [is] to do equal & impartial justice to all its citizens.

To Joseph Milligan, Monticello, April 6, 1816

Justice is the fundamental law of society.

To P. S. DuPont de Nemours, April 24, 1816

No man having a natural right to be the judge between himself and another, it is his natural duty to submit to the umpirage of an impartial third.

To Francis W. Gilmer, Monticello, June 7, 1816

Man was created for social intercourse; but social intercourse cannot be maintained without a sense of justice.

To Francis W. Gilmer, Monticello, June 7, 1816

Justness

History bears witness to the fact, that a just nation is taken on its word.

Second Inaugural Address, March 4, 1805

Language

I have been not a little disappointed, & made suspicious of my own judgment on seeing the Edinburgh Reviewers, the ablest Critics of the age, set their faces against the introduction of new words into the English language. They are particularly apprehensive that the writers of the United States will adulterate it. Certainly so great & growing a population, spread over such an extent of country, with such a variety of climates, of productions, of arts, must enlarge their language, to make it answer its purpose of expressing all ideas, the new as well as the old. The new circumstances under which we are placed, call for new words, new phrases, and for the transfer of old words to new objects. An American dialect will therefore be formed; so will a West-Indian and Asiatic, as a Scotch & an Irish are already formed. But whether will these adulterate, or enrich the English language? Has the beautiful poetry of Burns, or his Scottish dialect, disfigured it?

To John Waldo, Monticello, August 16, 1813

Law, medicine, chemistry, mathematics, every science has a language of its own, and Divinity not less than others.

To Peter Wilson, Monticello, January 20, 1816

Where brevity, perspicuity, & even euphony can be promoted by the introduction of a new word, it is an improvement of the language. It is thus the English language has been brought to what it is; one half of it having been innovations, made at different times, from the Greek, Latin, French, & other languages, and is it the worse for these?

To Joseph Milligan, Monticello, April 6, 1816

Nothing is more evident than that as we advance in the knowledge of new things, and of new combinations of old ones, we must have new words to express them.

To Joseph Milligan, Monticello, April 6, 1816

What do we not owe to Shakespeare for the enrichment of the language by his free and magical creation of words?

To Joseph Milligan, Monticello, April 6, 1816

Experience proves to us that the pronunciation of all languages changes, in their descent thro' time.

To Nathaniel Moore, Monticello, September 22, 1819

A language cannot be too rich. The more copious, the more susceptible of embellishment it will become.

To J. Evelyn Denison, Monticello, November 9, 1825

Classical Writers

To read the Latin & Greek authors in their original is a sublime luxury. . . . I enjoy Homer in his own language infinitely beyond Pope's translation of him, & both beyond the dull narrative of the same events by Dares Phrygius; & it is an innocent enjoyment. I thank on my knees him who directed my early education for having put into my possession this rich source of delight: and I would not exchange it for any thing which I could then have acquired & have not since acquired.

To Joseph Priestley, Philadelphia, January 27, 1800

Among the values of classical learning, I estimate the Luxury of reading the Greek & Roman authors in all the beauties of their originals. And why should not this innocent & elegant luxury take its preeminent stand ahead of all those addressed merely to the senses? I think myself more indebted to my father for this, than for all the other luxuries his cares and affections have placed within my reach.

To John Brazer, Poplar Forest, August 24, 1819

Foreign Languages

[Speaking of Smith's appointment as secretary to the American legation in Great Britain] You will have one disagreeable circumstance the less than we have here, that of speaking the language of the country you are in. No one can know the value of this advantage till he has experienced the want of it.

To William Stephens Smith, Paris, June 22, 1785

[Jefferson suggests France as the place to study politics, law and history] because you will at the same time be learning to speak the language of that country, [which will] become absolutely essential under our present circumstances. The best method of doing this would be to fix yourself in some family where there are women & children, in Passy, Auteuil or some other of the little towns in reach of Paris. The principal hours of the day you will attend to your studies, & in those of relaxation associate with the family. You will learn to speak better from women & children in three months, than from men in a year.

To Thomas Mann Randolph, Jr., Paris, July 6, 1787

With respect to modern languages, French, as I have before observed, is indispensable. Next to this the Spanish is most important to an American. Our connection with Spain is already important & will become daily more so. Besides this the ancient part of American history is written chiefly in Spanish. To a person who would make a point of reading & speaking French & Spanish, I should doubt the utility of learning Italian. These three languages, being all degeneracies from the Latin, resemble one another so much that I doubt the possibility of keeping in the head a distinct knowledge of them all. I suppose that he who learns them all will speak a compound of the three, & neither perfectly.

To Thomas Mann Randolph, Jr., Paris, July 6, 1787

The perplexities of a foreign language, the insulated state in which it places us in the midst of society & the embarrassment it occasions when speaking or spoken to, have added in your case a severe season & severe illness.

To Madame de Bréhan, Paris, May 9, 1788

This scrap of French reminds me that I ought to make an apology for not writing to you in your own language. But the little habit I had of explaining myself in that tongue, is entirely lost, and I have been forced to address you in English or to lose the benefit of doing it at all.

To Madame Plumard de Ballanger, Monticello,
April 25, 1794

As I think the learning French essential to the study of the law, I cannot help being anxious that you should do it, & that without loss of time, as for want of understanding it you must read every day is a disadvantage. I think if you could come & stay here one month, applying yourself solely & constantly to that object, you would acquire it sufficiently to pursue it afterwards by yourself.

To Dabney Carr, Monticello,
September 24, 1794

The difficulty of communicating my ideas justly in a foreign language often prevented my indulging myself in conversation with persons whose acquaintance I wished to cultivate.

To William Short, Philadelphia, May 1, 1798

I much regret that you do not speak our language with ease, as I know from experience how much that lessens the pleasures of society.

To P. S. Du Pont de Nemours, Philadelphia,
January 17, 1800

Did you ever know an instance of one who could write in a foreign language with the elegance of a native?

To P. S. Dupont de Nemours, Monticello, December 31, 1815

Grammar

My busy life has not permitted me to indulge in a pursuit to which I felt great attraction. While engaged in it however some ideas occurred for facilitating the study by simplifying its grammar, by reducing the infinite diversities of its unfixed orthography to single and settled forms, indicating at the same time the pronunciation of the word by its correspondence with the characters & powers of the English alphabet.

To Sir Herbert Croft, Monticello, October 30, 1798

Mine has been a life of business, of that kind which appeals to a man's conscience, as well as his industry, not to let it suffer; & the few moments allowed me from labor have been devoted to more attractive studies, that of Grammar having never been a favorite with me. The scanty foundation laid in at school has carried me thro' a life of much hasty writing, more indebted for style to reading & memory, than to rules of grammar. I have been pleased to see that in all cases you appeal to Usage, as the arbiter of language; & justly consider that as giving law to Grammar, & not Grammar to Usage. I concur entirely with you in opposition to the Purists, who would destroy all strength & beauty of style, by subjecting it to a rigorous compliance with their rules. Fill up all the Ellipses & Syllepses of Tacitus, Sallust, Livy, &c., and the elegance & force of their sententious brevity are extinguished.

To John Waldo, Monticello, August 16, 1813

Language Skills

Such is become the prostitution of language that sincerity has no longer distinct terms in which to express her own truths.

To George Washington, Philadelphia,
January 22, 1783

Style in writing or speaking is formed very early in life while the imagination is warm, & impressions are permanent.

To John Banister, Jr., Paris, October 15, 1785

Ingenious minds, availing themselves of the imperfection of language, have tortured the expressions out of their plain meaning in order to infer departures from them in practice.

To Isaac Story, Washington, December 5, 1801

Letters are not the first, but the last step in the progression from barbarism to civilization.

To James Pemberton, Washington, June 21, 1808

Dictionaries are but the depositories of words already legitimated by usage. Society is the work-shop in which new ones are elaborated. When an individual uses a new word, if ill formed it is rejected in society, if well formed, adopted, and, after due time, laid up in the depository of dictionaries.

To John Adams, Monticello, August 15, 1820

Nor am I a friend to a scrupulous purism of style. I readily sacrifice the niceties of syntax to euphony and strength. It is by boldly neglecting the rigorisms of grammar that Tacitus has made himself the strongest writer in the world. The Hypercritics call him barbarous; but I should be sorry to exchange his barbarisms for their wire-drawn purisms.

To Edward Everett, Monticello, February 24, 1823

Mottos

The beauty of a motto is to condense much matter in as few words as possible.

To George Wythe, Paris, August 13, 1786

Translations

I make it a rule never to read translations where I can read the original.

To Edmund Randolph, Monticello,
February 3, 1794

I say nothing of style, not doubting its merit, & conscious I am no judge of it in a foreign language. I believe it impossible, in any but our native tongue, to be so thoroughly sensible of the delicacies of style, which constitutes an essential merit in poetical composition, as to criticize them with correctness.

To Amelot de la Croix, Washington, February 3, 1809

Life

The most fortunate of us all in our journey through life frequently meet with calamities and misfortunes which may greatly afflict us; and to fortify our minds against the attacks of these calamities and misfortunes should be one of the principal studies and endeavors of our lives. The only method of doing this is to assure a perfect resignation to the divine will, to consider that whatever does happen, must happen, and that by our uneasiness we cannot prevent the blow before it does fall, but we may add to its force after it has fallen. These considerations and others such as these may enable us in some measure to surmount the difficulties thrown in our way, to bear up with a tolerable degree of patience under this burden of life, and to proceed with a pious and unshaken resignation till we arrive at our journey's end, where we may deliver up our trust into the hands of him who gave it, and receive such reward as to him shall seem proportioned to our merit.

To John Page, Shadwell, July 15, 1763

That your road, through life, may be covered with roses, is [my] sincere prayer.

To Madame de Tott, Paris,
February 28, 1787

Portrait of Jefferson by Thomas Sully, 1821.
(Monticello/Thomas Jefferson Foundation, Inc.)

Blessings of Life

The good things of this life are scattered so sparingly in our way that we must glean them up as we go.

To Abigail Adams, Paris, November 1786

That to the health of youth you may add an old age of vigor is the sincere prayer of
> Yours, affectionately.

To John Garland Jefferson, Monticello, January 25, 1810

The Broad Picture

General views are sometimes better taken at a distance than nearer. The working of the whole machine is sometimes better seen elsewhere than at its center.

To Joel Barlow, Monticello, April 16, 1811

Cycles of Life

Every thing has its beginning, its growth, and end.

To the Marquis de Lafayette, Monticello, October 9, 1824

Fatalism

We must take things as they come.

To John Adams, Monticello, April 8, 1816

Old Age

I find as I grow older, that I love those most whom I loved first.

To Mary Jefferson Bolling, Paris, July 23, 1787

While old men feel sensibly enough their own advance in years, they do not sufficiently recollect it in those whom they have seen young.

To William Short, Philadelphia, January 3, 1793

I know nothing so dreary in prospect as old age surviving its old friends and burdening its young ones.

To Elizabeth Wayles Eppes, Philadelphia, March 24, 1798

My health has been always so uniformly firm, that I have for some years dreaded nothing so much as the living too long.

To Benjamin Rush, Washington, December 20, 1801

Being very sensible of bodily decays from advancing years, I ought not to doubt their effect on the mental faculties. To do so would evince either great self-love or little observation of what passes under our eyes: and I shall be fortunate if I am the first to perceive and to obey this admonition of nature.

To Isaac Weaver, Jr., Washington, June 7, 1807

A longer period of life was less important, alloyed as the feeble enjoyments of that age are with so much pain.

To Joseph Bringhurst, Washington, February 24, 1808

I find in old age that the impressions of youth are the deepest & most indelible.

To David Campbell, Monticello, January 12, 1810

It is wonderful to me that old men should not be sensible that their minds keep pace with their bodies in the progress of decay. . . . Nothing betrays imbecility so much as the being insensible of it.

To Benjamin Rush, Poplar Forest, August 17, 1811

The hand of age is upon me. The decay of bodily faculties apprises me that those of the mind cannot be
unimpaired, had I not still better proofs. Every year
counts by increased debility, and departing faculties
keep the score. The last year it was the sight, this it is
the hearing, the next something else will be going,
until all is gone. . . . As a compensation for faculties
departed, nature gives me good health, & a perfect
resignation to the laws of decay which she has prescribed to all the forms & combinations of matter.

To William Duane, Monticello, October 1, 1812

Our machines have now been running for 70 or 80
years, and we must expect that, worn as they are,
here a pivot, there a wheel, now a pinion, next a
spring, will be giving way: and however we may
tinker them up for awhile, all will at length surcease
motion. Our watches, with works of brass and steel,
wear out within that period.

To John Adams, Monticello, July 5, 1814

To me every mail, in the departure of some Cotempo-
rary, brings warning to be in readiness myself also,
and to cease from new engagements. It is a warning of
no alarm. When faculty after faculty is retiring from
us, and all the avenues to cheerful sensation closing,
sight failing now, hearing next, then memory, debility
of body, trepitude of mind, nothing remaining but a
sickly vegetation, with scarcely the relief of a little
loco-motion, the last cannot be but a coup de grace.*

*the death blow; the stroke of mercy

To John Melish, Monticello, December 10, 1814

The regrets . . . of 72 at the loss of friends may be the less, as the time is shorter within which we are to meet again, according to the creed of our education.

To the Marquis de Lafayette, Monticello, February 14, 1815

A decline of health, at the age of 76 was naturally to be expected, and is a warning of an event which cannot be distant, and whose approach I contemplate with little concern. For indeed in no circumstance has nature been kinder to us, than in the soft gradations by which she prepares us to part willingly with what we are not destined always to retain. First one faculty is withdrawn and then another, sight, hearing, memory, accuracy, affections, & friends, filched one by one, till we are left among strangers, the mere monuments of times past, and specimens of antiquity for the observation of the curious.

To Horatio Gates Spafford, Monticello, May 11, 1819

A severe illness the last year, another from which I am just emerged, admonish me that repetitions may be expected, against which a declining frame cannot long bear up.

To Spencer Roane, Poplar Forest, September 6, 1819

My business is to beguile the wearisomeness of declining life, as I endeavor to do by the delights of classical reading and of mathematical truths and by the consolations of a sound philosophy, equally indifferent to hope & fear.

To William Short, Monticello, October 31, 1819

Great decline in the energies of the body impart naturally a corresponding wane of the mind, and a longing after tranquility as the last and sweetest asylum of age.

To Spencer Roane, Monticello, March 9, 1821

Man, like the fruit he eats, has his period of ripeness. Like that too, if he continues longer hanging to the stem, it is but an useless and unsightly appendage.

To Henry Dearborn, Monticello, August 17, 1821

The lapses of memory of an old man, are innocent subjects of compassion, more than of blame.

To John Campbell, Monticello, November 10, 1822

I do not write with the ease which your letter of Sept. 18 supposes. Crippled wrists and fingers make writing slow & laborious. But while writing to you, I lose the sense of these things in the recollection of ancient times, when youth & health made happiness out of every thing. I forget for a while the hoary winter of old age, when we can think of nothing but how to keep ourselves warm, and how to get rid of our heavy hours until the friendly hand of death shall rid us of all at once.

To John Adams, Monticello, October 12, 1823

The solitude in which we are left by the death of our friends is one of the great evils of protracted life. When I look back to the days of my youth, it is like

looking over a field of battle. All, all dead! and ourselves left alone amidst a new generation whom we
know not, and who know not us.

To Francis A. Van Der Kemp, Monticello,
January 11, 1825

I know how apt we are to consider those whom we
knew long ago, and have not since seen, to be exactly still what they were when we knew them; and to
have been stationary in body and mind as they have
been in our recollections.

To Edward Livingston, Monticello, March 25, 1825

Reliving One's Life

Putting to myself your question, Would I agree to
live my 73 years over again for ever? I hesitate to
say. With [Benjamin] Chew's limitations from 25
to 60, I would say Yes; and might go further back,
but not come lower down. For, at the latter period,
with most of us, the powers of life are sensibly on
the wane, sight becomes dim, hearing dull, memory
constantly enlarging its frightful blank and parting
with all we have ever seen or known, spirits evapo-
rate, bodily debility creeps on palsying every limb,
and so faculty after faculty quits us, and where then
is life? If, in its full vigor, of good as well as evil,
your friend [William] Vassall could doubt its value,
it must be purely a negative quantity when its evils
alone remain. Yet I do not go into his opinion entirely. I do not agree that an age of pleasure is no
compensation for a moment of pain. I think, with

you, that life is a fair matter of account, and the balance often nay generally in its favor. It is not indeed easy, by calculation of intensity and time, to apply a common measure, or to fix the par between pleasure and pain: yet it exists, and is measurable.

To John Adams, Monticello, August 1, 1816

Retirement

The independence of private life under the protection of republican laws will I hope yield me that happiness from which no slave is so remote as the minister of a Commonwealth.

To the Marquis de Lafayette, Monticello,
August 4, 1781

It is not easy to reconcile ourselves to the many useless miseries to which Providence seems to expose us. But his justice affords a prospect that we shall all be made even some day.

To Eliza House Trist, Annapolis, December 11, 1783

I look to that period with the longing of a waveworn mariner, who has at length the land in view, & shall count the days & hours which still lie between me & it.

To George Washington, Monticello,
September 9, 1792

I now contemplate the approach of that moment with the fondness of a sailor who has land in view.

To Thomas Pinckney, Philadelphia, November 8, 1792

The difference of my present & past situation is such as to leave me nothing to regret but that my retirement has been postponed four years too long.

To John Adams, Monticello, April 25, 1794

I have not been disappointed in the satisfaction I expected from the society of my family & occupations of my farms. The latter have engrossed my attentions beyond what I thought possible, and as I advance in the execution of my plans, I find myself more and more engaged by them, & new ones opening upon me. Master of my own time, my own operations & actions, secured by their innocence towards the world against the censures of the world, and against newspaper denunciations, I look back with wonder & regret over my useless waste of time in other employments.

To Robert Morris, Monticello, February 19, 1795

[Encouraging Alexander Donald to retire near to Monticello] Come then, since you cannot have Monticello, and fix yourself along side of it, and let us take our soup and wine together every day, and talk over the stories of our youth, and the tales of other times. We shall never see better. Only do not be too long in thinking yourself rich enough for retirement; otherwise we may both first make our great retirement to where there is neither soup nor wine, and where we are told that neither moth nor rust doth corrupt.

To Alexander Donald, Monticello, May 30, 1795

My books, my family, my friends, & my farm, furnish more than enough to occupy me the remainder of my life, & of that tranquil occupation most analogous to my physical & moral constitution.

To Monsieur Odit, Monticello, October 14, 1795

Your son . . . found me in a retirement I dote on, living like an Antediluvian patriarch among my children & grand children, and tilling my soil. . . . You hope I have not abandoned entirely the service of our country. After five & twenty years' continual employment in it, I trust it will be thought I have fulfilled my tour, like a punctual soldier, and may claim my discharge.

To Edward Rutledge, Monticello,
November 30, 1795

I had retired after five & twenty years of constant occupation in public affairs, and total abandonment of my own. I retired much poorer than when I entered the public service, and desired nothing but rest and oblivion.

To Edward Rutledge, Monticello, December 27, 1796

I leave to others the sublime delights of riding in the storm, better pleased with sound sleep & a warmer berth below it, encircled with the society of my neighbors, friends, & fellow laborers of the earth, rather than with spies & sycophants.

To John Adams, Monticello, December 28, 1796

It is now among my most fervent longings to be on my farm, which, with a garden & fruitery, will constitute my principal occupation in retirement.

To Robert R. Livingston, Washington, January 3, 1808

I derive great personal consolation from the assurances in your friendly letter that the electors of Massachusetts would still have viewed me with favor as a candidate for a 3d Presidential term. But the duty of retirement is so strongly impressed on my mind, that it is impossible for me to think of that. If I can carry into retirement the good will of my fellow citizens, nothing else will be wanting to my happiness.

To Governor James Sullivan, Washington, March 3, 1808

I am full of plans of employment when I get there, they chiefly respect the active functions of the body. To the mind I shall administer amusement chiefly. An only daughter and numerous family of grandchildren, will furnish me great resources of happiness.

To Charles Thomson, Washington, December 25, 1808

As the moment of my retirement approaches, I become more anxious for its arrival, and to begin at length to pass what yet remains to me of life & health in the bosom of my family & neighbors, & in communication with my friends, undisturbed by political concerns or passions.

To George Logan, Washington, December 27, 1808

You suppose I am "in the prime of life for rule." I am sensible I am not; and before I am so far declined as to become insensible of it, I think it right to put it out of my own power. I have the comfort too of knowing that the person whom the public choice has designated to receive the charge from me is eminently qualified as a safe depository by the endowments of integrity, understanding, & experience. On a review therefore of the reasons for my retirement, I think you cannot fail to approve them.

To Henry Guest, Washington, January 4, 1809

Within a few days I retire to my family, my books & farms; & having gained the harbor myself, I shall look on my friends still buffeting the storm, with anxiety indeed, but not with envy. Never did a prisoner, released from his chains, feel such relief as I shall on shaking off the shackles of power. Nature intended me for the tranquil pursuits of science, by rendering them my supreme delight. But the enormities of the times in which I have lived, have forced me to take a part in resisting them, and to commit myself on the boisterous ocean of political passions. I thank god for the opportunity of retiring from them without censure, and carrying with me the most consoling proofs of public approbation.

To P. S. Dupont de Nemours, Washington, March 2, 1809

I am held by the cords of love to my family & country, or I should certainly join you. Within a few days

I shall now bury myself in the groves of Monticello, & become a mere spectator of the passing events.

To Alexander von Humboldt, Washington, March 6, 1809

I am at length enjoying the never before luxury of employing myself for my own gratification only.

To Meriwether Lewis, Monticello, August 16, 1809

I am leading a life of considerable activity as a farmer, reading little & writing less. Something pursued with ardor is necessary to guard us from the tedium vitae,* and the active pursuits lessen most our sense of the infirmities of age.

*weariness of life

To John Garland Jefferson, Monticello, January 25, 1810

My occupations here are almost exclusively given to my farm & affairs. They furnish me exercise, health & amusement, and with the recreations of family & neighborly society, fill up most of my time, and give a tranquility necessary to my time of life.

To William Lambert, Monticello, July 16, 1810

Anxious, in my retirement, to enjoy undisturbed repose, my knowledge of my successor & late coadjutors, and my entire confidence in their wisdom and integrity, were assurances to me that I might sleep in security with such watchmen at the helm, and that whatever difficulties & dangers should assail our course, they would do what could be done to

avoid or surmount them. In this confidence, I enve-
lope myself, & hope to slumber on to my last sleep.

To William Duane, Monticello, August 12, 1810

There is a fullness of time when men should go, &
not occupy too long the ground to which others
have a right to advance.

To Benjamin Rush, Poplar Forest, August 17, 1811

In the scenes which are to ensue, I am to be but a
spectator. I have withdrawn myself from all political
intermeddlings, to indulge the evening of my life
with what have been the passions of every portion of
it, books, science, my farms, my family and friends.
To these every hour of the day is now devoted. I retain a good activity of mind, not quite as much of
body, but uninterrupted health. Still the hand of age
is upon me. All my friends are nearly gone.

To James Maury, Monticello, April 25, 1812

I think it a great blessing that I retain understanding enough to be sensible how much of it I have
lost, & to avoid exposing myself as a spectacle for
the pity of my friends: that I have surmounted the
difficult point of knowing when to retire. As a compensation for faculties departed, nature gives me
good health, & a perfect resignation to the laws of
decay which she has prescribed to all the forms &
combinations of matter.

To William Duane, Monticello, October 1, 1812

The summum bonum* with me is now truly Epicurian, ease of body and tranquility of mind; & to these I wish to consign my remaining days.

> *the supreme good

> To John Adams, Monticello, June 27, 1813

The swaggering on deck, as a passenger, is so much more pleasant than clambering the ropes as a seaman, & my confidence in the skill and activity of those employed to work the vessel is so entire, that I notice nothing en passant,* but how smoothly she moves.

> *in passing

> To John Wayles Eppes, Poplar Forest, September 11, 1813

I am now retired: I resign myself, as a passenger, with confidence to those at the present helm, and ask but for rest, peace and good will.

> To Samuel Kercheval, Monticello, July 12, 1816

Tranquility is the summum bonum* of age. I wish therefore to offend no man's opinions, nor to draw disquieting animadversions on my own. While duty required it I met opposition with a firm and fearless step. But loving mankind in my individual relations with them I pray to be permitted to depart in their peace; and like the superannuated soldier, "quadragenis stipendis emeritis,"** to hang my arms on the post.

> *the supreme good

> **with forty years of honorable service

> To Spencer Roane, Poplar Forest, September 6, 1819

Time

You are now old enough to know how very important to your future life will be the manner in which
you employ your present time. I hope therefore you
will never waste a moment of it.

To Peter Carr, Annapolis, December 11, 1783

It is to time I look as the surest remedy.

To William Short, Toulon, April 7, 1787

Time is sure, though slow.

Martha Jefferson Randolph, Philadelphia, August 18, 1793

In no course of life have I been ever more closely
pressed by business than in the present. Much of
this proceeds from my own affairs; much from the
calls of others; leaving little time for indulgence in
my greatest of all amusements, reading. Doctor
Franklin used to say that when he was young, and
had time to read, he had not books; and now when
he had become old and had books, he had no time.
Perhaps it is that, when habit has strengthened our
sense of duties, they leave no time for other things;
but when young, we neglect them, and this gives us
time for any thing.

To Abigail Adams, Monticello, August 22, 1813

Consider how little time is left you, and how much
you have to attain in it, and that every moment you
lose of it is lost for ever.

To Francis Eppes, Monticello, October 6, 1820

Time is now the most pressing and precious thing in the world to you, and the greatest injury which can possibly be done you is to waste what remains.

To Francis Eppes, Poplar Forest,
December 13, 1820

Youth

It is while we are young that the habit of industry is formed. If not then, it never is afterwards. The fortune of our lives therefore depends on employing well the short period of youth.

To Martha Jefferson, Aix en Provence, March 28, 1787

Life's Difficulties

I hope you will have better health, and still many years of life to enjoy it. I mean if you desire it; for I feel myself how possible it is that we may cease to desire to live. Every course of life doubtless has its difficulties.

To Carlo Bellini, Monticello, April 24, 1799

Bad Timing

A good cause is often injured more by ill timed efforts of its friends than by the arguments of its enemies.

To James Heaton, Monticello, May 20, 1826

Condolences

By this time I hope your mind has felt the good effects of time & occupation. They are slow physicians indeed, but they are the only ones. Their opiate influence lessens our sensibility tho their power does not extend to dry up the sources of sorrow.

To Eliza House Trist, Paris, August 18, 1785

I . . . sincerely condole with you on the great loss you have sustained. Experience, however, in the same bitter school has taught me that it is not condolence, but time and silence alone which can heal those wounds.

To Henry Remsen, Philadelphia, March 18, 1792

Condolences were but renewals of grief.

To Benjamin Rush, Monticello, January 16, 1811

[On the death of Abigail Adams] Tried myself, in the school of affliction, by the loss of every form of connection which can rive the human heart, I know well, and feel what you have lost, what you have suffered, are suffering, and have yet to endure. The same trials have taught me that, for ills so immeasurable, time and silence are the only medicines. I will not therefore, by useless condolences, open afresh the sluices of your grief nor, altho' mingling sincerely my tears with yours, will I say a word more, where words are vain, but that it is of some comfort to us both that the term is not very distant at which we are to deposit, in the same cerement, our sorrows and suffering bodies, and to ascend in essence to an ecstatic meeting with the friends we have loved and lost and whom we shall still love and never lose again. God bless you and support you under your heavy affliction.

To John Adams, Monticello, November 13, 1818

Defeat
Lamentations & invective were all that remained to them.

To Richard M. Johnson, Washington,
March 10, 1808

Failing Memory
Of all the faculties of the human mind that of Memory is the first which suffers decay from age.

To Benjamin Henry Latrobe, Monticello, July 12, 1812

A life of constant action leaves no time for recording. Always thinking of what is next to be done, what has been done is dismissed and soon obliterated from the memory.

To Horatio Gates Spafford, Monticello, May 11, 1819

Maladies
Calamity was our best physician.

To Richard Price, Paris, February 1, 1785

A malady of either body or mind once known is half cured.

To the Marquis de Chastellux, Paris, September 2, 1785

At your time of life the resources of nature are so powerful that, in a case which gives her time, they are infallible. In the whole course of my observations, I cannot recollect one instance of a chronic complaint in any person of your age not being surmounted, except in the case of consumption, which is not yours. One very disagreeable circumstance indeed is the effect of the disease on your spirits. But this is merely mechanical. It is not the result of reasoning on the known nature of your complaint. That I am satisfied is known to nobody. The wisest physicians agree in another fact, that there never was an instance of a chronic complaint relieved by medicine, even where the character of the disease is known. But where it is unknown, medicine is given at hap-hazard, and may do much mischief. Keep up your strength then, by such exercise as you find does not fatigue you, & by eating such things & in such quantities as you find you can digest. This will give time to the vis medicatrix naturae,* which, if it be not thwarted in its efforts by medicine, is infallible in its resources at your time of life. Its efforts would indeed be immensely aided if you could, by the force of reason & confidence in her, counteract the mechanical effects of the disease on your spirits. But if you cannot do this, still exercise moderately, eat soberly but sufficiently, and take no medicine, and your friends will have nothing to fear. I think we may strongly conjecture that your complaint is a gout, because no other disease is so long in declaring itself, and because you have a hereditary expectation of that. However if the symptoms be permitted to develop themselves, they will in time unfold the disease, and bring on that crisis which is contrived by nature to relieve it.

*the healing power of nature

To Thomas Mann Randolph, Jr., Monticello, January 18, 1796

There are ills in life as desperate as intolerable.

To Samuel Brown, Monticello, July 14, 1813

Obstacles

I have always found it best to remove obstacles first.

To Abigail Adams, Paris, June 21, 1785

Regrets

Put . . . aside vain regrets.

To Joel Barlow, Monticello, April 16, 1811

Restrictions

We are bound down by the laws of our situation.

To William Duane, Monticello, March 28, 1811

Senility

Of all human contemplations the most abhorrent is body without mind.

To John Adams, Monticello, August 1, 1816

The papers tell us that Genl. Starke is off at the age of 93. Charles Thomson still lives at about the same age, cheerful, slender as a grasshopper, and so much without memory that he scarcely recognizes the members of his household. An intimate friend of his called on him not long since: it was difficult to make him recollect who he was, and, sitting one hour, he told him the same story 4 times over. Is this life? . . . It is at most but the life of a cabbage; surely not worth a wish. When all our faculties have left, or are leaving us, one by one, sight, hearing, memory, every avenue of pleasing sensation is closed, and athumy, debility and malaise left in their places, when the friends of our youth are all gone, and a generation is risen around us whom we know not, is death an evil? . . . I have ever dreaded a doting old age; and my health has been generally so good, and is now so good, that I dread it still. The rapid decline of my strength during the last winter has made me hope sometimes that I see land. During summer I enjoy its temperature, but I shudder at the approach of winter, and wish I could sleep through it with the Dormouse, and only wake with him in spring, if ever.

To John Adams, Monticello, June 1, 1822

The misfortune of a weakened mind is an insensibility of its weakness.

To Edward Livingston, Monticello, March 25, 1825

Small Problems
Do not be discouraged by small difficulties.

To John Taylor, Monticello, November 26, 1798

Surviving Ordeals

It is pleasant for those who have just escaped threatened shipwreck, to hail one another when landed in unexpected safety.

To James Warren, Washington, March 21, 1801

Love

I wish they had formed us like the birds of the air, able to fly where we please. I would have exchanged for this many of the boasted preeminencies of man. I was so unlucky when very young, as to read the history of Fortunatus. He had a cap of such virtues that when he put it on his head, and wished himself anywhere, he was there. I have been all my life sighing for this cap. Yet if I had it, I question if I should use it but once. I should wish myself with you, and not wish myself away again.

To Maria Cosway, Paris, December 24, 1786

A great deal of love given to a few, is better than a little to many.

To Maria Cosway, Paris, July 27, 1788

If I love you more, it is because you deserve more.

To Maria Cosway, Paris, July 30, 1788

Maria Cosway. (Monticello/Thomas Jefferson Foundation, Inc.)

Let us be together in spirit. Preserve for me always a little corner in your affection in exchange for the spacious part you occupy in mine.

To Maria Cosway, Paris, January 14, 1789

Love is always a consolatory thing.

To Maria Cosway, Paris, May 21, 1789

When wafting on the bosom of the ocean I shall pray it to be as calm and smooth as yours to me.

To Maria Cosway, Paris, May 21, 1789

We think last of those we love most.

To Maria Cosway, Cowes, Isle of Wight, October 14, 1789

In truth whenever I think of you, I am hurried off on the wings of imagination into regions where fancy submits all things to our will.

To Maria Cosway, Monticello, September 8, 1795

The Military

Army

Our men are good, but our generals unqualified. Every failure we have incurred has been the fault of the general, the men evincing courage in every instance.

To Samuel Brown, Monticello, July 14, 1813

Military Command

Our war on the land has commenced most inauspiciously. I fear we are to expect reverses until we can find out who are qualified for command, & until these can learn their profession. The proof of a general, to know whether he will stand fire, costs a more serious price than that of a cannon.

To William Duane, Monticello, January 22, 1813

The creator has not thought proper to mark those in the forehead who are of stuff to make good generals. We are first therefore to seek them blindfold, and then let them learn the trade at the expense of great losses.

To Theodorus Bailey, Monticello, February 6, 1813

It is unfortunate that heaven has not set its stamp on the forehead of those whom it has qualified for military achievement. That it has left us to draw for them in a lottery of so many blanks to a prize, and where the blank is to be manifested only by the public misfortunes.

To John Armstrong, Monticello, February 8, 1813

Navy

Every rational citizen must wish to see an effective instrument of coercion, and should fear to see it on any other element but the water. A naval force can never endanger our liberties, nor occasion bloodshed; a land force would do both.

To James Monroe, Paris, August 11, 1786

At sea we have rescued our character.

To Samuel Brown, Monticello,
July 14, 1813

Morality

The great principles of right and wrong are legible to every reader; to pursue them requires not the aid of many counsellors.

A Summary View of the Rights of British America, 1774

Give up money, give up fame, give up science, give up the earth itself & all it contains rather than do an immoral act. And never suppose that in any possible situation or under any circumstances that it is best for you to do a dishonorable thing however slightly so it may appear to you. Whenever you are to do a thing tho' it can never be known but to yourself, ask yourself how you would act were all the world looking at you, & act accordingly.

To Peter Carr, Paris, August 19, 1785

Morals were too essential to the happiness of man, to be risked on the uncertain combinations of the head. She laid their foundation, therefore, in sentiment, not in science.

To Maria Cosway, Paris, October 12, 1786

We may well admit morality to be the child of the understanding rather than of the senses, when we observe that it becomes dearer to us as the latter weaken, & as the former grows stronger by time & experience till the hour arrives in which all other objects lose all their value.

To Richard Price, Paris, July 11, 1788

I know but one code of morality for man whether acting singly or collectively. He who says I will be a rogue when I act in company with a hundred others but an honest man when I act alone, will be believed in the former assertion, but not in the latter.

To James Madison, Paris, August 28, 1789

We are firmly convinced, and we act on that conviction, that with nations, as with individuals, our interests soundly calculated, will ever be found inseparable from our moral duties.

Second Inaugural Address, March 4, 1805

It has a great effect on the opinion of our people & the world to have the moral right on our side.

To President James Madison, Monticello, April 19, 1809

I never did, or countenanced, in public life, a single act inconsistent with the strictest good faith, having never believed there was one code of morality for a public, & another for a private man.

To Don Valentine de Foronda, Monticello,
October 4, 1809

I sincerely then believe with you in the general existence of a moral instinct. I think it the brightest gem with which the human character is studded; and the want of it as more degrading than the most hideous of the bodily deformities.

To Thomas Law, Poplar Forest, June 13, 1814

He [God] has formed us moral agents. Not that, in the perfection of his state, he can feel pain or pleasure from any thing we may do: he is far above our power; but that we may promote the happiness of those with whom he has placed us in society, by acting honestly towards all, benevolently to those who fall within our way, respecting sacredly their rights, bodily and mental, and cherishing especially their freedom of conscience, as we value our own.

To Miles King, Monticello, September 26, 1814

I fear, from the experience of the last 25 years that morals do not, of necessity, advance hand in hand with the sciences.

To José Correa da Serra, Monticello, June 28, 1815

The moral sense is as much a part of our constitution as that of feeling, seeing, or hearing.

To John Adams, Monticello, October 14, 1816

Aid

The laws of humanity make it a duty for nations, as well as individuals, to succor those whom accident & distress have thrown upon them.

To Albert Gallatin, Washington, January 24, 1807

Character

If pride of character be of worth at any time, it is when it disarms the efforts of malice.

To Thomas Nelson, Richmond, February 21, 1781

[I hope] to become acquainted with your father who must be good, because you are so. The fruit is a specimen of the tree.

Angelica Schuyler Church, Paris, August 17, 1788

The uniform tenor of a man's life furnishes better evidence of what he has said or done on any particular occasion than the word of any enemy.

To George Clinton, Washington, December 31, 1803

The only exact testimony of a man is his actions, leaving the reader to pronounce on them his own judgment.

To Louis H. Girardin, Monticello, March 27, 1815

Charity

I deem it the duty of every man to devote a certain proportion of his income for charitable purposes. . . . However disposed the mind may feel to unlimited good, our means having limits, we are necessarily circumscribed by them.

To Drs. Rogers and Slaughter, Washington, March 2, 1806

The aid we would be disposed to give to a promising enterprise would be very different from that we might offer to a desperate one.

To Jean de la Coste, Washington, May 24, 1807

We are all doubtless bound to contribute a certain portion of our income to the support of charitable & other useful public institutions. But it is a part of our duty also to apply our contributions in the most effectual way we can to secure their object. The question then is whether this will not be better done by each of us appropriating our whole contributions to the institutions within our own reach, under our own eye; & over which we can exercise some useful control? Or would it be better that each should divide the sum he can spare among all the institutions of his state, or of the United States? Reason, & the interest of these institutions themselves certainly decide in favor of the former practice. This question has been forced on me heretofore by the multitude of applications which have come to me from every quarter of the union on behalf of academies, churches, missions, hospitals, charitable establishments, &c. Had I parceled among them all the contributions which I could spare, it would have been for each too feeble a sum to be worthy of being either given or received. If each portion of the state, on the contrary will apply its aids & its attentions exclusively to those nearest around them, all will be better taken care of. Their support, their conduct, & the best administration of their funds, will be under the inspection & control of those most convenient to take cognizance of them, & most interested in their prosperity.

To Samuel Kercheval, Monticello, January 15, 1810

Private charities, as well as contributions to public purposes in proportion to every one's circumstances, are certainly among the duties we owe to society.

To Charles Christian, Monticello, March 21, 1812

Conscience

Never do nor say a bad thing. If ever you are about to say any thing amiss or to do any thing wrong, consider before hand. You will feel something within you which will tell you it is wrong & ought not to be said or done: this is your conscience, & be sure to obey it. Our maker has given us all, this faithful internal Monitor, and if you always obey it, you will always be prepared for the end of the world: or for a much more certain event which is death. This must happen to all: it puts an end to the world as to us, & the way to be ready for it is never to do a wrong act.

To Martha Jefferson, Annapolis, December 11, 1783

The moral sense, or conscience, is as much a part of man as his leg or arm. It is given to all human beings in a stronger or weaker degree, as force of members is given them in a greater or less degree. It may be strengthened by exercise, as may any particular limb of the body. This sense is submitted indeed in some degree to the guidance of reason; but it is a small stock which is required for this: even a less one than what we call Common sense. State a moral case to a ploughman & a professor. The former will decide it as well, & often better than the latter, because he has not been led astray by artificial rules.

To Peter Carr, Paris, August 10, 1787

Doing Good

I know that, to you, a consciousness of doing good is a luxury ineffable.

To George Wythe, Paris, September 16, 1787

You . . . will find that we are working for ourselves while we do good to others.

To Mary Jefferson Eppes, Philadelphia, February 12, 1800

Doing What Is Right

If ever you find yourself environed with difficulties & perplexing circumstances, out of which you are at a loss how to extricate yourself, do what is right, and be assured that that will extricate you the best out of the worst situations. Tho' you cannot see when you take one step, what will be the next, yet follow truth, justice, & plain dealing, & never fear their leading you out of the labyrinth in the easiest manner possible. The knot which you thought a Gordian one will untie itself before you.

To Peter Carr, Paris, August 19, 1785

If ever you find yourself in difficulty and doubt how to extricate yourself, do what is right, & you will find it the easiest way of getting out of the difficulty.

To Martha Jefferson, Toulon, April 7, 1787

My principle is to do whatever is right, and leave consequences to him who has the disposal of them.

To George Logan, Monticello, October 3, 1813

The End Justifies the Means
It is a maxim of our municipal law, and, I believe, of universal law, that he who permits the end, permits of course the means, without which the end cannot be effected.

To Albert Gallatin, Washington, March 23, 1808

Integrity
Rigid integrity is the first and most gainful qualification (in the long run) in every profession.

To John Garland Jefferson, Philadelphia,
February 5, 1791

I am sure that in estimating every man of value either in private or public life, a pure integrity is the quality we take first into calculation, and that learning and talents are only the second. After these come benevolence, good temper &c. But the first is always that sort of integrity which makes a man act in the dark as if it was in the open blaze of day.

To John Garland Jefferson, Philadelphia, June 15, 1792

Principles
When principles are well understood their application is less embarrassing.

To Gouverneur Morris, Philadelphia,
December 30, 1792

An unprincipled man, let his other fitnesses be what they will, ought never to be employed.

To George Gilmer, Philadelphia, June 28, 1793

I know my own principles to be pure, and therefore am not ashamed of them. On the contrary I wish them known, & therefore willingly express them to every one. They are the same I have acted on from the year 75 to this day, and are the same, I am sure, with those of the great body of the American people.

To Samuel Smith, Monticello, August 22, 1798

True wisdom does not lie in mere practice without principle.

To John Adams, Monticello, October 14, 1816

Repentance

When sins are dear to us we are but too prone to slide into them again. The act of repentance itself is often sweetened with the thought that it clears our account for a repetition of the same sin.

To Maria Cosway, Paris, November 19, 1786

Virtue

Encourage all your virtuous dispositions, & exercise them whenever an opportunity arises, being assured that they will gain strength by exercise as a limb of the body does, & that exercise will make them habitual. From the practice of the purest virtue you may be assured you will derive the most sublime

comforts in every moment of life, & in the moment
of death.

To Peter Carr, Paris, August 19, 1785

Virtues of the heart require time and trial [to dis-
cover].

To William Carmichael, Bourdeaux, May 26, 1787

That there is much vice & misery in the world, I
know: but more virtue & happiness I believe, at least
in our part of it.

To Abbé Salimankis, Monticello, March 14, 1810

Without virtue, happiness cannot be.

To Amos J. Cook, Monticello, January 21, 1816

The essence of virtue is in doing good to others.

To John Adams, Monticello, October 14, 1816

If no action is to be deemed virtuous for which malice can imagine a sinister motive, then there never
was a virtuous action; no, not even in the life of our
savior himself. But he has taught us to judge the
tree by its fruit, and to leave motives to him who can
alone see into them.

To Martin Van Buren, Monticello,
June 29, 1824

The Natural World

Botany

Botany is the school for patience, and its amateurs learn resignation from daily disappointments.

To Madame de Tessé, Paris,
April 25, 1788

Botany I rank with the most valuable sciences, whether we consider its subjects as furnishing the principal subsistence of life to man & beast, delicious varieties for our tables, refreshments from our orchards, the adornments of our flower-borders, shade and perfume of our groves, materials for our buildings, or medicaments for our bodies.

To Thomas Cooper, Monticello,
October 7, 1814

Chemistry

I think it on the contrary among the most useful of sciences, and big with future discoveries for the utility & safety of the human race. It is yet indeed a mere embryon. Its principles are contested. Experiments seem contradictory; their subjects are so minute as to escape our senses; and their result too fallacious to satisfy the mind.

To the Rev. James Madison, Paris,
July 19, 1788

Climate

How have you weathered this rigorous season, my dear friend? Surely it was never so cold before. To me who am an animal of a warm climate, a mere orangutan, it has been a severe trial.

To Maria Cosway, Paris, January 14, 1789

On the whole, I find nothing anywhere else, in point of climate, which Virginia need envy to any part of the world. . . . When we consider how much climate contributes to the happiness of our condition, by the fine sensations it excites, and the productions it is the parent of, we have reason to value highly the accident of birth in such a one as that of Virginia.

To Martha Jefferson Randolph, Lake Champlain, May 31, 1791

I think it more probable you should return to bask in the genial sunshine of this country, than that I should go to shiver under the frozen skies of the North.

To Horatio Gates, Monticello, February 3, 1794

Let us quit this, & turn to the fine weather we are basking in. We have had one of our tropical winters. Once only a snow of 3 inches deep, which went off the next day, & never as much ice as would have cooled a bottle of wine. And we have now but a month to go through of winter weather, for February always gives us good samples of the spring of which it is the harbinger.

To James Madison, Monticello, December 28, 1794

We have had this year such rains as never came I believe since Noah's flood.

To George Washington, Monticello, September 12, 1795

I have often wondered that any human being should live in a cold country who can find room in a warm one. I have no doubt but that cold is the source of more sufferance to all animal nature than hunger, thirst, sickness, & all the other pains of life & death itself put together. I live in a temperate climate, and under circumstances which do not expose me often to cold. Yet when I recollect on one hand all the sufferings I have had from cold, & on the other all my other pains, the former preponderate greatly. What then must be the sum of that evil if we take in the vast land & by sea, all the families of beasts, birds, reptiles, & even the vegetable kingdom! for that too has life, and where there is life there may be sensation.

To William Dunbar, Washington, January 12, 1801

Certainly it is a truth that climate is one of the sources of the greatest sensual enjoyment.

To Joseph Priestley, Washington, June 19, 1802

In no case, perhaps, does habit attach our choice or judgment more than in climate. The Canadian glows with delight in his sleigh & snow; the very idea of which gives me the shivers.

To the Comte de Volney, Washington, February 8, 1805

The change which has taken place in our climate, is one of those facts which all men of years are sensible of, & yet none can prove by regular evidence, they can only appeal to each other's general observation for the fact.

To Dr. Nathaniel Chapman, Monticello,
December 11, 1809

Emptiness

Where there is an absence of matter, I call it void, or nothing, or immaterial space.

To John Adams, Monticello, August 15, 1820

Flowers

Nothing new has happened in our neighborhood since you left us; the houses and the trees stand where they did; the flowers come forth like the belles of the day, have their short reign of beauty and splendor, and retire, like them, to the more interesting office of reproducing their like. The Hyacinths and Tulips are off the stage, the Irises are giving place to the Belladonnas, as these will to the Tuberoses, etc.; as your mamma has done to you, my dear Anne, as you will do to the sisters of little John, and as I shall soon and cheerfully do to you all in wishing you a long, long good-night.

To Anne C. Bankhead, Monticello, May 26, 1811

Natural History

Nobody can desire more ardently than myself to concur in whatever may promote useful science, and I view no science with more partiality than Natural history.

To Jean de la Coste, Washington, May 24, 1807

Nature

This is the fact. We know too little of the operations of Nature in the physical world to assign causes with any degree of confidence. Willing always however to guess at what we do not know, I have sometimes indulged myself with conjectures on the causes.

To Jean Baptiste Le Roy, Paris, November 13, 1786

Rainbows

I remark a rainbow of a great portion of the circle observed by you when on the line of demarcation. I live in a situation which has given me an opportunity of seeing more than the semicircle often. I am on a hill 500 ft. perpendicularly high. On the west side it breaks down abruptly to the base where a river passes through. A rainbow therefore about sunset, plunges one of its legs down to the river, 500 ft. below the level of the eye on the top of the hill. I have twice seen bows formed by the moon. They were of the color of the common circle round the moon, and were very near, being within a few paces of me in both instances.

To William Dunbar, Washington, January 12, 1801

Rocks

It is now generally agreed that rocks grow, and it seems that it grows in layers in every direction, as the branches of trees grow in all directions. . . . Every thing in nature decays. If it were not reproduced then by growth, there would be a chasm.

To Charles Thomson, Paris, September 20, 1787

Science

Besides the comfort of knowledge, every science is auxiliary to every other.

To Thomas Mann Randolph, Jr., Paris, August 27, 1786

What a field have we set at our doors to signalize ourselves in! The botany of America is far from being exhausted, its mineralogy is untouched, and its Natural History or Zoology totally mistaken and misrepresented. . . . It is the work to which the young men you are forming should lay their hands. We have spent the prime of our lives in procuring them the precious blessing of liberty. Let them spend theirs in showing that it is the great parent of science and virtue, and that a nation will be great in both always in proportion as it is free.

To Joseph Willard, March 24, 1789

The more ignorant we become the less value we set on science, and the less inclination we shall have to seek it.

To John Adams, Monticello, May 27, 1795

Our country offers to the lovers of science a rich field of the works of nature, but little explored, except in the department of botany.

To Marc Auguste Pictet, Monticello, October 14, 1795

I am for encouraging the progress of science in all its branches.

To Elbridge Gerry, January 26, 1799

There are other branches of science [besides mathematics] worth the attention of every man. Astronomy, botany, chemistry, natural philosophy, natural history, anatomy. Not indeed to be a proficient in them; but to possess their general principles & outlines, so as that we may be able to amuse and inform ourselves further in any of them as we proceed through life & have occasion for them. Some knowledge of them is necessary for our character as well as comfort.

To William Green Munford, June 18, 1799

It is impossible for a man who takes a survey of what is already known, not to see what an immensity in every branch of science yet remains to be discovered, & that too of articles to which our faculties seem adequate.

To William Green Munford, June 18, 1799

I have changed my circle here according to my wish; abandoning the rich, & declining their dinners & parties, and associating entirely with the class of science, of whom there is a valuable society here.

To Martha Jefferson Randolph, Philadelphia,
February 11, 1800

Every son of science feels a strong & disinterested desire of promoting it in every part of the earth.

To Marc Auguste Pictet, Washington, February 5, 1803

We certainly are not to deny whatever we cannot account for. A thousand phenomena present themselves daily which we cannot explain, but where facts are suggested, bearing no analogy with the laws of nature as yet known to us, their verity needs proofs proportioned to their difficulty. A cautious mind will weigh well the opposition of the phenomenon to everything hitherto observed, the strength of the testimony by which it is supported, and the errors & misconceptions to which even our senses are liable.

To Daniel Salmon, Washington, February 15, 1808

You know the just esteem which attached itself to Doctor Franklin's science, because he always endeavored to direct it to something useful in private life.

To Thomas Cooper, Monticello, July 10, 1812

But even in Europe a change has sensibly taken place in the mind of man. Science had liberated the ideas of those who read and reflect, and the American example had kindled feelings of right in the people. An insurrection has consequently begun, of science, talents, & courage, against rank and birth, which have fallen into contempt. It has failed in its first effort, because the mobs of the cities, the instrument used for its accomplishment, debased by ignorance, poverty, and vice, could not be restrained to rational action. But the world will recover from the panic of this first catastrophe. Science is progressive, and talents and enterprise on the alert.

To John Adams, October 28, 1813

Nature has, in truth, produced units only through all her works. Classes, orders, genera, species are not of her work. Her creation is of individuals. No two animals are exactly alike; no two plants, nor even two leaves or blades of grass; no two crystallizations. And if we may venture from what is within the cognizance of such organs as ours to conclude on that beyond their powers, we must believe that no two particles of matter are of exact resemblance. This infinitude of units or individuals being far beyond the capacity of our memory, we are obliged, in aid of that, to distribute them into masses, throwing into each of these all the individuals which have a certain degree of resemblance; to subdivide these again into smaller groups, according to certain points of dissimilitude observable in them; and so on until we have formed what we call a system of classes, orders, genera, and species.

To John Manners, February 22, 1814

I am not fond of reading what is merely abstract, and unapplied immediately to some useful science. Bonaparte, with his repeated derisions of Ideologists (squinting at this author) has by this time felt that true wisdom does not lie in mere practice without principle.

To John Adams, Monticello, October 14, 1816

When I contemplate the immense advances in science, and discoveries in the arts which have been made within the period of my life, I look forward with confidence to equal advances by the present generation; and have no doubt they will consequently be as much wiser than we have been, as we than our fathers were, and they than the burners of witches.

To Benjamin Waterhouse, Monticello, March 3, 1818

Soil

The soil is the gift of God to the living.

To John Wayles Eppes, Monticello, June 24, 1813

Springtime in the Mountains

The soft genial temperature of the season, just above the want of fire, enlivened by the reanimation of birds, flowers, the fields, forests & gardens, has been truly delightful & continues to be so. My peach & cherry trees blossomed on the 9th of March. . . . The fine temperate weather of spring continues here about two months. Indeed my experience of the different parts of America convinces me that these mountains are the Eden of the U.S. for soil, climate, navigation & health.

To the Comte de Volney, Monticello, April 9, 1797

Thermometer Readings

Fahrenheit's thermometer is the only one in use with us. I make my daily observations as early as possible in the morning & again about 4 o'clock in the afternoon, these generally showing the maxima of cold & heat in the course of 24 hours.

To Giovanni Fabbroni, Williamsburg, June 8, 1778

Trees

The Bois de Boulogne,* invites you earnestly to come and survey its beautiful verdure, to retire to its umbrage from the heats of the season. I was through it to-day, as I am every day. Every tree charged me with this invitation to you.

*the former royal hunting park in Paris

To Madame de Corny, Paris, June 30, 1787

I never before knew the full value of trees. My house is entirely embosomed in high plane trees, with good grass below, & under them I breakfast, dine, write, read, & receive my company. What would I not give that the trees planted nearest round the house at Monticello were full grown.

To Martha Jefferson Randolph, Philadelphia,
July 7, 1793

[Remembrance by Margaret Bayard Smith] I remember on one occasion (it was after he was President) his exclaiming "How I wish that I possessed the power of a despot." The company at [the] table stared at a declaration so opposed to his disposition and principles. "Yes," continued he, in reply to their inquiring looks, "I wish I was a despot that I might save the noble, the beautiful trees that are daily falling sacrifices to the cupidity of their owners, or the necessity of the poor."

Margaret Bayard Smith, Reminiscences, 1837

Occupations

❦

Interesting occupations are essential to happiness: indeed the whole art of being happy consists in the art of finding employment.

To Martha Jefferson Randolph, New York, April 26, 1790

Doctors

The followers of Esculapius are also numerous [like lawyers]. Yet I have remarked that wherever one sets himself down in a good neighborhood, not preoccupied, he secures to himself its practice, and, if prudent, is not long, in acquiring whereon to retire & live in comfort. The physician is happy in the attachment of the families in which he practices. All think he has saved some one of them, & he finds himself every where a welcome guest, a home in every house. If, to the consciousness of having saved some lives, he can add that of having at no time, from want of caution, destroyed the boon he was called to save, he will enjoy in age the happy reflection of not having lived in vain.

To David Campbell, Monticello, January 28, 1810

Lawyers

A lawyer without books would be like a workman without tools.

To Thomas Turpin, Shadwell, February 5, 1769

The law may be studied as well at one place as another; because it is a study of books alone; at least till near the close of it. Books can be read equally well at Williamsburg, at London, or Paris. The study of the law is an affair of 3 years.

To Thomas Mann Randolph, Sr., Paris, August 11, 1787

Law [as a profession] is quite overdone. It is fallen to the ground; and a man must have great powers to raise himself in it to either honor or profit. The mob of the profession get by it as little money & less respect, than they would by digging the earth. . . . [At his retirement] the lawyer has only to recollect, how many, by his dexterity, have been cheated of their right, and reduced to beggary.

To David Campbell, Monticello, January 28, 1810

It is not incumbent on lawyers to be learned.

To Isaac McPherson, Monticello, August 13, 1813

Merchants

Skill, punctuality, and integrity are the requisites in such a character.

To George Washington, Paris, November 14, 1786

Merchants have no country.

To Horatio G. Spafford, Monticello, March 17, 1814

Teachers

Do not be misled by others into an opinion that to oppose a tutor and to set him at defiance is showing a laudable spirit, on the contrary nothing can be more blamable, and nothing will discredit you more in the opinion of sensible men.

To Peter Carr, Annapolis, December 11, 1783

Pain and Pleasure

Head. Put into one scale the pleasures which any object may offer; but put fairly into the other the pains which are to follow, and see which preponderates. The making an acquaintance is not a matter of indifference. When a new one is proposed to you, view it all round. Consider what advantages it presents, and to what inconveniences it may expose you. Do not bite at the bait of pleasure till you know there is no hook beneath it. The art of life is the art of avoiding pain: and he is the best pilot who steers clearest of the rocks and shoals with which it is beset. Pleasure is always before us; but misfortune is at our side: while running after that, this arrests us. The most effectual means of being secure against pain is to retire within ourselves, and to suffice for our own happiness. Those, which depend on ourselves, are the only pleasures a wise man will count on: for nothing is ours which another may deprive us of. Hence the inestimable value of intellectual pleasures. Ever in our power, always leading us to something new, never cloying, we ride, serene and sublime, above the concerns of this mortal world, contemplating truth and nature, matter and motion, the laws which bind up their existence, and that eternal being who made and bound them up by these laws. Let this be our employ. Leave the bustle and tumult of society to those who have not talents to occupy themselves without them. Friendship is but another name for an alliance with the follies and the misfortunes of others. Our own share of miseries is sufficient: why enter then as volunteers into those of another? Is there so little gall poured into our own cup that we must needs help to drink that of our neighbor? A friend dies or leaves us: we feel as if a limb was cut off. He is sick: we must watch over him, and participate of his pains. His fortune is shipwrecked: ours must be laid under contribution. He loses a child, a parent or a partner: we must mourn the loss as if it was our own.

Heart. And what more sublime delight than to mingle tears with one whom the hand of heaven hath smitten! To watch over the bed of sickness, and to beguile its tedious and its painful moments! To share our bread with one to whom misfortune has left none! This world abounds indeed with misery: to lighten its burden we must divide it with one another. But let us now try the virtues of your mathematical balance, and as you have put into one scale the burdens of friendship, let me put its comforts into the other. When languishing then under disease, how grateful is the solace of our friends!

How are we penetrated with their assiduities and attentions! How much are we supported by their encouragements and kind offices! When Heaven has taken from us some object of our love, how sweet is it to have a bosom whereon to recline our heads, and into which we may pour the torrent of our tears! Grief, with such a comfort, is almost a luxury! . . .

We have no rose without its thorn; no pleasure without alloy. It is the law of our existence, and we must acquiesce. It is the condition annexed to all our pleasures, not by us who receive, but by him who gives them.

To Maria Cosway, Paris, October 12, 1786

I do not agree that an age of pleasure is no compensation for a moment of pain.

To John Adams, Monticello, August 1, 1816

Grief

Deeply practiced in the school of affliction, the human heart knows no joy which I have not lost, no sorrow of which I have not drunk! Fortune can present no grief of unknown form to me! Who then can so softly bind up the wound of another as he who has felt the same wound himself?

To Maria Cosway, Paris, October 12, 1786

I have ever found time & silence the only medicine, and these but assuage, they never can suppress, the deep-drawn sigh which recollection for ever brings up, until recollection and life are extinguished together.

To John Adams, Monticello, October 12, 1813

I have often wondered for what good end the sensations of Grief could be intended. All our other passions, within proper bounds, have an useful object. And the perfection of the moral character is, not in a Stoical apathy, so hypocritically vaunted, and so untruly too, because impossible; but in a just equilibrium of all the passions. I wish the pathologists then would tell us what is the use of grief in the economy, and of what good it is the cause, proximate or remote.

To John Adams, Monticello, April 8, 1816

I see that, with the other evils of life, it is destined to temper the cup we are to drink.

To John Adams, Monticello, August 1, 1816

Peace

Peace and friendship with all mankind is our wisest policy: and I wish we may be permitted to pursue them. But the temper and the folly of our enemies may not leave this in our choice.

To C.W.F. Dumas, Paris, May 6, 1786

We love & we value peace: we know its blessings from experience. We abhor the follies of war, & are not untried in its distresses & calamities.

To William Carmichael and William Short, Philadelphia, June 30, 1793

For myself, I wish for peace, if it can be preserved, salva fide et honore.*

*with safety to one's honor

To James Monroe, Monticello, April 24, 1794

I confess to you I have seen enough of one war never to wish to see another.

To John Adams, Monticello, April 25, 1794

As to myself, I love peace, and I am anxious that we should give the world still another useful lesson, by showing to them other modes of punishing injuries than by war, which is as much a punishment to the punisher as to the sufferer.

To Tench Coxe, Monticello, May 1, 1794

The newspapers tell us France is beating the world into peace. The world will gain more by defeats leading to peace, than victories leading to war. God send us peace.

To Joseph Mussi, Monticello, January 21, 1795

Peace is our passion.

To Sir John Sinclair, Washington, June 30, 1803

My hope of preserving peace for our country is not founded in the greater principles of non-resistance under every wrong, but in the belief that a just & friendly conduct on our part will procure justice & friendship from others.

> To the Earl of Buchan, Washington, July 10, 1803

We ask for peace & justice from all nations.

> To James Monroe, Washington, May 4, 1806

Altho' our prospect is peace, our policy & purpose is to provide for defense by all those means to which our resources are competent.

> To James Bowdoin, Washington, July 10, 1806

Peace ... has been our principle, peace is our interest, and peace has saved to the world this only plant of free and rational government now existing in it.

> To Tadeusz Kosciusko, Monticello, April 13, 1811 [1816?]

When peace becomes more losing than war, we may prefer the latter on principles of pecuniary calculation. But for us to attempt, by war, to reform all Europe, & bring them back to principles of morality & a respect for the equal rights of nations, would show us to be only maniacs of another character. We should, indeed, have the merit of the good intentions, as well as of the folly of the hero of La Mancha.

> To William Wirt, Monticello, May 3, 1811

Peace is better for us all.

> To Francis C. Gray, Monticello, March 4, 1815

I pray ... for peace, as best for all the world, best for us, and best for me, who have already lived to see three wars, and now pant for nothing more than to be permitted to depart in peace.

To Thomas Leiper, Monticello, June 12, 1815

Peace & justice shall be the polar stars of the American societies.

To José Correa da Serra, Monticello, October 24, 1820

Peace and neutrality seem to be our duty and interest.

To President James Monroe, Monticello, June 11, 1823

The People

Our people in a body are wise, because they are under the unrestrained and unperverted operation of their own understanding.

To Joseph Priestley, Washington, June 19, 1802

Delusion of

The delusion of the people is necessary to the dominant party. I see the extent to which that delusion has been already carried, and I see there is no length to which it may not be pushed by a party in possession of the revenues & the legal authorities of the U.S. for a short time indeed, but yet long enough to admit much particular mischief. There is no event therefore, however atrocious, which may not be expected.

To Samuel Smith, Monticello, August 22, 1798

Population

A century's experience has shown that we double our numbers every twenty or twenty-five years. No circumstance can be foreseen at this moment which will lessen our rate of multiplication for centuries to come.

To the Comte de Montmorin, Paris, July 23, 1787

Self-Government

I have no fear that the result of our experiment will be that men may be trusted to govern themselves without a master. Could the contrary of this be proved, I should conclude either that there is no god, or that he is a malevolent being.

To David Hartley, Paris, July 2, 1787

It was by the sober sense of our citizens that we were safely and steadily conducted from monarchy to republicanism, and it is by the same agency alone we can be kept from falling back.

To Arthur Campbell, Monticello, September 1, 1797

I will never believe that man is incapable of self-government; that he has no resources but in a master, who is but a man like himself, and generally a worse man, inasmuch as power tends to deprave him.

To Everard Meade, Philadelphia, April 8, 1800

The will of the people ... is the only legitimate foundation of any government.

To Benjamin Waring and others, Washington,
March 23, 1801

The people of every country are the only safe guardians of their own rights, and are the only instruments which can be used for their destruction. And certainly they would never consent to be so used were they not deceived. To avoid this, they should be instructed, to a certain degree.

To John Wyche, Monticello, May 19, 1809

No man has greater confidence than I have, in the spirit of the people, to a rational extent. Whatever they can, they will.

To James Monroe, Monticello, October 16, 1814

The right of nations to self-government being my polar star, my partialities are steered by it.

To José Correa da Serra, Monticello, June 28, 1815

Politics

My private business can never call me elsewhere, and certainly politics will not, which I have ever hated both in theory & practice.

To Horatio Gates, Monticello, February 3, 1794

Political conversations I really dislike, & therefore avoid where I can without affectation.

To George Washington, Monticello, June 19, 1796

If the game runs sometimes against us at home, we must have patience, till luck turns, & then we shall have an opportunity of winning back the principles we have lost. For this is a game where principles are the stake.

To John Taylor, Philadelphia, June 4, 1798

Politics are such a torment that I would advise every one I love not to mix with them.

To Martha Jefferson Randolph, Philadelphia,
February 11, 1800

The scene passing here makes me pant to be away from it—to fly from the circle of cabal, intrigue, and hatred, to one where all is love and peace.

To Mary Jefferson Eppes, Washington, February 15, 1801

Party Spirit

Politics & party hatreds destroy the happiness of every being.

To Martha Jefferson Randolph, Philadelphia,
May 17, 1798

Every word which goes from me, whether verbally or in writing, becomes the subject of so much malignant distortion, & perverted construction, that I am obliged to caution my friends against admitting the possibility of my letters getting into the public papers, or a copy of them to be taken under any degree of confidence.

To Edward Dowse, Washington, April 19, 1803

So inveterate is the rancor of party spirit among us, that nothing ought to be credited but what we hear with our own ears. . . . Little is to be believed which interests the prevailing passions, and happens beyond the limits of our own senses.

To James Monroe, Washington, March 10, 1808

Political Abuse
Unmerited abuse wounds, while unmerited praise has not the power to heal. These are hard wages for the services of all the active & healthy years of one's life.

To Edward Rutledge, Monticello, December 27, 1796

Political Civility
I feel extraordinary gratification indeed in addressing this letter to you, with whom shades of difference in political sentiment have not prevented the interchange of good opinion, nor cut off the friendly offices of society & good correspondence. This political tolerance is the more valued by me who consider social harmony as the first of human felicities, & the happiest moments those which we are given to the effusions of the heart.

To John Henry, Philadelphia,
December 31, 1797

If we can once more get social intercourse restored to its pristine harmony, I shall believe we have not lived in vain.

To Thomas Lomax, Washington, February 25, 1801

It will be a great blessing to our country if we can once more restore harmony and social love among its citizens. I confess, as to myself, it is almost the first object of my heart and one to which I would sacrifice every thing but principle. With the people I have hopes of effecting it.

To Elbridge Gerry, Washington, March 29, 1801

Political Compromise

I think an Editor [of a newspaper] should be independent, that is, of personal influence, & not be moved from his opinions on the mere authority of any individual. But, with respect to the general opinion of the political section with which he habitually accords, his duty seems very like that of a member of Congress. Some of these indeed think that independence requires them to follow always their own opinion, without respect for that of others. This has never been my opinion, nor my practice, when I have been of that, or any other body. Differing, on a particular question, from those whom I knew to be of the same political principles with myself, and with whom I generally thought & acted, a consciousness of the fallibility of the human mind, & of my own in particular, with a respect for the accumulated judgment of my friends, has induced me to suspect erroneous impressions on myself, to suppose my own opinion wrong, & to act with them on theirs.

To William Duane, Monticello, April 30, 1811

Political Dissension
There are many who think that not to support the Executive is to abandon Government.

To Thomas Bell, Philadelphia, May 18, 1797

Political dissension is doubtless a less evil than the lethargy of despotism, but still it is a great evil, and it would be as worthy the efforts of the patriot as of the philosopher, to exclude its influence, if possible, from social life. . . . Whether we shall ever be able so far to perfect the principles of society, as that political opinions shall, in its intercourse, be as inoffensive as those of philosophy, mechanics, or any other, may be well doubted.

To Thomas Pinckney, Philadelphia, May 29, 1797

Political Enemies
It has been a source of great pain to me to have met with so many among our opponents who had not the liberality to distinguish between political & social opposition, who transferred at once to the person the hatred they bore to his political opinions. I suppose indeed that in public life, a man whose political principles have any decided character, and who has energy enough to give them effect, must always expect to encounter political hostility from those of adverse principles.

To Richard M. Johnson, Washington, March 10, 1808

Their malice I have long learned to disregard, their censures to deem praise.

To John Hollins, Washington, February 19, 1809

Let them have justice, and protection against personal violence, but no favor. Powers & preeminences conferred on them are daggers put into the hands of assassins, to be plunged into our own bosoms in the moment the thrust can go home to the heart. Moderation can never reclaim them. They deem it timidity, & despise without fearing the tameness from which it flows.

To Henry Dearborn, Poplar Forest, August 14, 1811

Men of energy of character must have enemies: because there are two sides to every question, and taking one with decision, and acting on it with effect, those who take the other will of course be hostile in proportion as they feel that effect.

To John Adams, Monticello, May 5, 1817

I never suffered a political to become a personal difference.

To Timothy Pickering, Monticello, February 27, 1821

Political Incivility

The passions are too high at present to be cooled in our day. You & I have formerly seen warm debates and high political passions. But gentlemen of different politics would then speak to each other, & separate the business of the senate from that of society.

It is not so now. Men who have been intimate all their lives cross the streets to avoid meeting, & turn their heads another way, lest they should be obliged to touch their hat. This may do for young men, with whom passion is enjoyment. But it is afflicting to peaceable minds.

To Edward Rutledge, Philadelphia, June 24, 1797

One piquing thing said draws on another, that a third, and always with increasing acrimony, until all restraint is thrown off, and it becomes difficult for yourselves to keep clear of the toils in which your friends will endeavor to interlace you, and to avoid the participation in their passions which they will endeavor to produce.

To James Monroe, Washington, February 18, 1808

[Speaking of the 1790s] Public discussions ... whether relating to men, measures, or opinions, were conducted by the parties with an animosity, a bitterness, and an indecency, which had never been exceeded. All the resources of reason, and of wrath, were exhausted by each party in support of its own, and to prostrate the adversary opinions. The one party was upbraided with receiving the Antifederalists, the other the old tories & refugees into their bosoms. Of this acrimony the public papers of the day exhibit ample testimony in the debates of Congress, of state legislatures, of stump orators, in addresses, answers, and news-paper essays. And to these, without question may be added the private

correspondencies of individuals; and the less guard-
ed in these, because not meant for the public eye, not
restrained by the respect due to that; but poured
forth from the overflowings of the heart into the bosom of a friend, as a momentary easement of our feelings. In this way, and in answers to addresses, you &
I could indulge ourselves. We have probably done it,
sometimes with warmth, often with prejudice, but
always, as we believed, adhering to truth.

To John Adams, Monticello, June 27, 1813

Political Parties

I am not a Federalist, because I never submitted the
whole system of my opinions to the creed of any party
of men whatever in religion, in philosophy, in politics,
or in any thing else where I was capable of thinking
for myself. Such an addiction is the last degradation
of a free and moral agent. If I could not go to heaven
but with a party, I would not go there at all.

To Francis Hopkinson, Paris, March 13, 1789

Our citizens are divided into two political sects. One
which fears the people most, the other the government.

To the Comte de Volney, Monticello, December 9, 1795

Were parties here divided merely by a greediness for
office, as in England, to take a part with either would
be unworthy of a reasonable or moral man. But
where the principle of difference is as substantial and
as strongly pronounced as between the republicans

& the Monocrats of our country I hold it as honorable to take a firm & decided part, and as immoral to pursue a middle line, as between the parties of Honest men, & Rogues, into which every country is divided.

To William Branch Giles, Monticello,
December 31, 1795

In every free and deliberating society, there must, from the nature of man, be opposite parties and violent dissensions and discords; and one of these, for the most part, must prevail over the other for a longer or shorter time. Perhaps this party division is necessary to induce each to watch and delate to the people the proceedings of the other.

To John Taylor, Philadelphia, June 1, 1798

Both of our political parties, at least the honest portion of them, agree conscientiously in the same object, the public good: but they differ essentially in what they deem the means of promoting that good. One side believes it best done by one composition of the governing powers, the other by a different one. One fears most the ignorance of the people; the other the selfishness of rulers independent of them.

To Abigail Adams, Monticello, September 11, 1804

The same political parties which now agitate the U.S. have existed thro' all time. Whether the power of the people, or that of the aristocrats should prevail, were questions which kept the states of Greece & Rome in eternal convulsions; as they now schismatize every people whose minds and mouths are not shut up by the gag of a despot. And in fact the terms of whig & tory belong to Natural history, as well as to civil.

To John Adams, Monticello, June 27, 1813

For in truth, the parties of Whig and Tory are those of nature. They exist in all countries, whether called by these names, or by those of Aristocrats and democrats, coté droite and coté gauche,* Ultras and Radicals, Serviles, and Liberals. The sickly, weakly, timid man fears the people, and is a tory by nature. The healthy strong and bold cherishes them, and is formed a whig by nature.

*the right side and the left side

To the Marquis de Lafayette, Monticello,
November 4, 1823

Men by their constitutions are naturally divided into two parties: 1. Those who fear and distrust the people, and wish to draw all powers from them into the hands of the higher classes. 2nly. Those who identify themselves with the people, have confidence in them, cherish and consider them as the most honest & safe, altho' not the most wise depository of the public interests. In every country these two parties exist, and in every one where they are free to think, speak, and write, they will declare themselves. Call them therefore liberals and serviles, Jacobins and Ultras, whigs and tories, republicans and federalists, aristocrats & democrats, or by whatever name you please, they are the same parties still, and pursue the same object. The last appellation of aristocrats and democrats is the true one expressing the essence of all.

To Henry Lee, Monticello, August 10, 1824

Political Peacemaking

Sincerely the friend of all the parties, I ask of none why they have fallen out by the way, and would gladly infuse the oil & wine of the Samaritan into all their wounds. I hope that time, the assauger of all evils, will heal these also; and I pray from them all a continuance of their affection, & to be permitted to bear to all the same unqualified esteem.

To John Hollins, Monticello, May 5, 1811

Pork-Barreling

[Pork-barreling in Congress] will be a source of eternal scramble among the members who can get the most money wasted in their state, and they will always get most who are meanest.

To James Madison, Monticello, March 6, 1796

Public Censure

My great wish is to go on in a strict but silent performance of my duty: to avoid attracting notice & to keep my name out of newspapers, because I find the pain of a little censure, even when it is unfounded, is more acute than the pleasure of much praise.

To Francis Hopkinson, Paris, March 13, 1789

Public Opinion

The advantage of public opinion; is like that of the weather gauge in a naval action.

> To James Monroe, Monticello, January 1, 1815

When public opinion changes, it is with the rapidity of thought.

> To Charles Yancey, Monticello, January 6, 1816

The Press

Our citizens may be deceived for a while, & have been deceived; but as long as the presses can be protected, we may trust to them for light.

> To Archibald Stuart, Monticello, May 14, 1799

I deplore with you the putrid state into which our newspapers have passed, and the malignity, the vulgarity, & mendacious spirit of those who write for them.

> To Walter Jones, Monticello, January 2, 1814

If a nation expects to be ignorant & free, in a state of civilization, it expects what never was & never will be. The functionaries of every government have propensities to command at will the liberty & property of their constituents. There is no safe deposit for these but with the people themselves; nor can they be safe with them without information. Where the press is free and every man able to read, all is safe.

To Charles Yancey, Monticello, January 6, 1816

The only security of all is in a free press. The force of public opinion cannot be resisted, when permitted freely to be expressed. The agitation it produces must be submitted to. It is necessary to keep the waters pure.

To the Marquis de Lafayette, Monticello,
November 4, 1823

Freedom of the Press

Our liberty depends on the freedom of the press, and that cannot be limited without being lost.

To James Currie, Paris, January 28, 1786

No government ought to be without censors: & where the press is free, no one ever will.

To George Washington, Monticello, September 9, 1792

The abuses of the freedom of the press here have been carried to a length never before known or borne by any civilized nation. But it is so difficult to draw a clear line of separation between the abuse and the wholesome use of the press, that as yet we have found it better to trust the public judgment, rather than the magistrate, with the discrimination between truth & falsehood. And hitherto the public judgment has performed that office with wonderful correctness.

To Marc Auguste Pictet, Washington, February 5, 1803

No experiment can be more interesting than that we are now trying, & which we trust will end in establishing the fact that man may be governed by reason and truth. Our first object should therefore be to leave open to him all the avenues to truth. The most effectual hitherto found is the freedom of the press.

To John Tyler, Washington, June 28, 1804

The press, confined to truth, needs no other legal restraint; the public judgment will correct false reasonings and opinions, on a full hearing of all parties; and no other definite line can be drawn between the inestimable liberty of the press and its demoralizing licentiousness.

Second Inaugural Address, March 4, 1805

As to myself, conscious that there was not a truth on earth which I feared should be known, I have lent myself willingly as the subject of a great experiment, which was to prove that an administration, conducting itself with integrity & common understanding, cannot be battered down, even by the falsehoods of a licentious press, and consequently still less by the press, as restrained within the legal and wholesome limits of truth. This experiment was wanting for the world to demonstrate the falsehood of the pretext that freedom of the press is incompatible with orderly government. I have never therefore even contradicted the thousands of calumnies so industriously propagated against myself. But the fact being once established, that the press is impotent when it abandons itself to falsehood, I leave to others to restore it to its strength, by recalling it within the pale of truth. Within that it is a noble institution, equally the friend of science & of civil liberty.

To Thomas Seymour, Washington, February 11, 1807

I have from the beginning determined to submit myself as the subject on whom may be proved the impotency of a free press in a country like ours, against those who conduct themselves honestly, and enter into no intrigue. I admit at the same time that restraining the press to truth as the present laws do, is the only way of making it useful. But I have thought necessary first to prove it can never be dangerous.

To William Short, Monticello, September 6, 1808

Newspapers

I am persuaded myself that the good sense of the people will always be found to be the best army. . . . The basis of our governments being the opinion of the people, the very first object should be to keep that right; and were it left to me to decide whether we should have a government without newspapers, or newspapers without a government, I should not hesitate a moment to prefer the latter.

To Edward Carrington, Paris, January 16, 1787

At a very early period of my life, I determined never to put a sentence into any newspaper. I have religiously adhered to the resolution through my life, and have great reason to be contented with it. Were I to undertake to answer the calumnies of the newspapers, it would be more than all my own time, & that of 20 aids could effect. For while I should be answering one, twenty new ones would be invented. I have thought it better to trust to the justice of my countrymen, that they would judge me by what they see of my conduct on the stage where they have placed me, & what they knew of me before the epoch since which a particular party has supposed it might answer some view of theirs to vilify me in the public eye.

To Samuel Smith, Monticello, August 22, 1798

A coalition of sentiments is not for the interest of the printers. They, like the clergy, live by the zeal they can kindle & the schisms they can create.

To Elbridge Gerry, Washington, March 29, 1801

Newspapers . . . serve as chimneys to carry off noxious vapors and smoke.

To Tadeusz Kosciusko, Washington, April 2, 1802

Newspapers for the most part, present only the caricatures of disaffected minds.

To Marc Auguste Pictet, Washington, February 5, 1803

Nothing can now be believed which is seen in a newspaper. Truth itself becomes suspicious by being put into that polluted vehicle. The real extent of this state of misinformation is known only to those who are in situations to confront facts within their knowledge with the lies of the day. I really look with commiseration over the great body of my fellow citizens, who, reading newspapers live & die in the belief that they have known something of what has been passing in the world in their time; whereas the accounts they have read in newspapers are just as true a history of any other period of the world as of the present, except that the real names of the day are affixed to their fables. General facts may indeed be collected from them, such as that Europe is now at war, that Bonaparte has been a successful warrior, that he has subjected a great portion of Europe to his will, &c., &c.; but no details can be relied on. I will add that the man who never looks into a newspaper is better informed than he who reads them; inasmuch as he who knows nothing is nearer to truth than he whose mind is filled with falsehoods & errors. He who reads nothing will still learn the great facts, and the details are all false.

To John Norvell, Washington, June 11, 1807

The newspapers indeed had said so, but I yield little faith to them.

To Robert Smith, Monticello, April 30, 1811

I have given up newspapers in exchange for Tacitus & Thucydides, for Newton & Euclid; & I find myself much the happier.

To John Adams, Monticello, January 21, 1812

I deplore with you the putrid state into which our newspapers have passed, & the malignity, the vulgarity, and mendacious spirit of those who write them.

To Walter Jones, Monticello, January 2, 1814

A truth now and then projecting into the ocean of newspaper lies, serves like headlands to correct our course. Indeed my skepticism as to every thing I see in a newspaper makes me indifferent whether I ever see one.

To James Monroe, Monticello, January 1, 1815

We perceive the English passions to be high also, nourished by the newspapers, that first of all human contrivances for generating war. But it is the office of the rulers on both sides to rise above these vulgar vehicles of passion; to assuage angry feelings, and by examples and expressions of mutual regard in their public intercourse, to lead their citizens into good temper with each other.

To James Maury, Monticello, June 15, 1815

From 40 years experience of the wretched guess work of the newspapers of what is not done in open daylight, and of their falsehood even as to that, I rarely think them worth reading, & almost never worth notice.

To James Monroe, Monticello, February 4, 1816

This formidable censor of the public functionaries, by arraigning them at the tribunal of public opinion,

produces reform peaceably, which must otherwise
be done by revolution.

To Adamantios Coray, Monticello, October 31, 1823

Preservation of Public Records

The question is, what means will be the most effectual for preserving these remains [i.e., old Virginia
laws] from future loss? All the care I can take of
them, will not preserve them from the worm, from
the natural decay of the paper, from the accidents of
fire, or those of removal when it is necessary for any
public purposes, as in the case of those now sent
you. Our experience has proved to us that a single
copy, or a few, deposited in manuscript in the public
offices cannot be relied on for any great length of
time. The ravages of fire and of ferocious enemies
have had but too much part in producing the very
loss we are now deploring. How many of the precious works of antiquity were lost while they were
preserved only in manuscript? Has there ever been
one lost since the art of printing has rendered it
practicable to multiply & disperse copies? This
leads us then to the only means of preserving those
remains of our laws now under consideration, that
is, a multiplication of printed copies. I think therefore that there should be printed at public expense,
an edition of all the laws ever passed by our legislatures which can now be found; that a copy should be
deposited in every public library in America, in the
principal public offices within the State, and some
perhaps in the most distinguished public libraries of

Europe, and that the rest should be sold to individuals, towards reimbursing the expenses of the edition.

To George Wythe, Monticello,
January 16, 1796

Printing

While the art of printing is left to us, science can never be retrograde; what is once acquired of real knowledge can never be lost. To preserve the freedom of the human mind then & freedom of the press, every spirit should be ready to devote itself to martyrdom; for as long as we may think as we will, & speak as we think, the condition of man will proceed in improvement.

To William Green Munford,
June 18, 1799

The art of printing secures us against the retrogradation of reason & information.

To Pierre Paganel, Monticello,
April 15, 1811

The light which has been shed on mankind by the art of printing has eminently changed the condition of the world.

To John Adams, Monticello,
September 4, 1823

Racism

Deep-rooted prejudices entertained by the whites; ten thousand recollections, by the blacks, of the injuries they have sustained; new provocations; the real distinctions which nature has made; and many other circumstances, will divide us into parties, and produce convulsions, which will probably never end but in the extermination of the one or the other race.

Notes on the State of Virginia, 1782

African Americans

No body wishes more than I do to see such proofs as you exhibit, that nature has given to our black brethren, talents equal to those of the other colors of men, & that the appearance of a want of them is owing merely to the degraded condition of their existence both in Africa & America. I can add with truth that no body wishes more ardently to see a good system commenced for raising the condition both of their body & mind to what it ought to be, as fast as the imbecility of their present existence, and other circumstances which cannot be neglected, will admit.

To Benjamin Banneker, Philadelphia,
August 30, 1791

Religion

Believing with you that religion is a matter which lies solely between Man & his God, that he owes account to none other for his faith or his worship, that the legitimate powers of government reach actions only, & not opinions, I contemplate with sovereign reverence that act of the whole American people which declared that their legislature should "make no law respecting an establishment of religion, or prohibiting the free exercise thereof," thus building a wall of separation between Church & State. Adhering to this expression of the supreme will of the nation in behalf of the rights of conscience, I shall see with sincere satisfaction the progress of those sentiments which tend to restore to man all his natural rights, convinced he has no natural right in opposition to his social duties.

To the Baptist Association of Danbury, Conn.,
January 1, 1802

As to myself, my religious reading has long been confined to the moral branch of religion, which is the same in all religions; while in that branch which consists of dogmas, all differ, all have a different set. The former instructs us how to live well and worthily in society; the latter are made to interest our minds in the support of the teachers who inculcate them. Hence, for one sermon on a moral subject, you hear ten on the dogmas of the sect. However, religion is not the subject for you & me; neither of us know the religious opinions of the other; that is a matter between our maker & ourselves.

To Thomas Leiper, Washington, January 21, 1809

The subject of religion, a subject on which I have ever been most scrupulously reserved, I have considered it as a matter between every man and his maker, in which no other, & far less the public had a right to intermeddle.

To Richard Rush, Monticello, May 31, 1813

For, dispute as long as we will on religious tenets, our reason at last must ultimately decide, as it is the only oracle which god has given us to determine between what really comes from him & the phantasms of a disordered or deluded imagination. When he means to make a personal revelation he carries conviction of its authenticity to the reason he has bestowed as the umpire of truth. . . . Hitherto I have been under the guidance of that portion of reason which he has thought proper to deal out to me. I have followed it faithfully in all important cases, to such a degree at least as leaves me without uneasiness; and if on minor occasions I have erred from its dictates, I have trust in him who made us what we are, and know it was not his plan to make us always unerring. . . . I must ever believe that religion substantially good which produces an honest life, and we have been authorized by one, whom you and I equally respect, to judge of the tree by its fruit.

Our particular principles of religion are a subject of accountability to our god alone. I inquire after no man's, and trouble none with mine: nor is it given to us in this life to know whether yours or mine; our friends or our foes, are exactly the right. Nay, we have heard it said that there is not a quaker or a baptist, a presbyterian or an episcopalian, a catholic or a protestant in heaven: that, on entering that gate, we leave those badges of schism behind, and find ourselves united in those principles only in which god has united us all. Let us not be uneasy then about the different roads we may pursue, as believing them the shortest, to that our last abode; but, following the guidance of a good conscience, let us be happy in the hope that, by these different paths, we shall all meet in the end.

To Miles King, Monticello, September 26, 1814

I have ever thought religion a concern purely between our god and our consciences, for which we were accountable to him, and not to the priests. I never told my own religion, nor scrutinized that of another. I never attempted to make a convert, nor wished to change another's creed. . . . It is in our lives, and not from our words, that our religion must be read.

To Margaret Bayard Smith, Monticello, August 6, 1816

The result of your 50 or 60 years of religious reading in the four words "be just and good" is that in which all our enquiries must end.

To John Adams, Monticello, January 11, 1817

Say nothing of my religion; it is known to my god and myself alone. Its evidence before the world is to be sought in my life. If that has been honest and dutiful to society, the religion which has regulated it cannot be a bad one. It is singular anxiety which some people have that we should all think alike. Would the world be more beautiful were all our faces alike? Were our tempers, our talents, our tastes, our forms, our wishes, aversions, and pursuits cast exactly in the same mould? If no varieties existed in the animal, vegetable, or mineral creation, but all were strictly uniform, catholic and orthodox, what a world of physical & moral monotony would it be! These are the absurdities into which those run who usurp the throne of god, & dictate to him what he should have done.

To John Adams, Monticello, January 11, 1817, and to Charles Thomson, January 29, 1817

If, by religion, we are to understand Sectarian dogmas, in which no two of them agree, then your exclamation on that hypothesis is just, "that this would be the best of all possible worlds, if there were no religion in it."

To John Adams, Monticello, May 5, 1817

Were I to be the founder of a new sect, I would call them Apiarians, and after the example of the bees, advise them to extract the honey of every sect. My fundamental principle would be the reverse of Calvin's, that we are to be saved by our good works which are within our power, and not by our faith which is not within our power.

To Thomas B. Parker, Monticello, May 15, 1819

In that branch of religion which regards the moralities of life, and the duties of a social being, which teaches us to love our neighbors as ourselves, and to do good to all men, I am sure that you & I do not differ. We probably differ on that which relates to the dogmas of theology, the foundation of all sectarianism, and on which no two sects dream alike; for if they did they would then be of the same. You say you are a Calvinist. I am not. I am of a sect by myself, as far as I know.

To Ezra Stiles, Monticello, June 25, 1819

If the freedom of religion, guaranteed to us by law in theory, can ever rise in practice under the overbearing inquisition of public opinion, truth will prevail over fanaticism and the genuine doctrines of Jesus, so long perverted by his pseudo-priests, will again be restored to their original purity.

To Jared Sparks, Monticello, November 4, 1820

I can never join Calvin in addressing his god. He was indeed an Atheist, which I can never be.

To John Adams, Monticello, April 11, 1823

Christianity

The Christian religion, when divested of the rags in which they have enveloped it, and brought to the

original purity and simplicity of its benevolent insti-
tutor, is a religion of all others most friendly to liberty, science, and the freest expansion of the human
mind.

To Moses Robinson, Washington, March 23, 1801

In some of the delightful conversations with you, in
the evenings of 1798–99 & which served as an Ano-
dyne to the afflictions of the crisis through which
our country was then laboring, the Christian religion was sometimes our topic: and I then promised
you that one day or other, I would give you my
views of it. They are the result of a life of inquiry &
reflection, & very different from that Anti-Christian
system imputed to me by those who know nothing
of my opinions. To the corruptions of Christianity, I
am indeed opposed; but not to the genuine precepts
of Jesus himself. I am a Christian in the only sense
in which he wished any one to be; sincerely attached
to his doctrines, in preference to all others; ascrib-
ing to himself every human excellence; & believing
he never claimed any other.

To Benjamin Rush, Washington, April 21, 1803

But a short time elapsed after the death of the great
reformer of the Jewish religion before his principles
were departed from by those who professed to be his
special servants, & perverted into an engine for enslaving mankind, and aggrandizing their oppressors
in church & state: that the purest system of morals
ever before preached to man has been adulterated &

sophisticated by artificial constructions, into a mere contrivance to filch wealth & power to themselves, that rational men not being able to swallow their impious heresies, in order to force them down their throats, they raise the hue & cry of infidelity, while themselves are the greatest obstacles to the advancement of the real doctrines of Jesus, and do in fact constitute the real Anti-Christ.

To Samuel Kercheval, Monticello, January 19, 1810

I am a real Christian; that is to say, a disciple of the doctrines of Jesus.

To Charles Thomson, Monticello, January 9, 1816

Had the doctrines of Jesus been preached always as purely as they came from his lips, the whole civilized world would now have been Christian.

To Benjamin Waterhouse, Monticello, June 26, 1822

The Creation

[In speaking of writers on the Creation] They all suppose the earth a created existence. They must suppose a creator then; and that he possessed power and wisdom to a great degree. As he intended the earth for the habitation of animals and vegetables is it reasonable to suppose he made two jobs of his creation? That he first made a chaotic lump and set it into rotary motion, and then waiting the millions of ages necessary to form itself, that when it had done this he stepped in a second time to create the animals and plants which were to inhabit it? As the hand of a creator is to be called in, it may as well be called in at one stage of the process as another. We may as well suppose he created the earth at once nearly in the state in which we see it, fit for the preservation of the beings he placed on it.

To Charles Thomson, Paris, December 17, 1786

The movements of the heavenly bodies, so exactly held in their course by the balance of centrifugal and centripetal forces, the structure of our earth itself, with its distribution of lands, waters and atmosphere, animal and vegetable bodies, examined in all their minutest particles, insects mere atoms of life, yet as perfectly organized as man or mammoth, the mineral substances, their generation and uses, it is impossible, I say, for the human mind not to believe that there is, in all this, design, cause, and effect, up to an ultimate cause, a fabricator of all things from matter and motion, their preserver and regulator while permitted to exist in their present forms, and their regenerator into new and other forms.

To John Adams, Monticello, April 11, 1823

The dreams about the modes of creation, enquiries whether our globe has been formed by the agency of fire or water, how many millions of years it has cost Vulcan or Neptune to produce what the fiat of the Creator would effect by a single act of will, is too idle to be worth a single hour of any man's life.

To John P. Emmet, Monticello, May 2, 1826

End of the World

I hope you will have good sense enough to disregard those foolish predictions that the world is to be at an end soon. The almighty has never made known to any body at what time he created it, nor will he tell any body when he means to put an end to it, if ever he means to do it. As to preparations for that event, the best way is for you to be always prepared for it.

To Martha Jefferson, Annapolis, December 11, 1783

Freedom of Religion

Section I. Well aware that the opinions and belief of men depend not on their own will, but follow involuntarily the evidence proposed to their minds; that Almighty God hath created the mind free, and manifested his supreme will that free it shall remain by making it altogether insusceptible of restraint; that all attempts to influence it by temporal punishments, or burdens, or by civil incapacitations, tend only to beget habits of hypocrisy and meanness, and are a departure from the plan of the holy author of our religion, who being lord both of body and mind, yet chose not to propagate it by coercions on either, as was in his Almighty power to do, but to extend it by its influence on reason alone; that the impious presumption of legislators and rulers, civil as well as ecclesiastical, who, being themselves but fallible and uninspired men, have assumed dominion over the faith of others, setting up their own opinions and modes of thinking as the only true and infallible, and as such endeavoring to impose them on others, xx H. 90a. 84

A BILL for establishing RELIGIOUS FREEDOM, printed for the consideration of the PEOPLE.

WELL aware that the opinions and belief of men depend not on their own will, but follow involuntarily the evidence proposed to their minds, that Almighty God hath created the mind free, and manifested his Supreme will that free it shall remain, by making it altogether insusceptible of restraint: That all attempts to influence it by temporal punishments or burthens, or by civil incapacitations, tend only to beget habits of hypocrisy and meanness, and are a departure from the plan of the holy author of our religion, who being Lord both of body and mind, yet chose not to propagate it by coercions on either, as was in his Almighty power to do, but to extend it by its influence on reason alone: That the impious presumption of legislators and rulers, civil as well as ecclesiastical, who, being themselves but fallible and uninspired men, have assumed dominion over the faith of others, setting up their own opinions and modes of thinking, as the only true and infallible, and as such, endeavouring to impose them on others, hath established and maintained false religions over the greatest part of the world, and through all time: That to compel a man to furnish contributions of money for the propagation of opinions which he disbelieves and abhors, is sinful and tyrannical: That even the forcing him to support this or that teacher of his own religious persuasion, is depriving him of the comfortable liberty of giving his contributions to the particular pastor whose morals he would make his pattern, and whose powers he feels most persuasive to righteousness, and is withdrawing from the Ministry those temporal rewards which, proceeding from an approbation of their personal conduct, are an additional incitement to earnest and unremitting labour for the instruction of mankind: That our civil rights have no dependance on our religious opinions, any more than on our opinions in physicks or geometry: That therefore the proscribing any citizen as unworthy the publick confidence, by laying upon him an incapacity of being called to offices of trust and emolument, unless he profess or renounce this or that religious opinion, is depriving him injuriously of those privileges and advantages to which, in common with his fellow citizens he has a natural right: That it tends also to corrupt the principles of that very religion it is meant to encourage, by bribing with a monopoly of worldly honours and emoluments, those who will externally profess and conform to it: That though indeed these are criminal who do not withstand such temptation, yet neither are those innocent who lay the bait in their way: That the opinions of men are not the object of civil government, nor under its jurisdiction: That to suffer the civil Magistrate to intrude his powers into the field of opinion, and to restrain the profession or propagation of principles on supposition of their ill tendency, is a dangerous fallacy, which at once destroys all religious liberty; because he being of course Judge of that tendency will make his own opinions the rule of judgment, and approve or condemn the sentiments of others only as they shall square with, or differ from his own: That it is time enough for the rightful purposes of civil government far its officers to interfere when principles break out into overt acts against peace and good order: And finally, that truth is great and will prevail if left to herself; that she is the proper and sufficient antagonist to errour, and has nothing to fear from the conflict, unless by human interposition, disarmed of her natural weapons, free argument and debate; errours ceasing to be dangerous when it is permitted freely to contradict them.

WE the General Assembly of Virginia do enact, that no man shall be compelled to frequent or support any religious Worship place or Ministry whatsoever, nor shall be enforced, restrained, molested, or burthened in his body or goods, nor shall otherwise suffer on account of his religious opinions or belief, but that all men shall be free to profess, and by argument to maintain their opinions in matters of religion, and that the same shall in no wise diminish, enlarge, or affect their civil capacities.

AND though we well know that this Assembly, elected by the people for the ordinary purposes of legislation only, have no power to restrain the acts of succeeding Assemblies, constituted with powers equal to our own, and that therefore to declare this act irrevocable would be of no effect in law; yet we are free to declare, and do declare, that the rights hereby asserted are of the natural rights of mankind, and that if any act shall be hereafter passed to repeal the present, or to narrow its operation, such act will be an infringement of natural right.

c

Broadside of *A Bill for Establishing Religious Freedom*, drafted by Jefferson in 1779 and enacted by the Virginia General Assembly in 1786.

hath established and maintained false religions over the greatest part of the world and through all time: That to compel a man to furnish contributions of money for the propagation of opinions which he disbelieves and abhors, is sinful and tyrannical; that even the forcing him to support this or that teacher of his own religious persuasion, is depriving him of the comfortable liberty of giving his contributions to the particular pastor whose morals he would make his pattern, and whose powers he feels most persuasive to righteousness; and is withdrawing from the ministry those temporary rewards, which proceeding from an approbation of their personal conduct, are an additional incitement to earnest and unremitting labors for the instruction of mankind; that our civil rights have no dependence on our religious opinions, any more than our opinions in physics or geometry; that therefore the proscribing any citizen as unworthy the public confidence by laying upon him an incapacity of being called to offices of trust and emolument, unless he profess or renounce this or that religious opinion, is depriving him injuriously of those privileges and advantages to which, in common with his fellow citizens, he has a natural right; that it tends also to corrupt the principles of that very religion it is meant to encourage, by bribing, with a monopoly of worldly honors and emoluments, those who will externally profess and conform to it; that though indeed these are criminal who do not withstand such temptation, yet neither are those innocent who lay the bait in their way; that the opinions of men are not the object of civil government, nor under its jurisdiction; that to suffer the civil magistrate to intrude his powers into the field of opinion and to restrain the profession or propagation of principles on supposition of their ill tendency is a dangerous fallacy, which at once destroys all religious liberty, because he being of course judge of that tendency will make his opinions the rule of judgment, and approve or condemn the sentiments of others only as they shall square with or differ from his own; that it is time enough for the rightful purposes of civil government for its officers to interfere when principles break out into overt acts against peace and good order; and finally, that truth is great and will prevail if left to herself; that she is the proper and sufficient antagonist to error, and has nothing to fear from the conflict unless by human interposition disarmed of her natural weapons, free argument and debate; errors ceasing to be dangerous when it is permitted freely to contradict them.

Sect. II. We the General Assembly of Virginia do enact that no man shall be compelled to frequent or support any religious worship, place, or ministry whatsoever, nor shall be enforced, restrained, molested, or burdened in his body or goods, nor shall otherwise suffer, on account of his religious opinions or belief; but that all men shall be free to profess, and by argument to maintain, their opinions in matters of religion, and that the same shall in no wise diminish, enlarge, or affect their civil capacities.

A Bill for Establishing Religious Freedom, January 19, 1786

God

I think you give a just outline of the theism of the three religions when you say that the principle of the Hebrew was the fear, of the Gentile the honor, & of the Christian the love of God.

To John Adams, Monticello, October 12, 1813

We are not in a world ungoverned by the laws and the power of a superior agent. Our efforts are in his hands, and directed by it; and he will give them their effect in his own time.

To David Barrow, Monticello, May 1, 1815

God's Will

It is not easy to reconcile ourselves to the many useless miseries to which Providence seems to expose us. But his justice affords a prospect that we shall all be made even some day.

To Eliza House Trist, Annapolis, December 11, 1783

But whatever is to be our destiny, wisdom, as well as duty, dictates that we should acquiesce in the will of him whose it is to give and to take away, and be contented in the enjoyment of those who are still permitted to be with us.

To John Page, Washington, June 25, 1804

I shall obey it [God's revelation] with the same fidelity with which I would obey his known will in all cases. Hitherto I have been under the guidance of that portion of reason which he has thought proper to deal

out to me. I have followed it faithfully in all important
cases, to such a degree at least as leaves me without
uneasiness; and if on minor occasions I have erred
from its dictates, I have trust in him who made us
what we are, and knows it was not his plan to make
us always unerring. He has formed us moral agents.
Not that, in the perfection of his state, he can feel pain
or pleasure in any thing we may do: he is far above
our power: but that we may promote the happiness of
those with whom he has placed us in society, by acting honestly towards all, benevolently to those who
fall within our way, respecting sacredly their rights,
bodily and mental, and cherishing especially their
freedom of conscience, as we value our own.

To Miles King, Monticello, September 26, 1814

Heaven

An eloquent preacher of your religious society,
Richard Motte, in a discourse of much emotion and
pathos, is said to have exclaimed aloud to his con-
gregation that he did not believe there was a Quaker, Presbyterian, Methodist or Baptist in heaven,
having paused to give his audience time to stare and
to wonder; he added, that, in heaven, God knew no
distinctions, but considered all good men as his children and as brethren of the same family. I believe,
with the Quaker preacher, that he who steadily observes those moral precepts in which all religions
concur, will never be questioned, at the gates of
heaven, as to the dogmas in which they all differ.
That on entering there, all these are left behind

us. . . . Of all the systems of morality, ancient or modern, which have come under my observation, none appear to me so pure as that of Jesus. He who follows this steadily need not, I think, be uneasy.

To William Canby, Monticello, September 18, 1813

The Hereafter

It is not for me to pronounce on the hypothesis you present of a transmigration of souls from one body to another in certain cases. The laws of nature have withheld from us the means of physical knowledge of the country of spirits and revelation has, for reasons unknown to us, chosen to leave us in the dark as we were. When I was young I was fond of the specula- tions which seemed to promise some insight into that hidden country, but observing at length that they left me in the same ignorance in which they had found me, I have for very many years ceased to read or to think concerning them, and have reposed my head on that pillow of ignorance which a benevolent creator has made so soft for us, knowing how much we should be forced to use it. I have thought it better, by nourishing the good passions, & controlling the bad, to merit an inheritance in a state of being of which I can know so little, and to trust for the future to him who has been so good for the past.

To Isaac Story, Washington, December 5, 1801

Jesus

In extracting the pure principles which he taught, we should have to strip off the artificial vestments in which they have been muffled by priests, who have travestied them into various forms, as instruments of riches and power to them. . . . There will be found remaining the most sublime and benevolent code of morals which has ever been offered to man. I have performed this operation for my own use, by cutting, verse by verse, out of the printed book, and arranging, the matter which is evidently his, and which is as easily distinguishable as diamonds in a dunghill. The result is . . . 46 pages of pure and unsophisticated doctrines, such as were professed & acted on by the unlettered apostles, the Apostolic fathers, and the Christians of the 1st century.

To John Adams, Monticello,
October 12, 1813

In the New testament there is internal evidence that parts of it have proceeded from an extraordinary man; and that other parts are of the fabric of very inferior minds. It is as easy to separate those parts, as to pick out diamonds from dunghills. The matter of the first was such as would be preserved in the memory of the hearers, and handed on by tradition for a long time; the latter such stuff as might be gathered up, imbedding it, any where, and at any time.

To John Adams, Monticello,
January 24, 1814

The doctrines which flowed from the lips of Jesus himself are within the comprehension of a child.

To John Adams, July 5, 1814

I too have made a wee little book from the same materials, which I call the Philosophy of Jesus. It is a paradigma of his doctrines, made by cutting the texts out of the book and arranging them on the pages of a blank book in a certain order of time or subject. A more beautiful or precious morsel of ethics I have never seen. It is a document in proof that I am a real Christian, that is to say, a disciple of the doctrines of Jesus.

To Charles Thomson, January 6, 1816

I hold the precepts of Jesus, as delivered by himself, to be the most pure, benevolent, and sublime which have ever been preached to man. I adhere to the principles of the first age; and consider all subsequent innovations as corruptions of his religion, having no foundation in what came from him.

To Jared Sparks, Monticello, November 4, 1820

No one sees with greater pleasure than myself the progress of reason in its advances towards rational Christianity. When we shall have done away the incomprehensible jargon of the Trinitarian arithmetic, that three are one, and one is three; when we shall have knocked down the artificial scaffolding, reared to mask from view the simple structure of Jesus; when, in short, we shall have unlearned every thing which has been taught since his day, and got back to the pure and simple doctrines he inculcated, we shall then be truly and worthily his disciples: and my opinion is that if nothing had ever been added to

what flowed purely from his lips, the whole world
would at this day have been Christian.

To Timothy Pickering, Monticello, February 27, 1821

The doctrines of Jesus are simple, and tend all to
the happiness of man.

1. That there is one only God, & he all perfect.

2. That there is a future state of rewards & punishments.

3. That to love God with all thy heart & thy
neighbor as thyself, is the sum of religion. These
are the great points on which he endeavored to
reform the religion of the Jews.

To Benjamin Waterhouse, Monticello, June 26, 1822

Missionaries

These incendiaries, finding that the days of fire and
faggot are over in the Atlantic hemisphere, are now
preparing to put the torch to the Asiatic regions.
What would they say were the Pope to send annually
to this country colonies of Jesuit priests with car-
goes of their Missal and translations of their Vul-
gate, to be put gratis into the hands of every one
who would accept them?

To John Adams, Poplar Forest, November 25, 1816

I think with them on many points, and especially on
missionary and Bible societies. While we have so
many around us, within the same social pale, who
need instruction and assistance, why carry to a distance, and to strangers what our own neighbors

need? It is a duty certainly to give our sparings to those who want: but to see also that they are faithfully distributed, & duly apportioned to the respective wants of those receivers. And why give thro' agents whom we know not, to persons whom we know not, and in countries from which we get no account, when we can do it at short hand, to objects under our eye, thro' agents we know, and to supply wants we see? I do not know that it is a duty to disturb by missionaries the religion and peace of other countries, who may think themselves bound to extinguish by fire and fagot the heresies to which we give the name of conversions, and quote our own example for it. Were the Pope, or his Holy allies to send in mission to us some thousands of Jesuit priests to convert us to their Orthodoxy, I suspect that we should deem and treat it as a National aggression on our peace and faith.

To Michael Megear, Monticello, May 29, 1823

Quakers
It seems to be well understood, that their attachment to England is stronger than to their principles or their country.

To James Madison, Philadelphia, March 29, 1798

You expect that your book will have some effect on the prejudices which the society of friends entertain against the present & late administrations. In this I think you will be disappointed. The Friends are men, formed with the same passions, & swayed by the same natural principles & prejudices as others.

In cases where the passions are neutral, men will display their respect for the religious professions of their sect. But where their passions are enlisted, these professions are no obstacle. You observe very truly that both the late & present administration conducted the government on principles professed by the Friends. Our efforts to preserve peace, our measures as to the Indians, as to slavery, as to religious freedom, were all in consonance with their professions. Yet I never expected we should get a vote from them, & in this I was neither deceived nor disappointed. There is no riddle in this to those who do not suffer themselves to be duped by the professions of religious sectarians. The theory of American Quakerism is a very obvious one. The Mother society is in England. Its members are English by birth & residence, devoted to their own country as good citizens ought to be. The Quakers of these states are colonies or filiations from the mother society, to whom that society sends its yearly lessons. On these, the filiated societies model their opinions, their conduct, their passions & attachments. A Quaker is essentially an Englishman, in whatever part of the earth he is born or lives.

To Samuel Kercheval, Monticello, January 19, 1810

Religious Intolerance
Your sect by its sufferings has furnished a remarkable proof of the universal spirit of religious intolerance, inherent in every sect, disclaimed by all while feeble and practiced by all when in power. Our laws

have applied the only antidote to this vice, protecting our religious, as they do our civil rights by putting them all on an equal footing. But more remains to be done, for altho' we are free by the law, we are not so in practice.

To Mordecai Manuel Noah, May 28, 1818

Religious Tolerance

Our rulers can have authority over such natural rights only as we have submitted to them. The rights of conscience we never submitted, we could never submit. We are answerable for them to our God. The legitimate powers of government extend to such acts only as are injurious to others. But it does me no injury for my neighbor to say there are twenty gods or no god. It neither picks my pocket nor breaks my leg. If it be said, his testimony in a court of Justice cannot be relied on; reject it then and be the stigma on him. Constraint may make him worse by making him a hypocrite, but it will never make him a truer man. It may fix him obstinately in his errors, but will not cure them. Reason and free enquiry are the only effectual agents against error.

Notes on the State of Virginia, 1782

The Soul

It requires one effort only to admit the single incomprehensibility of matter endowed with thought: and two to believe, 1st. that of an existence called Spirit, of which we have neither evidence nor idea, and then

2dly. how that spirit which has neither extension nor solidity, can put material organs into motion. These are things which you and I may perhaps know ere long.

To John Adams, Monticello, March 14, 1820

Unitarianism

That this will ere long be the religion of the majority from North to South, I have no doubt.

To Thomas Cooper, Monticello, November 2, 1822

Slavery

Can the liberties of a nation be thought secure when we have removed their only firm basis, a conviction in the minds of the people that these liberties are of the gift of god? That they are not to be violated but with his wrath? Indeed I tremble for my country when I reflect that god is just; that his justice cannot sleep forever.

Notes on the States of Virginia, 1782

There must doubtless be an unhappy influence on the manners of our people produced by the existence of slavery among us. The whole commerce between master and slave is a perpetual exercise of the most boisterous passions, the most unremitting despotism on the one part, and degrading submissions on the other.

Notes on the State of Virginia, 1782

Virginia. This is the next state to which we may turn our eyes for the interesting spectacle of justice in conflict with avarice & oppression: a conflict wherein the sacred side is gaining daily recruits from the influx into office of young men grown & growing up. These have sucked in the principles of liberty as it were with their mother's milk, and it is to them I look with anxiety to turn the fate of this question.

To Richard Price, Paris, August 7, 1785

What a stupendous, what an incomprehensible machine is man! Who can endure toil, famine, stripes, imprisonment or death itself in vindication of his own liberty, and the next moment be deaf to all those motives whose power supported him thro' his trial, and inflict on his fellow men a bondage, one hour of which is fraught with more misery than ages of that which he rose in rebellion to oppose. But we must await with patience the workings of an overruling providence, and hope that that is preparing the deliverance of these our suffering brethren. When the measure of their tears shall be full, when their groans shall have involved heaven itself in darkness, doubtless a god of justice will awaken to their distress, and by diffusing light and liberality among their oppressors, or at length by his exterminating thunder, manifest his attention to the things of this world, and that they are not left to the guidance of a blind fatality.

To Jean Nicolas Démeunier, Paris, June 26, 1786

I congratulate you, my dear friend, on the law of your state for suspending the importation of slaves, and for the glory you have justly acquired by endeavoring to prevent it for ever. This abomination must have an end, and there is a superior bench reserved in heaven for those who hasten it.

To Edward Rutledge, Paris, July 14, 1787

Whatever may have been the circumstances which influenced our forefathers to permit the introduction of personal bondage into any part of these states, & to participate in the wrongs committed on an unoffending quarter of the globe, we may rejoice that such circumstances, & such a sense of them, exist no longer. It is honorable to the nation at large that their legislature availed themselves of the first practicable moment for arresting the progress of this great moral & political error:* and I sincerely pray with you, my friends, that all the members of the human family may, in the time prescribed by the Father of us all, find themselves securely established in the enjoyments of life, liberty, & happiness.

> *The Constitution provided that Congress could not prohibit the foreign slave trade before 1808. Acting on the request of President Jefferson, Congress on March 2, 1807, passed an act prohibiting

the importation of slaves from Africa after January 1, 1808.

To Messrs. Thomas, Ellicot, and others,
November 13, 1807

I have received the favor of your letter of August 17 and with it the Volume you were so kind as to send me on the Literature of Negroes. Be assured that no person living wishes more sincerely than I do, to see a complete refutation of the doubts I have myself entertained and expressed on the grade of understanding allotted to them by nature, and to find that in this respect they are on a par with ourselves. My doubts were the result of personal observation on the limited sphere of my own State, where the opportunities for the development of their genius were not favorable, and those of exercising it still less so. I expressed them therefore with great hesitation, but whatever be their degree of talent it is no measure of their rights. Because Sir Isaac Newton was superior to others in understanding he was not therefore Lord of the person or property of others. On this subject they are gaining daily in the Opinions of nations, & hopeful advances are making towards their re-establishment on an equal footing with the other colors of the human family. I pray you therefore to accept my thanks for the many instances you have enabled me to observe of respectable intelligence in that race of men, which cannot fail to have effect in hastening the day of their relief.

To Henri Gregoire, Washington, February 25, 1809

The love of justice & the love of country plead equally the cause of these people, and it is a mortal reproach to us that they should have pleaded it so long in vain, and should have produced not a single effort, nay I fear not much serious willingness to relieve them & ourselves from our present condition of moral and political reprobation.

To Edward Coles, Monticello, August 25, 1814

My opinion has ever been that, until more can be done for them, we should endeavor, with those whom fortune has thrown on our hands, to feed and clothe them well, protect them from ill usage, require such reasonable labor only as it is performed voluntarily by freemen, and be led by no repugnancies to abdicate them and our duties to them.

To Edward Coles, Monticello, August 25, 1814

There is nothing I would not sacrifice to a practicable plan of abolishing every vestige of this moral and political depravity.

To Thomas Cooper, Monticello, September 10, 1814

I can say with conscious truth that there is not a man on earth who would sacrifice more than I would to relieve us from this heavy reproach, in any practicable way. The cession of that kind of property, for so it is misnamed, is a bagatelle which would not cost me a second thought, if, in that way, a general emancipation and expatriation could be effected: and, gradually, and with due sacrifices, I think it might be. But as it is, we have the wolf by the ear, and we can neither hold him, nor safely let him go. Justice is in one scale, and self-preservation in the other.

To John Holmes, Monticello, April 22, 1820

Nothing is more certainly written in the book of fate than that these people are to be free; nor is it less certain that the two races, equally free, cannot live in the same government. Nature, habit, opinion have drawn indelible lines of distinction between them. It is still in our power to direct the process of emancipation and deportation peaceably, and in such slow degree, as that the evil will wear off insensibly and their place be, pari passu,* filled up by free white laborers. If, on the contrary, it is left to force itself on, human nature must shudder at the prospect held up.

*equally and simultaneously

Autobiography, 1821

Our only blot is becoming less offensive by the great improvement in the condition and civilization of that race, who can now more advantageously compare their situation with that of the laborers of Europe. Still it is a hideous blot, as well from the heteromorph peculiarities of the race, as that, with them, physical compulsion to action must be substituted for the moral necessity which constrains the free laborers to work equally hard. We feel & deplore it morally and politically, and we look without entire despair to some redeeming means not yet specifically foreseen. I am happy in believing that the conviction of the necessity of removing this evil gains ground with time. Their emigration to the Westward lightens the difficulty by dividing it and renders it more practicable on the whole. And the neighborhood of a government of their color promises a more accessible asylum than that from whence they came.

To William Short, Monticello, September 8, 1823

The abolition of the evil is not impossible; it ought never therefore to be despaired of. Every plan should be adopted, every experiment tried, which may do something towards the ultimate object.

To Frances Wright, Monticello, August 7, 1825

Travel

I duly received your favor dated Antwerp. . . . I was much entertained with it. It revived my inclination to travel, an inclination which always lies uppermost.

To John Trumbull, Paris, October 13, 1786

I was alone thro the whole, & think one travels more usefully when they travel alone, because they reflect more.

To John Banister, Jr., Paris, June 19, 1787

Traveling . . . makes men wiser, but less happy.

To Peter Carr, Paris, August 10, 1787

Be good, be learned, & be industrious, & you will not want the aid of traveling, to render you precious to your country, dear to your friends, happy within yourself.

To Peter Carr, Paris, August 10, 1787

My journey has been little entertaining. A country of corn & pastures affords little interesting to an American who has seen in his own country so much of that, and who travels to see the country & not its towns.

To William Short, The Hague, March 10, 1788

[After taking the grand tour, Thomas Lee Shippen] will return charged, like a bee, with the honey of wisdom, a blessing to his country and honor and comfort to his friends.

To William Shippen, Jr., Paris, May 8, 1788

Traveling is good for your health and necessary for your amusement.

To Angelica Schuyler Church, Paris,
September 21, 1788

Time is every day adding to the improbabilities of my undertaking long journeys.

To Janet Livingston Montgomery, Monticello,
September 4, 1798

We have however the traveler's consolation. Every step shortens the distance we have to go; the end of our journey is in sight.

To John Page, Washington, June 25, 1804

Bon Voyage
Heaven bless you, Madame, & guard you under all circumstances: give you smooth waters, gentle breezes, & clear skies, hushing all its elements into peace, and leading with its own hand the favored bark, till it shall have safely landed its precious charge on the shores of our new world.

To Madame de Bréhan, Paris, October 9, 1787

Homesickness
[Away from America] I am burning the candle of life without present pleasure, or future object.

To Eliza House Trist, Paris, December 15, 1786

The distance to which I am removed has given a new value to all I valued before in my own country, and the day of my return to it will be the happiest I expect to see in this life.

To Mary Jefferson Bolling, Paris, July 23, 1787

Time, absence, & comparison render my own country much dearer, and give a luster to all it contains which I did not before know that it merited.

To Wilson Miles Cary, Paris, August 12, 1787

Insulated & friendless on this side the globe, with such an ocean between me and every thing to which

I am attached the days will seem long which are to be counted over before I too am to rejoin my native country. Young poets complain often that life is fleeting & transient. We find in it seasons & situations however which move heavily enough.

To Abigail Adams, Paris, February 2, 1788

Nothing in this country can make amends for what one loses by quitting their own.

To Randolph Jefferson, Paris, January 11, 1789

Sightseeing

[Traveling to Amsterdam] The few moments of leisure which I might have, I would employ in seeing things rather than men.

To C.W.F. Dumas, Paris, February 13, 1788

When you are doubting whether a thing is worth the trouble of going to see, recollect that you will never again be so near it, that you may repent the not having seen it, but can never repent having seen it. But there is an opposite extreme too. That is, the seeing too much. A judicious selection is to be aimed at, taking care that the indolence of the moment have no influence on the decision. Take care particularly not to let the porters of churches, cabinets &c. lead you thro' all the little details in their possession, which will load the memory with trifles, fatigue the attention and waste that and your time. It is difficult to confine these people to the few objects worth seeing and remembering. They wish for

your money, and suppose you give it more willingly
the more they detail for you.

Travelling Notes for Mr. Rutledge and Mr. Shippen,
Paris, June 3, 1788

Traveling by Ship

Though navigation by water is attended with frequent accidents, and in its infancy must have been
attended with more, yet these are now so familiar
that we think little of them [compared with recent
accidents by balloonists].

To Joseph Jones, Paris, June 19, 1785

I must now repeat my wish to have Polly* sent to
me next summer. This, however, must depend on
the circumstances of a good vessel sailing from Virginia in the months of April, May, June, or July. I
would not have her set out sooner or later on account of the equinoxes. The vessel should have performed one voyage at least, but not be more than
four or five years old. We do not attend to this circumstance till we have been to sea, but there the
consequence of it is felt. I think it would be found
that all the vessels which are lost are either on their
first voyage or after they are five years old; at least
there are few exceptions to this. . . . I will only
add that I would rather live a year longer without
her than have her trusted to any but a good ship and
a summer passage.

*Jefferson's youngest daughter, Mary

To Francis Eppes, August 30, 1785

The season of the year makes me fear a very disagreeable passage for Mrs. Adams & yourself, tho we have sometimes fine weather in these months. Nobody will pray more sincerely than myself for your passage, that it may be short, safe and agreeable.

To John Adams, Paris, February 20, 1788

[After arriving safely in Virginia from Europe] Our captain is as bold a sailor as a judicious one should be.

To Nathaniel Cutting, Lynhaven Bay, November 21, 1789

Your repugnance to the sea forbids all hope in us that you may come to repose under the shade of our Magnolias. . . . Promise us therefore that when you can be safely wafted in a balloon, so as to avoid the nausea of sea sickness, you will come over.

To Madame de Tessé, Monticello, September 6, 1795

War

A coward is much more exposed to quarrels than a man of spirit.

To James Monroe, Paris, February 6, 1785

The most successful war seldom pays for its losses.

To Edmund Randolph, Paris, September 20, 1785

[In dealing with Algiers] I acknowledge I very early thought it would be best to effect a peace thro' the medium of war. . . . If it be admitted however that war, on the fairest prospects, is still exposed to - incertainties, I weigh against this the greater incertainty of the duration of a peace bought with money.

To John Adams, Paris, July 11, 1786

In the present state of Europe a spark dropped any where must kindle the whole.

To John Bondfield, Paris, September 9, 1787

No nation makes war now-a-days but by the aid of loans.

To John Jay, Paris, November 3, 1787

This [potential European] war I think will catch from nation to nation till it becomes general.

To John Rutledge, Jr., Paris, August 12, 1788

I abhor war, and view it as the greatest scourge of mankind.

To Elbridge Gerry, Philadelphia, May 13, 1797

War is not the best engine for us to resort to, nature has given us one in our commerce, which, if properly managed, will be a better instrument for obliging the interested nations of Europe to treat us with justice.

To Thomas Pinckney, Philadelphia, May 29, 1797

Our people must consent to small occasional sacrifices, to avoid the greater evil of war.

To Edward Stevens, Philadelphia, June 14, 1797

It is our duty still to endeavor to avoid war; but if it shall actually take place, no matter by whom brought on, we must defend ourselves. If our house be on fire, without inquiring whether it was fired from within or without, we must try to extinguish it. In that I have no doubt we shall act as one man.

To James Lewis, Jr., Philadelphia, May 9, 1798

We are here struggling hard to avert war: till that point we are a divided people, because some wish to bring it on. If it actually takes place, we shall defend ourselves as one man. When our house is on fire, it matters little whether fired from without or within, or both. The first object is to extinguish it.

To St. George Tucker, Philadelphia, May 9, 1798

If we are forced into war, we must give up political differences of opinion, & unite as one man to defend our country. But whether at the close of such a war, we should be as free as we are now, god knows.

To Tadeusz Kosciusko, Philadelphia,
February 21, 1799

Whensoever hostile aggressions ... require resort to war, we must meet our duty and convince the world that we are just friends and brave enemies.

To Andrew Jackson, Washington, December 3, 1806

You may expect further information as we receive it, & tho' I expect it will be such as will place us at our ease, yet we must not place ourselves so until it be certain, but act on the possibility that the resources of our enemy may be greater & deeper than we are yet informed.

To James Wilkinson, Washington, January 3, 1807

Always a friend to peace, & believing it to promote eminently the happiness & prosperity of nations, I am ever unwilling that it should be disturbed, until greater & more important interests call for an appeal to force. Whenever that shall take place, I feel a perfect confidence that the energy & enterprise displayed by my fellow citizens in the pursuits of peace, will be equally eminent in those of war.

To John Shee, Washington, January 14, 1807

We have borne patiently a great deal of wrong, on the consideration that if nations go to war for every degree of injury, there would never be peace on earth.

To Madame de Stael de Holstein, Washington,
July 16, 1807

Trophies obtained by the blood-stained steel, or the tattered flags of the tented field, will never be envied.

To the republican citizens of Washington County,Maryland, Monticello, March 31, 1809

In times of peace, the people look most to their representatives; but in war, to the Executive solely.

To Caesar A. Rodney, Monticello, February 10, 1810

The maxim of war . . . not to leave an enemy in the rear; & especially where an insurrectionary flame is known to be under the embers, merely smothered, and ready to burst at every point.

To John Langdon, Monticello, March 5, 1810

Today we are at peace; tomorrow war. The curtain of separation is drawing between us.

To James Maury, Monticello, April 25, 1812

All men know that War is a losing game to both parties.

To William Short, Monticello, November 28, 1814

American Civil War

But this momentous question [the Missouri Compromise], like a fire bell in the night, awakened and filled me with terror. I considered it at once as the knell of the Union. It is hushed indeed for the moment. But this is a reprieve only, not a final sentence. A geographical line,* coinciding with a marked principle, moral and political, once conceived and held up to the angry passions of men, will never be obliterated; and every new irritation will mark it deeper and deeper.

> *The Missouri Compromise of 1820 prohibited slavery from the territory acquired in the Louisiana Purchase north of a line 36° 30'.

To John Holmes, Monticello, April 22, 1820

All, I fear, do not see the speck in our horizon which is to burst on us as a tornado, sooner or later. The line of division lately marked out, between different portions of our confederacy, is such as will never, I fear, be obliterated.

To James Breckenridge, Monticello, February 15, 1821

Defense

Weakness provokes insult & injury, while a condition to punish it often prevents it.

To John Jay, the secretary for foreign affairs, Paris, August 23, 1785

I am satisfied the good sense of the people is the strongest army our governments can ever have, & that it will not fail them.

To William Carmichael, Paris, December 26, 1786

Whatever enables us to go to war, secures our peace.

To James Monroe, New York, July 11, 1790

Were armies to be raised whenever a speck of war is visible in our horizon, we never should have been without them. Our resources would have been exhausted on dangers which have never happened, instead of being reserved for what is really to take place.

Sixth Annual Message to Congress, December 2, 1806

Insurrections

I know no danger so dreadful and so probable as that of internal contests.

To Edmund Randolph, Baltimore, February 15, 1783

Necessity

Necessity is Law, in times of war most especially.

To Matthew Pope, Charlottesville, May 21, 1781

Rebellion as a Good Thing

The commotions which have taken place in America, as far as they are yet known to me, offer nothing threatening. They are a proof that the people have liberty enough, and I would not wish them less than they have. If the happiness of the mass of the people can be secured at the expense of a little tempest now & then, or even of a little blood, it will be a precious purchase. Malo libertatum periculosum quam quietam servitutem.*

*I prefer dangerous liberty to a quiet servitude.

To Ezra Stiles, Paris, December 24, 1786

I hold it that a little rebellion now and then is a good thing, & as necessary in the political world as storms in the physical. Unsuccessful rebellions indeed generally establish the encroachments on the rights of the people which have produced them. An observation of this truth should render honest republican governors so mild in their punishment of rebellions, as not to discourage them too much. It is a medicine necessary for the sound health of government.

To James Madison, Paris, January 30, 1787

The spirit of resistance to government is so valuable on certain occasions, that I wish it to be always kept alive. It will often be exercised when wrong, but better so than not to be exercised at all. I like a little rebellion now & then. It is like a storm in the Atmosphere.

To Abigail Adams, Paris, February 22, 1787

God forbid we should ever be 20 years without such a rebellion. The people can not be all, & always, well informed. The part which is wrong will be discontented in proportion to the importance of the facts they misconceive. If they remain quiet under such misconceptions, it is lethargy, the forerunner of death to the public liberty. We have had 13 states independent for 11 years. There has been one rebellion [Shays's Rebellion]. That comes to one rebellion in a century and a half for each state. What country before ever existed a century & a half without a rebellion? & what country can preserve its liberties, if their rulers are not warned from time to time that their people preserve the spirit of resistance? Let them take arms. The remedy is to set them right as to facts, pardon & pacify them. What signify a few lives lost in a century or two? The tree of liberty must be refreshed from time to time with the blood of patriots & tyrants. It is its natural manure.

To William Stephens Smith, Paris, November 13, 1787

Resistance

When patience has begotten false estimates of its motives, when wrongs are pressed because it is believed they will be borne, resistance becomes morality.

To Madame de Stael de Holstein, Washington,
July 16, 1807

Vigilance

Let the eye of vigilance never be closed.

To Spencer Roane, Monticello, March 9, 1821

Women
ᑖ᙮ᑐ

Nothing can be more unmanly than to treat a lady superciliously.

To Peter Carr, Annapolis, December 11, 1783

Wisdom, I know, is social. She seeks her fellows. But Beauty is jealous, and illy bears the presence of a rival.

To Abigail Adams, Paris, September 25, 1785

I am in hopes that Mrs. Monroe will soon have on her hands domestic cares of the dearest kind, sufficient to fill her time and ensure her against the tedium vitae;* that she will find that the distractions of a town, and waste of life under these, can bear no comparison with the tranquil happiness of domestic life. If her own experience has not yet taught her this truth, she has in its favor the testimony of one who has gone through the various scenes of business, of bustle, of office, of rambling, and of quiet retirement, and who can assure her that the latter is the only point upon which the mind can settle at rest. Tho not clear of inquietudes, because no earthly situation is so, they are fewer in number, and mixed with more objects of contentment than in any other mode of life.

*tedium of life

To James Monroe, Paris, December 18, 1786

Mr. Jefferson has the honor to present his compliments to Mrs. Smith and to send her the two pair of Corsets she desired. He wishes they may be suitable, as Mrs. Smith omitted to send her measure. . . . Should they be too small however, she will be so good as to lay them by a while. There are ebbs as well as flows in this world. When the mountain refused to come to Mahomet, he went to the mountain.

To Abigail Adams Smith, Paris, January 15, 1787

Men, in a civilized country, never expose their wives and children to labor above their force or sex, as long as their own labor can protect them from it.

Notes of a Tour into the Southern Parts of France,
March 4, 1787

Music, drawing, books, invention and exercise will be so many resources to you against ennui. But there are others which to this object add that of utility. These are the needle, and domestic economy. The latter you cannot learn here, but the former you may. In the country life of America there are many moments when a woman can have recourse to nothing but her needle for employment. In a dull company and in dull weather for instance. It is ill manners to read; it is ill manners to leave them; no card-playing there among genteel people; that is abandoned to black-guards. The needle is then a valuable resource. Besides without knowing to use it herself, how can the mistress of a family direct the works of her servants?

To Martha Jefferson, Aix en Provence, March 28, 1787

Mr. Rucker, who is arrived here, gives me a terrible account of the luxury of our ladies in the article of dress. He says that they began to be sensible of the excess of it themselves, and to think a reformation necessary. That proposed is the adoption of a national dress. I fear however they have not resolution enough for this. I rejoice in the character of the lady who accompanies the Count de Moustier to America, and who is calculated to reform these excesses as far as her example can have weight. Simple beyond example in her dress, tho neat, hating parade & etiquette, affable, engaging, placid, & withal beautiful, I cannot help hoping a good effect from her example.

To Abigail Adams, Paris, August 30, 1787

The women here [in The Netherlands], as in Germany do all sorts of work. While one considers them as useful and rational companions, one cannot forget that they are also objects of our pleasures. Nor can they ever forget it. While employed in dirt and drudgery some tag of a ribbon, some ring or bit of bracelet, earbob or necklace, or something of that kind will show that the desire of pleasing is never suspended in them. How valuable is that state of society which allots to them internal employments only, and external to the men. They are formed by nature for attentions and not for hard labor. A woman never forgets one of the numerous train of little offices which belong to her; a man forgets often.

Notes on a Tour through Holland, March 1788

We have now need of something to make us laugh, for the topics of the times are sad & eventful. The gay & thoughtless Paris is now become a furnace of Politics. All the world is run politically mad. Men, women, children talk nothing else; & you know that naturally they talk much, loud, & warm. Society is spoiled by it, at least for those who, like myself, are but lookers on.—You too have had your political fever. But our good ladies, I trust, have been too wise to wrinkle their foreheads with politics. They are contented to soothe & calm the minds of their husbands returning ruffled from political debate. They have the good sense to value domestic happiness above all other, and the art to cultivate it beyond all others. There is no part of the earth where so much of this is enjoyed as in America. You agree with me in this: but you think that the pleasures of Paris more than supply its want: in other words that a Parisian is happier than an American. You will change your opinion, my dear Madam, and come over to mine in the end. Recollect the women of this capital, some on foot, some on horses, & some in carriages hunting pleasure in the streets, in routs & assemblies, and forgetting that they have left it behind them in their nurseries; compare them with our own countrywomen occupied in the tender & tranquil amusements of domestic life, and confess that it is a comparisons of Amazons and Angels.

> To Anne Willing Bingham, Paris, May 11, 1788

The tender breasts of ladies were not formed for political convulsion; and the French ladies miscalculate much their own happiness when they wander from the true field of their influence into that of politics.

> To Angelica Schuyler Church, Paris,
> September 21, 1788

You will preserve from temper & inclination the happy privilege of the ladies to leave to the rougher sex, & to the newspapers their party-squabbles & reproaches.

> To Angelica Schuyler Church, Philadelphia,
> May 24, 1797

The appointment of a woman to office is an innovation for which the public is not prepared, nor am I.

> To Albert Gallatin, January 13, 1807

Thomas Jefferson Describes
His Contemporaries

John Adams

To James Madison, Baltimore,
February 14, 1783

From what you mention in your letter I suppose the newspapers must be wrong when they say that Mr. Adams had taken up his abode with Dr. Franklin. I am nearly at a loss to judge how he will act in the negotiation [of the peace treaty with England]. He hates Franklin, he hates Jay, he hates the French, he hates the English. To whom will he adhere? His vanity is a lineament in his character which had entirely escaped me. His want of taste I had observed. Notwithstanding all this he has a sound head on substantial points, and I think he has integrity. I am glad therefore that he is of the commission & expect he will be useful in it. His dislike of all parties, and all men, by balancing his prejudices, may give the same fair play to his reason as would a general benevolence of temper. At any rate honesty may be extracted even from poisonous weeds.

To John Adams, Paris, July 7, 1785

I shall be happy to receive your corrections of these ideas as I have found in the course of our joint services that I think right when I think with you.

To James Madison, Paris, January 30, 1787

You know the opinion I formerly entertained of my friend Mr. Adams. Yourself & the governor were the first who shook that opinion. I afterwards saw proofs which convicted him of a degree of vanity, and of a blindness to it, of which no germ had appeared in Congress. A 7 months intimacy with him here and as many weeks in London have given me opportunities of studying him closely. He is vain, irritable and a bad calculator of the force and probable effect of the motives which govern men. This is all the ill which can possibly be said of him. He is as disinterested as the being which made him: he is profound in his views: and accurate in his judgment except where knowledge of the world is necessary to form a judgment. He is so amiable, that I pronounce you will love him if ever you become acquainted with him. He would be, as he was, a great man in Congress.

To James Madison, Paris, May 25, 1788

Of rigorous honesty, and careless of appearances he lived for a considerable time as an economical private individual. . . . His pecuniary affairs were under the direction of *Mrs. Adams*, one of the most estimable characters on earth, and the most attentive & honorable economists. Neither had a wish to lay up a copper, but both wished to make both ends meet. I suspect however, from an expression dropped in conversation, that they were not able to do this, and that a deficit in their accounts appeared in their winding up.

To William Short, Washington, June 12, 1807

He has a better heart than head.

To Benjamin Rush, Monticello,
January 16, 1811

I think it a part of his character to suspect foul play in those of whom he is jealous, and not easily to relinquish his suspicions.

To Benjamin Rush, Poplar Forest,
December 5, 1811

Changing a single word only in Dr. Franklin's character of him, I knew him to be always an honest man, often a great one, but sometimes incorrect & precipitate in his judgments; and it is known to those who have ever heard me speak of Mr. Adams, that I have ever done him justice myself, and defended him when assailed by others, with the single exception as to political opinions.

Conversation with Daniel Webster, 1824

John Adams was our Colossus on the floor. He was not graceful, nor elegant, nor remarkably fluent; but he came out occasionally with a power of thought & expression, that moved us from our seats.

Samuel Adams

To Samuel Adams, Philadelphia, February 26, 1800

Your principles have been tested in the crucible of time, & have come out pure. You have proved that it was monarchy, & not merely British monarchy, you opposed.

To Benjamin Waterhouse, Monticello, January 31, 1819

I was the youngest man but one in the old Congress, and he the oldest but one; as I believe. His only senior, I suppose, was Stephen Hopkins. . . . Altho' my high reverence for Samuel Adams was returned by habitual notices from him which highly flattered me, yet the disparity of age prevented intimate and confidential communications. I always considered him as more than any other member [in Congress] the fountain of our important measures. And altho' he was neither an eloquent nor easy speaker, whatever he said was sound and commanded the profound attention of the House. In the discussions on the floor of Congress he reposed himself on our main pillar in debate, Mr. John Adams. These two gentlemen were verily a host in our councils. Comparisons with their associates, Northern and Southern, would answer no profitable purpose, but they would suffer by comparison with none.

To Samuel Adams Wells, Monticello,
May 12, 1819

I can say that he was truly a great man, wise in council, fertile in resources, immovable in his purposes, and had, I think, a greater share than any other member, in advising and directing our measures, in the Northern war especially. As a speaker he could not be compared with his living colleague and namesake, whose deep conceptions, nervous style,* and undaunted firmness, made him truly our bulwark in debate, But Mr. Samuel Adams, altho' not of fluent elocution, was so rigorously logical, so clear in his views, abundant in good sense, and master always of his subject that he commanded the most profound attention whenever he rose in an assembly by which the froth of declamation was heard with the most sovereign contempt. I sincerely rejoice that the record of his worth is to be undertaken by one so much disposed as you will be to hand him down fairly to that posterity for whose liberty and happiness he was so zealous a laborer.

    *strong, powerful

Conversation with Daniel Webster, 1824

For depth of purpose, zeal, & sagacity, no man in Congress *exceeded*, if any equalled Sam Adams; & none did more than he, to originate & sustain revolutionary measures in Congress. But he could not speak, he had a hesitating grunting manner.

Aaron Burr

The Anas, 1804

I had never seen Colo. Burr till he came as a member of the Senate. His conduct very soon inspired me with distrust. I habitually cautioned Mr. Madison against trusting him too much. I saw afterwards that under Genl. W's and Mr. A's administrations, whenever a great military appointment or a diplomatic one was to be made, he came post to Philadelphia to show himself & in fact that he was always at market, if they had wanted him. He was indeed told by [Jonathan] Dayton in 1800 he might be Secretary at War; but this bid was too late. His election as V.P. was then foreseen. With these impressions of Colo. Burr there never had been any intimacy between us, and but little association. When I destined him for a high appointment, it was out of respect for the favor he had obtained with the republican party by his extraordinary exertions and successes in the N.Y. election in 1800.

To Robert R. Livingston, Washington, March 24, 1807

Burr has indeed made a most inglorious exhibition of his much over-rated talents. He is now on his way to Richmond for trial.

To William Branch Giles, Monticello,
April 20, 1807

Against Burr, personally, I never had one hostile
sentiment. I never indeed thought him an honest,
frank-dealing man, but considered him as a crooked
gun or other perverted machine whose aim or stroke
you could never be sure of. Still, while he possessed
the confidence of the nation, I thought it my duty to
respect in him their confidence, & to treat him as if
he deserved it.

John Dickinson

To François Soulés, September 13–18, 1786

Mr. Dickinson, a lawyer of more ingenuity than
sound judgment, and still more timid than ingenious.

To Joseph Bringhurst, Washington,
February 24, 1808

I have to acknowledge the receipt of your letter of
the 16th. It gave me the first information of the
death of our distinguished fellow-citizen, John
Dickinson. A more estimable man, or truer patriot,
could not have left us. Among the first of the advocates for the rights of his country when assailed by
Great Britain, he continued to the last the orthodox
advocate of the true principles of our new government, and his name will be consecrated in history as
one of the great worthies of the revolution. We

ought to be grateful for having been permitted to retain the benefit of his counsel to so good an old age; still the moment of losing it, whenever it arises, must be a moment of deep-felt regret. For himself, perhaps, a longer period of life was less important, alloyed as the feeble enjoyments of that age are with so much pain. But to his country every addition to his moments was interesting. A junior companion of his labors in the early part of our revolution, it has been a great comfort to me to have retained his friendship to the last moments of his life.

Benjamin Franklin

To the Reverend William Smith, Philadelphia,
February 19, 1791

I can only therefore testify in general that there appeared to me more respect & veneration attached to the character of Doctor Franklin in France, than to that of any other person in the same country, foreign or native. I had opportunities of knowing particularly how far these sentiments were felt by the foreign ambassadors & ministers at the court of Versailles. The fable of his capture by the Algerines, propagated by the English newspapers, excited no uneasiness; as it was seen at once to be a dish cooked up to the palate of their readers. But nothing could exceed the anxiety of his diplomatic brethren, on a subsequent report of his death, which, tho' premature, bore some marks of authenticity.

I found the ministers of France equally impressed with the talents & integrity of Doctor Franklin. The Comte de Vergennes particularly gave me repeated & unequivocal demonstrations of his entire confidence in him. . . .

His death was an affliction which was to happen to us at some time or other. We had reason to be thankful he was so long spared: that the most useful life, should be the longest also; that it was protracted so far beyond the ordinary span allotted to man, as to avail us of his wisdom in the establishment of our own freedom, & to bless him with a view of its dawn in the east, where they seemed, till now, to have learned every thing, but how to be free.

The succession to Dr. Franklin, at the court of France, was an excellent school of humility. On being presented to any one as the Minister of America, the common-place question used in such cases was *"c'est vous, Monsieur, qui remplace le Docteur Franklin?"* "it is you, sir, who replaces Doctor Franklin?" I generally answered—"no one can replace him, Sir: I am only his successor."

To Samuel Smith, Monticello,
August 22, 1798

The greatest man & ornament of the age and country in which he lived.

To Thomas Jefferson Randolph, Washington, November 24, 1808

It was one of the rules which above all others made Doctor Franklin the most amiable of men in society, "never to contradict any body." If he was urged to announce an opinion, he did it rather by asking questions, as if for information, or by suggesting doubts.

To Robert Walsh, Monticello, December 4, 1818

As to the charge of subservience to France, besides the evidence of his friendly colleagues before named [Arthur Lee and John Adams], two years of my own service with him at Paris, daily visits, and the most friendly and confidential conversations, convince me it had not a shadow of foundation. He possessed the confidence of that government in the highest degree, insomuch that it may truly be said that they were more under his influence, than he under theirs. The fact is that his temper was so amiable and conciliatory, his conduct so rational, never urging impossibilities, or even things unreasonably inconvenient to them, in short so moderate and attentive to their difficulties, as well as our own, that what his enemies called subserviency, I saw was only that reasonable disposition, which, sensible that advantages are not all to be on one side, yielding what is just and liberal, is the more certain of obtaining liberality and justice. Mutual confidence produces of course mutual influence, and this was all which subsisted between Dr. Franklin & the government of France.

Albert Gallatin

To William Duane, Monticello,
March 28, 1811

I believe Mr. Gallatin to be of as pure integrity, and as zealously devoted to the liberties and interests of our country as its most affectionate native citizen. Of this his courage in Congress, in the days of terror, gave proofs which nothing can obliterate from the recollection of those who were witnesses of it. . . . An intercourse, almost daily, of eight years with him has given me opportunities of knowing his character more thoroughly than perhaps any other man living.

Alexander Hamilton

To James Madison, September 8, 1793

Hamilton is ill of the fever as is said. He had two physicians out at his house the night before last. His family think him in danger, & he puts himself so by his excessive alarm. He had been miserable several days before from a firm persuasion he should catch it [i.e., yellow fever]. A man as timid as he is on the water, as timid on horseback, as timid in sickness, would be a phenomenon if the courage of which he has the reputation in military occasions were genuine.

Portrait of Alexander Hamilton by John Trumbull.
(Metropolitan Museum of Art, New York.)

To James Madison, Monticello,
September 21, 1795

Hamilton is really a colossus to the antirepublican
party. Without numbers, he is an host within himself. They have got themselves into a defile, where
they might be finished; but too much security on

the Republican part, will give time to his talents &
indefatigableness to extricate them. We have had
only middling performances to oppose him. In
truth, when he comes forward there is nobody but
yourself who can meet him. His adversaries having
begun the attack, he has the advantage of answering
them, & remains unanswered himself. . . . For god's
sake take up your pen, and give a fundamental reply
to Curtius & Camillus.

To Benjamin Rush, Monticello,
January 16, 1811

I received a letter from President Washington, then
at Mount Vernon, desiring me to call together the
heads of departments, and to invite Mr. Adams to
join us (which, by the bye, was the only instance of
that being done) in order to determine on some measure which required despatch; and he desired me to
act on it, as decided, without again recurring to him.
I invited them to dine with me, and after dinner, sitting at our wine, having settled our question, other
conversation came on, in which a collision of opinion
arose between Mr. Adams & Colo. Hamilton, on the
merits of the British constitution, Mr. Adams giving
it as his opinion that, if some of its defects & abuses
were corrected, it would be the most perfect constitution of government ever devised by man. Hamilton, on the contrary, asserted that, with its existing
vices, it was the most perfect model of government

that could be formed; & that the correction of its vices would render it an impracticable government. And this you may be assured was the real line of difference between the political principles of these two gentlemen. Another incident took place on the same occasion which will further delineate Hamilton's political principles. The room being hung around with a collection of the portraits of remarkable men, among them were those of Bacon, Newton & Locke, Hamilton asked me who they were. I told him they were my trinity of the three greatest men the world had ever produced, naming them. He paused for some time: "the greatest man," said he, "that ever lived was Julius Caesar." Mr. Adams was honest as a politician, as well as a man; Hamilton honest as a man, but, as a politician, believing in the necessity of either force or corruption to govern man.

The Anas, 1818

Hamilton was indeed a singular character. Of acute understanding, disinterested, honest, and honorable in all private transactions, amiable in society, and duly valuing virtue in private life, yet so bewitched & perverted by the British example, as to be under thorough conviction that corruption* was essential to the government of a nation.

> *Corruption in the eighteenth century meant *influence* or *favoritism*.

Patrick Henry

To George Rogers Clark, November 26, 1782

I was not a little surprised however to find one person hostile to you as far as he has personal courage to show hostility to any man. Who he is you will probably have heard, or may know him by this description as being all tongue without either head or heart. In the variety of his crooked [i.e., devious or tortured] schemes however, his interests may probably veer about so as to put it in your power to be useful to him; in which case he certainly will be your friend again if you want him.

To William Wirt, Monticello,
April 12, 1812

Mr. Henry's ravenous avarice [was] the only passion paramount to his love of popularity.

To William Wirt, Monticello,
April 12, 1812

In ordinary business [in the House of Burgesses] he was a very inefficient member. He could not draw a bill on the most simple subject which would bear legal criticism, or even the ordinary criticism which looks to correctness of style & ideas, for indeed there was no accuracy of idea in his head. His imagination was copious, poetical, sublime, but vague also. He said the strongest things in the finest language, but without logic, without arrangement, desultorily.

Autobiography, 1821

Mr. Pendleton, . . . who, taken all in all, was the ablest man in debate I have ever met with. He had not indeed the poetical fancy of Mr. Henry, his sublime imagination, his lofty and overwhelming diction. . . .

When the famous Resolutions of 1765, against the Stamp-act, were proposed, I was yet a student of law in Williamsburg. I attended the debate however at the door of the lobby of the H. of Burgesses, & heard the splendid display of Mr. Henry's talents as a popular orator. They were great indeed; such as I have never heard from any other man. He appeared to me to speak as Homer wrote.

. . . He was the laziest man in reading I ever knew.

Conversation with Daniel Webster, 1824

Patrick Henry was originally a bar-keeper. He was married very young, & going into some business on his own account, was a bankrupt before the year was out. . . .

He was as well suited to the times as any man ever was, & it is not now easy to say, what we should have done without Patrick Henry. He was far before all, in maintaining the spirit of the Revolution. His influence was most extensive, with the Members from the Upper Counties, & *his* boldness & their votes overawed & controlled the more cool, or the more timid Aristocratic gentlemen of the lower part of the State. His eloquence was peculiar; if indeed it

should be called eloquence, for it was impressive &
sublime beyond what can be imagined. Although it
was difficult when he had spoken, to tell what he had
said, yet while he was speaking, it always seemed directly to the point. When he had spoken in opposition to *my* opinion, had produced a great effect, & I
myself been highly delighted & moved, I have asked
myself when he ceased, "What the devil has he said,"
& could never answer the enquiry.

His person was of full size, & his manner &
voice free & manly. His utterance neither very fast nor
very slow. His speeches generally short from a quarter to an half hour. His pronunciation, was vulgar &
vicious, but it was forgotten while he was speaking.

He was a man of very little knowledge of any
sort, he read nothing & had no books. Returning one
November from Albemarle Court, he borrowed of
me Hume's Essays, in two vols. saying he should
have leisure in the winter for reading. In the Spring
he returned them, & declared he had not been able to
go farther than twenty or thirty pages, in the first volume. He wrote almost nothing, he *could not* write.
The resolutions of '75 which have been ascribed to
him, have by many, been supposed to have been written by Mr. [Thomas] Johnson, who acted as his second, on that occasion. But if they were written by
Henry himself, they are not such as to prove any power of composition. Neither in politicks nor in his profession was he a man of business, he was a man for
debate only. His biographer [William Wirt] says,
that he read Plutarch every year,—I doubt whether

he ever read a volume of it in his life. His temper was excellent, & he generally observed decorum in debate.

On one or two occasions I have seen him *angry*—and his anger was terrible. Those who witnessed it, were not disposed to rouse it again. In his opinions he was yielding & practicable, & not disposed to differ from his friends. In private conversation he was agreeable, & facetious & while in genteel society appeared to understand all the decencies & proprieties of it; but in his *heart*, he preferred low society, & sought it as often as possible. He would hunt in the pine woods of Fluvannah, with overseers, & people of that description, living in a camp for a fortnight at a time without a change of raiment. I have often been astonished at his command of proper language; how he obtained the knowledge of it, I never could find out, as he read so little & conversed little with educated men.

After all, it must be allowed that he was our leader, in the measures of the Revolution, in Virginia. In that respect more is due to HIM than to any other person. If we had not had *him*, we probably have got on pretty well, as you did by a number of men of nearly equal talents, but he left us all far behind.

David Humphreys

To Elbridge Gerry, Paris, May 7, 1786

I am induced from my own feelings to recommend Colo. Humphreys to your care. He is sensible, prudent, & honest, and may be very firmly relied on in any office which requires these talents.

To William Short, Paris, February 9, 1789

Colo. Humphreys is attacked in the papers for his French airs, for bad poetry, bad prose, vanity, &c. It is said his dress in so gay a style gives general disgust against him.

Andrew Jackson

Conversation with Daniel Webster, 1824

I feel much alarmed at the prospect of seeing General Jackson, President. He is one of the most unfit men, I know of for such a place. He has had very little respect for Laws or Constitutions,—& is in fact an able military chief. His passions are terrible. When I was President of the Senate, he was a Senator; & he could never speak from the *rashness* of his feelings. I have seen him attempt it repeatedly, & as often choke with rage. His passions are no doubt cooler now;—he has been much tried since I knew him—but he is a *dangerous man.*

John Paul Jones

To Edward Carrington, Paris, May 27, 1788

Paul Jones is invited into the Empress's service with the rank of rear admiral, & to have a separate command. I wish it corresponded with the views of Congress to give him that rank from the taking of the Serapis. [I look to] this officer as our great future dependence on the sea, where alone we should think of ever having a force. He is young enough to see the day when we shall be more populous than the whole British dominions and able to fight them ship to ship. We should procure him then every possible opportunity of acquiring experience.

Henry Knox

The Anas, 1793

Knox joined Hamilton in everything.

To Martin Van Buren, Monticello,
June 29, 1824

General Knox, a man of parade . . .

The Marquis de Lafayette

To James Madison, Paris, March 18, 1785

Your character of the M. Fayette is precisely agreeable to the idea I had formed of him. I take him to be of unmeasured ambition but that the means he uses are virtuous. He is returned [to France from America] fraught with affection to America and disposed to render every possible service.

To James Madison, Paris, January 30, 1787

The Marquis de Lafayette is a most valuable auxiliary to me. His zeal is unbounded, & his weight with those in power great. His education having been merely military, commerce was an unknown field to him. But his good sense enabling him to comprehend perfectly whatever is explained to him. His agency has been very efficacious. He has a great deal of sounder genius is well remarked by the king & rising in popularity. He [i.e., the king] has nothing against him but the suspicion [of] republican principles. I think he will one day be of the ministry. His foible is a canine appetite for popularity and fame. But he will get above this.

Richard Henry Lee

To John Adams, Monticello, August 22, 1813

[On his style of writing] His was loose, vague, frothy, rhetorical. He was a poorer writer than his brother Arthur.

To John Adams, Monticello, December 18, 1825

I presume you have received a copy of the life of Richd. H. Lee from his grandson of the same name, author of the work. You and I know that he merited much during the revolution. Eloquent, bold, and ever watchful at his post, of which his biographer omits no proof. I am not certain whether the friends of George Mason, of Patrick Henry, yourself, and even of Genl. Washington may not reclaim some feathers of the plumage given him, notable as was his proper and original coat.

Meriwether Lewis

To Dr. Barton, Washington,
February 27, 1803

You know we have been many years wishing to have the Missouri explored, & whatever river, heading with that, runs into the Western ocean. Congress, in some secret proceedings, have yielded to a proposition I made them for permitting me to have it done: It is to be undertaken immediately, with a party of about ten, & I have appointed Capt. Lewis, my secretary, to conduct it. It was impossible to find a character who to a complete science in botany, natural history, mineralogy, & astronomy, joined the firmness of constitution and character, prudence, habits adapted to the woods, and familiarity with the Indian manners & character, requisite for this undertaking. All the latter qualifications, Capt. Lewis has. Altho' no regular botanist &c., he possesses a remarkable store of accurate observation on all the subjects of the three kingdoms, & will therefore readily single out whatever presents itself new to him in either; and he has qualified himself for taking the observations of longtitude & latitude necessary to fix the geography of the line he passes through.

James Madison

To Peter Carr, Annapolis, December 11, 1783

If you can find means to attract the notice and acquaintance of my friend Mr. Madison lately returned to your neighborhood from Congress he will be a most valuable patron to you. His judgment is so sound and his heart so good that I would wish you to respect every advice he would be so kind as to give you, equally as if it came from me.

To James Madison, Paris, March 18, 1785

Late letters tell us you are nominated for the court of Spain. . . . I need not tell you how much I shall be pleased with such an event. Yet it has its displeasing sides also. I want you in the Virginia Assembly and also in Congress yet we cannot have you everywhere. We must therefore be contended to have you where you choose.

To Thomas C. Flourney, Monticello,
October 1, 1812

You probably do not know Mr. Madison personally, or at least intimately as I do. I have known him from 1779, when he first came into the public councils; and from three & thirty years' trial, I can say conscientiously that I do not know in the world a man of purer integrity, more dispassionate, disinterested & devoted to genuine republicanism; nor could I, in the whole scope of America & Europe point out an abler head. He may be illy seconded by others, betrayed by the Hulls & Arnolds of our country, for such there are in every country, and with sorrow & suffering we know it. But what man can do will be done by Mr. Madison.

To John Adams, Monticello, May 5, 1817

I do not entertain your apprehensions for the happiness of our brother Madison in a state of retirement. Such a mind as his, fraught with information, and with matter for reflection, can never know ennui. Besides, there will always be work enough cut out for him to continue his active usefulness to his country.

Autobiography, 1821

Mr. Madison came into the House in 1776. A new member and young; which circumstances, concurring with his extreme modesty, prevented his venturing himself in debate before his removal to the Council of State in Nov. 77. From thence he went to Congress, then consisting of few members. Trained in these successive schools, he acquired a habit of self-possession which placed at ready command the rich resources of his luminous and discriminating mind, & of his extensive information, and rendered him the first of every assembly afterwards of which he became a member. Never wandering from his subject into vain declamation, but pursuing it closely in language pure, classical, and copious, soothing always the feelings of his adversaries by civilities and softness of expression, he rose to the eminent station which he held in the great National convention of 1787, and in that of Virginia which followed, he sustained the new constitution in all its parts, bearing off the palm against the logic of George Mason, and the fervid declamation of Mr. Henry. With these consummate powers were united a pure and spotless virtue which no calumny has ever attempted to sully. Of the powers and polish of his pen, and of the wisdom of his administration in the highest office of the nation, I need say nothing. They have spoken, and will forever speak for themselves.

John Marshall

*To James Madison, Philadelphia,
June 29, 1792*

I learn that he [i.e., Alexander Hamilton] has expressed the strongest desire that Marshall should come into Congress from Richmond, declaring there is no man in Virginia whom he so much wishes to see there, and I am told that Marshall has expressed half a mind to come. Hence I conclude that Hamilton has plied him well with flattery and solicitation, and I think nothing better could be done than to make him a judge.

To James Madison, Monticello,
November 26, 1795

Though Marshall will be able to embarrass the Republican party in the assembly a good deal, yet upon the whole, his having gone into it will be of service. He has been hitherto able to do more mischief, acting under the mask of republicanism than he will be able to do after throwing it plainly off. His lax lounging manners have made him popular with the bulk of the people of Richmond, and a profound hypocrisy with many thinking men in our country.

To Albert Gallatin, Monticello,
September 27, 1810

The Judge's inveteracy is profound, and his mind of that gloomy malignity which will never let him forego the opportunity of satiating it on a victim. His decisions, his instructions to a jury, his allowances & disallowances & garblings of evidence, must all be subjects of appeal.

To William Johnson, Monticello,
June 12, 1823

This practice of Judge Marshall of traveling out of his case to prescribe what the law would be in a moot case not before the court, is very irregular and very censurable.

George Mason

Autobiography, 1821

In giving an account of the laws of which I was my-self the mover & draftsman, I by no means mean to claim to myself the merit of obtaining their passage. I had many occasional and strenuous coadjutors in debate, and one most steadfast, able, and zealous; who was himself a host. This was George Mason, a man of the first order of wisdom among those who acted on the theatre of the Revolution, of expansive mind, profound judgment, cogent in argument, learned in the lore of our former constitution, and earnest for the republican change on democratic principles. His elocution was neither flowing nor smooth, but his language was strong, his manner most impressive, and strengthened by a dash of bit-ing cynicism when provocation made it seasonable.

John Francis Mercer

To James Madison, Annapolis,
April 25, 1784

Mercer is acting a very extraordinary part. He is a candidate for the secretaryship of foreign affairs and tho' he will not get the vote of one state, I believe he expects the appointment. . . . Vanity & ambition seem to be the ruling passions of this young man and as his objects are impure so also are his means. Intrigue is a principal one on particular occasions as party attachment is in the general. He takes now about one half of the time of Congress to himself, & in conjunction with [Jacob] Read and Spaight obstruct business inconceivably.

Autobiography, 1821

My colleague Mercer was one of those afflicted with the morbid rage of debate. Of an ardent mind, prompt imagination, and copious flow of words, he heard with impatience any logic which was not his own.

James Monroe

To James Madison, Annapolis, May 8, 1784

I think Colonel Monroe will be of the Committee of the states. He wishes a correspondence with you; and I suppose his situation will render him an useful one to you. The scrupulousness of his honor will make you safe in the most confidential communications. A better man there cannot be.

To William Temple Franklin, Paris, May 7, 1786

You have formed a just opinion of Monroe. He is a man whose soul might be turned wrong side outwards without discovering a blemish to the world.

To Philip Mazzei, Monticello,
April 24, 1796

Colo. Monroe is our M.P. [minister plenipotentiary]
at Paris a most worthy patriot & honest man.

To William Duane, Monticello,
October 1, 1812

I clearly think with you on the competence of Monroe to embrace great views of action. The decision of
his character, his enterprise, firmness, industry, &
unceasing vigilance, would, I believe, secure, as I am
sure it would merit, the public confidence, and give
us all the success which our means can accomplish.

Gouverneur Morris

To Maria Cosway, Paris, July 25, 1789

Receive then into your peace and grace the bearer
hereof Mr. Morris, a countryman and friend of mine
of great consideration in his own country, and who
deserves to be so everywhere. Peculiarly gifted with
fancy and judgment, he will be qualified to taste the
beauties of your canvas.

The Anas, 1792

The fact is, that Gouverneur Morris, a high flying
monarchy-man, shutting his eyes & his faith to every
fact against his wishes, & believing everything he

desires to be true, has kept the President's [i.e. Washington's] mind constantly poisoned with his forebodings [respecting the French Revolution].

Thomas Paine

To Francis Eppes, Monticello,
January 19, 1821

You ask my opinion of Lord Bolingbroke and Thomas Paine. They were alike in making bitter enemies of the priests & Pharisees of their day. Both were honest men; both advocates for human liberty. Paine wrote for a country which permitted him to push his reasoning to whatever length it would go. . . . These two persons differed remarkably in the style of their writing, each leaving a model of what is most perfect in both extremes of the simple and the sublime. No writer has exceeded Paine in ease and familiarity of style, in perspicuity of expression, happiness of elucidation, and in simple and unassuming language. In this he may be compared with Dr. Franklin; and indeed his Common Sense was, for awhile, believed to have been written by Dr. Franklin, and published under the borrowed name of Paine, who had come over with him from England.

To John Cartwright, Monticello,
June 5, 1824

Paine . . . thought more than he read.

Edmund Pendleton

Autobiography, 1821

Mr. Pendleton, . . . who, taken all in all, was the ablest man in debate I have ever met with. He had not indeed the poetical fancy of Mr. Henry, his sublime imagination, his lofty and overwhelming diction; but he was cool, smooth and persuasive; his language flowing, chaste & embellished, his conceptions quick, acute and full of resource; never vanquished; for if he lost the main battle, he returned upon you, and regained so much of it as to make it a drawn one, by dexterous maneuvers, skirmishes in detail, and the recovery of small advantages which, little singly, were important altogether. You never knew when you were clear of him, but were harassed by his perseverance until the patience was worn down of all who had less of it than himself. Add to this that he was one of the most virtuous & benevolent of men, the kindest friend, the most amiable & pleasant of companions, which ensured a favorable reception to whatever came from him.

Timothy Pickering

To Martin Van Buren, Monticello,
June 29, 1824

I could not have believed that, for as many years, and to such a period of advanced age, he could have nourished passions so vehement and viperous. It appears that, for 30 years past, he has been industriously collecting materials for vituperating the characters he had marked for his hatred; some of whom, certainly, if enmities towards him had ever existed, had forgotten them all, or buried them in the grave with themselves. As to myself, there never had been any thing personal between us, nothing but the general opposition of party sentiment; and our personal intercourse had been that of urbanity, as himself says. But it seems he has been all this time brooding over an enmity which I had never felt, and yet that with respect to myself, as well as others, he has been writing far and near, and in every direction, to get hold of original letters, where he could, copies where he could not, certificates and journals, catching at every gossiping story he could hear of in any quarter, supplying by suspicions what he could find no where else, and then arguing on this motley farrago as if established on gospel evidence. . . .

He arraigns me on two grounds, my actions and my motives. The very actions however which he arraigns have been such as the great majority of my fellow citizens have approved. The approbation of Mr. Pickering, and of those who thought with him, I had no right to expect. My motives he chooses to ascribe to hypocrisy; to ambition, and a passion for popularity. Of these the world must judge between us. It is no office of his or mine. To that tribunal I have ever submitted my actions and motives, without ransacking the union for certificates, letters, journals and gossiping tales to justify myself and weary them. . . . I leave to its fate the libel of Mr. Pickering, with the thousands of others like it, to which I have given no other answer than a steady course of similar action.

Edmund Randolph

Record of conversation with President Washington,
August 6, 1793

I asked him [Washington] whether some person could not take my office par interim, till he should make an appointment? as Mr. Randolph for instance. Yes, says he, but there you would raise the expectation of keeping it, and I do not know that he is fit for it nor what is thought of Mr. Randolph. I avoided noticing the last observation, & he put the question to me directly. I then told him that I went into society so little as to be unable to answer it: I knew that the embarrassments in his private affairs had obliged him to use expedients which had injured him with the merchants & shop-keepers & affected his character of independence; that these embarrassments were serious, & not likely to cease soon.

To James Madison, Philadelphia,
August 11, 1793

I can by this confidential conveyance speak more freely of R. He is the poorest Cameleon I ever saw having no color of his own, & reflecting that nearest him. When he is with me he is a whig, when with H. [Alexander Hamilton] he is a tory, when with the P. [President Washington] he is what he thinks will please him. The last is his strongest hue, tho' the 2nd tinges him very strongly. The first is what I think he would prefer in his heart if he were in the woods where he could see nobody, or in a society of *all whigs.* . . . It is not the less true that his opinion always makes the majority [in the Cabinet], & that the President acquiesces *always* in the majority; consequently that the government is now solely directed by him. As he is not yet openly thrown off by the whig party, it gives to the public a false security that fair play is given to the whiggism of the Pr[esident] by an equal division of whig & tory among his counselors. I have kept on terms of strict friendship with him hitherto, that I might make some good out of him, & because he has really some good private qualities. But he is in a station infinitely too important for his understanding, his firmness, or his circumstances.

To William Branch Giles, Monticello,
December 31, 1795

Tho he mistakes his own political character in the aggregate, yet he gives it to you in the detail. Thus, he supposes himself a man of no party, that his opinions not containing any systematic adherence to party, fall sometimes on one side and sometimes on the other. . . . Whether his conduct is to be ascribed to a superior view of things, an adherence to right without regard to party, as he pretends, or to an anxiety to trim between both, those who know his character & capacity will decide.

To James Monroe, March 2, 1796

The resignation or rather removal of R. you will have learnt. His vindication bears hard on the executive in the opinions of this quarter, and tho' it clears him in their judgment of the charge of bribery, it does not give them high ideas of his wisdom or steadiness.

To Philip Mazzei, Monticello, April 24, 1796

E.R. is bankrupt, or tantamount to it.

David Rittenhouse

*To David Rittenhouse, Monticello,
July 19, 1778*

Writing to a philosopher, I may hope to be pardoned for intruding some thoughts of my own tho' they relate to him personally. Your time for two years past has I believe been principally employed in the civil government of your country. . . . I doubt not there are in your country many persons equal to the task of conducting government: but you should consider that the world has but one Rittenhouse, & that it never had one before. The amazing mechanical representation

of the solar system which you conceived & executed, has never been surpassed by any but the work
of which it is a copy. Are those powers then, which
being intended for the erudition of the world are,
like air & light, the world's common property, to be
taken from their proper pursuit to do the common-
place drudgery of governing a single state, a work
which may be executed by men of an ordinary
stature, such as are always & every where to be
found?

Notes on the State of Virginia, 1782

We have supposed Mr. Rittenhouse second to no astronomer living: that in genius he must be the first,
because he is self-taught. As an artist he has exhibited as great a proof of mechanical genius as the
world has ever produced. He has not indeed made a
world; but he has by imitation approached nearer
its Maker than any man who has lived from creation
to this day.

Benjamin Rush

To John Adams, Monticello, May 27, 1813

Another of our friends of 76 is gone, my dear Sir,
another of the Co-signers of the independence of
our country. And a better man, than Rush, could not
have left us, more benevolent, more learned, of finer
genius, or more honest.

To Richard Rush, Monticello, May 31, 1813

No one has taken a more sincere part than myself in the affliction which has lately befallen your family, by the loss of your inestimable and ever to be lamented father. His virtues rendered him dear to all who knew him, and his benevolence led him to do to all men every good in his power. Much he was able to do, and much therefore will be missed. My acquaintance with him began in 1776. It soon became intimate, and from that time a warm friendship has been maintained by a correspondence of unreserved confidence.

To Joseph Delaplaine, Monticello, May 3, 1814

I thank you for the print of Dr. Rush. He was one of my early & intimate friends, and among the best of men.

John Trumbull

To Ezra Stiles, Paris, September 1, 1786

Another countryman of yours, Mr. Trumbull, has paid us a visit here, & brought with him two pictures which are the admiration of the Connoisseurs. His natural talents for this art seem almost unparalleled.

To John Trumbull, Paris, June 18, 1789

I think you undervalue too much your art, which is a most noble one when possessed so eminently as it is by you. I fear much that our country is not yet rich enough to encourage you as you deserve.

George Washington

To Benjamin Harrison, Philadelphia,
November 11, 1783

I had the happiness of seeing Genl. Washington the other day after an interval of 7 years. He has more health in his countenance than I ever saw in it before.

To George Washington, Annapolis,
April 16, 1784

The moderation & virtue of a single character has probably prevented this revolution from being closed as most others have been by a subversion of that liberty it was intended to establish; that he is not immortal, & his successor or some of his successors be led by false calculation into a less certain road to glory.

To William Short, Philadelphia, March 16, 1791

To overdo a thing with him is to undo it.

To William Branch Giles, Monticello,
December 31, 1795

[The President] errs as other men do, but errs with integrity.

To Archibald Stuart, Monticello,
January 4, 1797

In answer to your favor of Dec. 31 & to the question whether advisable to address the P[resident] on the subject of war against France, I shall speak explicitly because I know I may do it safely to you. Such is the popularity of the President that the people will support him in whatever he will do or will not do, without appealing to their own reason or to any thing but their feelings towards him: his mind had been so long used to unlimited applause that it could not brook contradiction, or even advice offered without asking. To advice, when asked, he is very open. I have long thought therefore it was best for the republican interest to soothe him by flattery where they could approve his measures, & to be silent, where they disapprove, that they may not render him desperate as to their affection; & and entirely indifferent to their wishes; in short to lie on their oars while he remains at the helm, & let the bark drift at his will & a superintending providence shall direct.

To the Earl of Buchan, Washington,
July 10, 1803

I feel a pride in the justice which your lordship's sentiments render to the character of my illustrious countryman, Washington. The moderation of his desires, & the strength of his judgment, enabled him to calculate correctly, that the road to that glory which never dies is to use power for the support of the laws & liberties of our country, not for their destruction; & his will accordingly survives the wreck of every thing now living.

To Walter Jones, Monticello, January 2, 1814

I think I knew General Washington intimately and thoroughly; and were I called on to delineate his character it should be in terms like these.

His mind was great and powerful, without being of the very first order; his penetration strong, tho' not so acute as that of a Newton, Bacon or Locke; and as far as he saw, no judgment was ever sounder. It was slow in operation, being little aided by invention or imagination, but sure in conclusion. . . . He was incapable of fear, meeting personal dangers with the calmest unconcern. Perhaps the strongest feature in his character was prudence, never acting until every circumstance, every consideration was maturely weighed; refraining if he saw a doubt, but, when once decided, going through with his purpose whatever obstacles opposed. His integrity was most pure, his justice the most inflexible I have ever known, no motives of interest or consanguinity, of friendship or hatred, being able to bias his decision. He was, indeed, in every sense of the words, a wise, a good, & a great man. His temper was naturally irritable and high toned; but reflection & resolution had obtained a firm and habitual ascendancy over it. If ever however it broke its bonds he was most tremendous in his wrath. In his expenses he was honorable, but exact; liberal in contributions to whatever promised utility; but frowning and unyielding on all visionary projects and all unworthy calls on his charity. His heart was not warm in its affections; but he exactly calculated every man's value, and gave him a solid esteem proportioned to it. His person, you know, was fine, his stature exactly what one would wish, his deportment easy, erect and noble; the best horseman of his age, and the most graceful figure that could be seen on horseback. Altho' in the circle of his friends, where he might be unreserved with safety, he took a free share in conversation, his colloquial talents were not above mediocrity, possessing neither copiousness of ideas, nor fluency of words. In public, when called on for a sudden opinion, he was unready, short and embarrassed. Yet he wrote readily, rather diffusely, in an easy & correct style. This he had acquired by conversation with the world, for his education was merely reading, writing and common arithematic, to which he added surveying at a later day. His time was employed in action chiefly, reading little, and that only in Agriculture and English history. His correspondence became necessarily extensive, and with journalizing his agricultural proceedings, occupied most of his leisure hours within doors. On the whole, his character was, in its mass, perfect, in nothing bad, in few points indifferent; and it may truly be said that never did nature and fortune combine more perfectly to make a man great, and to place him in the same constellation with whatever worthies have merited from man an everlasting remembrance. . . . For his was the singular destiny and merit of leading the armies of his country successfully thro' an arduous war, for the establishment of its independence, of conducting its councils thro' the birth of a government, new in its forms & principles, until it had settled down into a quiet and orderly train; and of scrupulously obeying the laws through the whole of his career, civil and military, of which the history of the world furnishes no other example.

. . . He was no monarchist from preference of his judgment. The soundness of that gave him correct views of the rights of man, and his severe justice devoted him to them. He has often declared to me that he considered our new constitution as an experiment on the practicability of republican government, and with what dose of liberty man could be trusted for his own good; that he was determined the experiment should have a fair trial, and would lose the last drop of his blood in support of it.

. . . I felt on his death, with my countrymen, that "verily a great man hath fallen this day in Israel."

George Wythe

To Peter Carr, Paris, August 10, 1787

I have received your two letters . . . and am happy to find by them, as well as by letters from Mr. Wythe, that you have been so fortunate as to attract his notice

& good will: I am sure you will find this to have been one of the most fortunate events of your life, as I have ever been sensible it was of mine.

To John Saunderson, August 31, 1820

George Wythe was born about the year 1727 or 1728, of a respectable family in the county of Elizabeth city on the shores of the Chesapeake. He inherited from his father a fortune sufficient for independence & ease. He had not the benefit of a regular education in the schools, but acquired a good one of himself, and without assistance; insomuch, as to become the best Latin and Greek scholar in the state. It is said that while reading the Greek Testament, his mother held an English one to aid him in rendering the Greek text conformably with that. He also acquired by his own reading a good knowledge of Mathematics, of natural and moral philosophy. He engaged in the study of the law under the direction of a Mr. Lewis of that profession, and went early to the bar of the General Court, then occupied by men of great ability, learning, & dignity in their profession. He soon became eminent among them, and, in the process of time, the first at the bar, taking into consideration his superior learning, correct elocution, and logical style of reasoning; for in pleading he never indulged himself with an useless or declamatory thought or word; and became as distinguished by correctness and purity of conduct in his profession, as he was by his industry & fidelity to those who employed him. He was early elected to the House of Representatives, then called the House of Burgesses, and continued in it until the revolution. On the first dawn of that, instead of higgling on half way principles, as others did who feared to follow their reason, he took his stand on the solid ground that the only link of political union between us and Great Britain was the identity of our Executive; that that nation and its parliament had no more authority over us than we had over them, and that we were co-ordinate nations with Great Britain and Hanover. . . .

No man ever left behind him a character more venerated than G. Wythe. His virtue was of the purest tint; his integrity inflexible, and his justice exact; of warm patriotism, and, devoted as he was to liberty, and the natural and equal rights of man, he might truly be called the Cato of his country, without the avarice of the Roman; for a more disinterested person never lived. Temperance and regularity in all his habits gave him general good health, and his unaffected modesty and suavity of manners endeared him to every one. He was of easy elocution, his language chaste, methodical in the arrangement of his matter, learned and logical in the use of it, and of great urbanity in debate; not quick of apprehension, but, with a little time, profound in penetration, and sound in conclusion. In his philosophy he was firm, and neither troubling, nor perhaps trusting, any one with his religious creed, he left to the world to the conclusion, that that religion must be good which could produce a life of such exemplary virtue.

His stature was of the middle size, well formed and proportioned, and the features of his face were manly, comely, and engaging. Such was George Wythe, the honor of his own, and model of future times.

Thomas Jefferson Described by His Contemporaries

John Adams, Diary, October 25, 1775

[James] Duane says that Jefferson is the greatest Rubber off of Dust that he has met with, that he has learned French, Italian, Spanish and wants to learn German.

John Adams, Autobiography, 1776
(written in 1802)

Mr. Jefferson had been now about a Year a Member of Congress, but had attended his Duty in the house but a very small part of the time and when there had never spoken in public: and during the whole Time I sat with him in Congress, I never heard him utter three Sentences together. The most of a Speech he ever made in my hearing was a gross insult on Religion, in one or two Sentences, for which I gave him immediately the Reprehension, which he richly merited. It will naturally be inquired, how it happened that he was appointed on a Committee of such importance. There were more reasons than one. Mr. Jefferson had the Reputation of a masterly Pen. He had been chosen a Delegate in Virginia, in consequence of a very handsome public Paper which he had written for the house of Burgesses, which had given him the Character of a fine Writer. Another reason was that Mr. Richard Henry Lee was not beloved by the most of his Colleagues, from Virginia, and Mr. Jefferson was set up to rival and supplant him. This could be done only by the Pen, for Mr. Jefferson could stand no competition with him or any one else in Elocution and public debate. . . . The Committee had several meetings, in which were proposed the Articles of which the declaration was to consist, and minutes made of them. The Committee then appointed Mr. Jefferson and me, to draw them up in form, and clothe them in a proper Dress. The Sub Committee met, and considered the Minutes, making such Observations on them as then occurred; when Mr. Jefferson desired me to take them to my Lodgings and make the Draft. This I declined and gave several reasons for declining. 1. That he was a Virginian and I a Massachusettsian. 2. that he was a southern Man and I a northern one. 3. That I had been so obnoxious for my early and constant Zeal in promoting the Measure, that any draft of mine, would undergo a more severe Scrutiny and Criticism in Congress, than one of his composition. 4thly and lastly and that would be reason enough if there were no other, I had a great Opinion of the Elegance of his pen and none at all of my own. I therefore insisted that no hesitation should be made on his part. He accordingly took the Minutes and in a day or two produced to me his Draft. Whether I made or suggested any corrections I remember not. The Report was made to the Committee of five, by them examined, but whether altered or corrected in any thing I cannot recollect. But in substance at least it was reported to Congress where, after a severe Criticism, and striking out several of the most oratorical Paragraphs it was adopted on the fourth of July 1776, and published to the World.

Jacob Rubsamen to Unknown, December 1, 1780

The Governor [i.e., Jefferson] possesses a Noble Spirit of Building, he is now finishing an elegant building projected according to his own fancy. In his parlor he is creating on the Ceiling a Compass of his own invention by which he can Know the strength as well as Direction of the Winds. I have promised to paint the Compass for it. . . . As all Virginians are fond of Music, he is particularly so. You will find in his House an Elegant Harpsichord Piano forte and some Violins. The latter he performs well upon himself, the former his Lady touches very skillfully and who, is in all Respects a very agreeable Sensible and Accomplished Lady.

The Marquis de Chastellux, Travels in North-America, in the Years 1780, 1781, and 1782

Let me describe to you a man, not yet forty, tall, and with a mild and pleasing countenance, but whose mind and understanding are ample substitutes for every exterior grace. An American, who without ever having quitted his own country, is at once a musician, skilled in drawing; a geometrician, an astronomer, a natural philosopher, legislator, and statesman. A senator of America, who sat for two years in that famous

Congress which brought about the revolution; and which is never mentioned without respect, though unhappily not without regret: a governor of Virginia, who filled this difficult station during the invasions of Arnold, of Philips, and of Cornwallis; a philosopher, in voluntary retirement, from the world, and public business, because he loves them, inasmuch only as he can flatter himself with being useful to mankind; and the minds of his countrymen are not yet in a condition either to bear the light, or to suffer contradiction. A mild and amiable wife, charming children, of whose education he himself takes charge, a house to embellish, great provisions to improve, and the arts and sciences to cultivate; these are what remain to Mr. Jefferson, after having played a principal character on the theater of the new world, and which he preferred to the honorable commission of Minister Plenipotentiary in Europe. The visit which I made him was not unexpected, for he had long since invited me to come and pass a few days with him, in the center of the mountains; notwithstanding which I found his first appearance serious, nay even cold; but before I had been two hours with him we were as intimate as if we had passed our whole lives together; walking, books, but above all, a conversation always varied and interesting, always supported by that sweet satisfaction experienced by two persons, who in communicating their sentiments and opinions, are invariably in unison, and who understand each other at the first hint, made four days pass away like so many minutes.

*Edmund Randolph to James Madison, Richmond,
September 20, 1782*

Mrs. Jefferson has at last shaken off her tormenting pains by yielding to them,* and has left our friend inconsolable. I ever thought him to rank domestic happiness in the first class of the chief good; but I scarcely supposed, that his grief would be so violent, as to justify the circulating report, of his swooning away, whenever he sees his children.

        *Martha Jefferson died on September 6, 1782.

*James Madison to Edmund Randolph,
September 30, 1782*

I conceive very readily the affliction & anguish which our friend at Monticello must experience at his irreparable loss. But his philosophical temper renders the circulating rumor which you mention altogether incredible. Perhaps this domestic catastrophe may prove in its operation beneficial to his country by weaning him from those attachments which deprived it of his services. The vacancy occasioned by his refusal of a particular service,* you need not be informed, still subsists. As soon as his sensibility will bear a subject of such a nature, will you undertake to obtain his sentiments thereupon, and let me know whether or not his aversion is still insuperable?

        *as a peace commissioner

François Barbé de Marbois to Joseph-Matthais
Gérard de Rayneval, Philadelphia,
August 24, 1784

Mr. Jefferson is an upright, just man, who belongs to no party, and his representations will have the greatest weight on the general Congress.

Abigail Adams to Cotton Tufts, March 8, 1785

Mr. Adams's Colleague Mr. Jefferson is an Excellent Man. Worthy of his station and will do honor to his Country.

John Adams to Richard Cranch, Auteuil, France,
April 27, 1785

I shall part with Mr. Jefferson, with great Regret, but as he will no doubt be placed at Versailles, I shall be happy in a Correspondence of Friendship, Confidence and Affection with the Minister at this Court, which is a very fortunate Circumstance, both for me, and the public.

John Quincy Adams, Diary, May 4, 1785

He is a man of great Judgment.

Abigail Adams to Mary Smith Cranch, May 8, 1785

I shall really regret to leave Mr. Jefferson, he is one of the choice ones of the Earth.

Abigail Adams to Thomas Jefferson, London,
June 6, 1785

Mr. Adams has already written you that we arrived
in London upon the 27 of May. We journey'd slowly
and sometimes silently. I think I have somewhere
met with the observation that nobody ever leaves
Paris but with a degree of tristness. I own I was
loath to leave my garden because I did not expect to
find its place supplied. I was still more loath on account of the increasing pleasure, and intimacy which
a longer acquaintance with a respected Friend promised, to leave behind me the only person with whom
my Companion could associate with perfect freedom,
and unreserve: and whose place he had no reason to
expect supplied in the Land to which he is destined.

Abigail Adams to Mary Smith Cranch, London,
October 1, 1785

In Mr. Jefferson he [i.e., Adams] has a firm and faithful Friend, with whom he can consult and advise, and
as each of them have no object but the good of their
Country in view, they have an unlimited confidence in
each other, and they have only to lament that the
Channel divides their more frequent intercourse.

The Marquis de Lafayette to James McHenry, Paris,
December 3, 1785

No better minister could be sent to France. He is
everything that is good, upright, enlightened, and

clever, and is respected and beloved by everyone that knows him.

John Adams to Henry Knox, London,
December 15, 1785

You can Scarcely have heard a Character too high of my Friend and Colleague Mr. Jefferson, either in point of Power or Virtues. My Fellow Laborer in Congress, eight or nine years ago, upon many arduous Trials, particularly in the draft of our Declaration of Independence and in the formation of our Code of Articles of War, and Laws for the Army. I have found him uniformly the same wise and prudent Man and Steady Patriot. I only fear that his unquenchable Thirst for knowledge may injure his Health.

The Marquis de Lafayette to George Washington,
Paris, February 6, 1786

Words cannot sufficiently express to you how much I am pleased with Mr. Jefferson's public conduct— He unites every ability that can recommend him with the ministers, and at the time possesses accomplishments of the mind and the heart which cannot but give him many friends.

Lucy Ludwell Paradise to Thomas Jefferson,
London, May 5, 1786

[Refers to Jefferson as] the First Character in Our State, and I shall add, the First in the Continent of North America.

*The Marquis de Lafayette to
George Washington, Paris,
October 26, 1786*

Mr. Jefferson is a Most able and Respected Representative, and Such a Man as Makes me Happy to Be His Aid de Camp—Congress Have Made a choice Very favorable to their affairs.

*Alexander Donald to
Thomas Jefferson, Richmond,
November 12, 1787*

Your old school Companion W[arner] Lewis, of Warner Hall was here staying with me when I had the pleasure of receiving your letter. It was so Friendly, and so very Flattering to my Pride, that I could not resist the vanity of showing it to him. He added to my Pride, by declaring (what I was pretty much convinced of before) that of all the Men he ever knew in his Life, he believed you to be the most sincere in your profession of Friendship. I am free to say, that when we used to pass some jovial days together at Hanover Town, I did not then imagine, that at this time you would be in Paris, Ambassador to the Court of Versailles. Some People in your High Character would be very apt to forget their old acquaintance, but you are not, and I must be allowed to do myself the justice to declare, I never entertained an Idea that you would.

The Marquis de Lafayette to George Washington,
Paris, January 1, 1788

I am More and More pleased with Mr. Jefferson.
His abilities, His Virtues, His temper, Every thing
of Him Commands Respect and Attracts Affection.
He Enjoys Universal Regard, and does the Affairs
of America to perfection. It is the Happiest choice
that Could Be Made.

Gouverneur Morris to Robert Morris, Paris,
July 21, 1789

An American Minster at this Court gains more than
he looses by preserving his Originality—for the
Rest, Mr. Jefferson lives well keeps a good Table
and excellent Wines which he distributes freely and
by his Hospitality to his Countrymen here possesses
very much their good Will.

Edmund Randolph, History of Virginia,
post-1810

As yet Thomas Jefferson had not attained a marked
grade in politics. Until about the age of twenty-five
years he had pursued general science, with which he
mingled the law, as a profession, with an eager industry and unabated thirst. His manners could never
be harsh, but they were reserved toward the world
at large. To his intimate friends he showed a peculiar sweetness of temper and by them was admired
and beloved. In mathematics and experimental

philosophy, he was a proficient, assiduously taught by Dr. Small of William and Mary College, whose name was not concealed among the literati of Europe. He panted after the fine arts and discovered a taste in them not easily satisfied with such scanty means as existed in a colony whose chief ambition looked to the general system of education in England as the ultimate point of excellence. But it constituted a part of Mr. Jefferson's pride to run before the times in which he lived. Prudent himself, he did not waste his resources in gratifications to which they were incompetent, but being an admirer of elegance and convenience, and venerated by his contemporaries who were within the scope of his example, he diffused a style of living much more refined than that which had been handed down to them by his and their ancestors. He had been ambitious to collect a library, not merely amassing NUMBERS of books, but distinguishing authors of merit and assembling them in subordination to every art and science; and notwithstanding losses by fire, this library was at this time more happily calculated than any other private one to direct to objects of utility and taste, to present to genius the scaffolding upon which its future eminence might be built, and to reprove the restless appetite, which is too apt to seize the mere gatherer of books.

The theories of human rights he had drawn from Locke, Harrington, Sidney, English history, and Montesquieu he had maturely investigated in all their aspects, and was versed in the republican doctrines and effusions which conducted the first Charles to the scaffold. With this fund of knowledge, he was ripe for stronger measures than the public voice was conceived to demand. But he had not gained a sufficient ascendancy to quicken or retard the progress of the popular current.

Indefatigable and methodical in whatever he undertook, he spoke with ease, perspicuity, and elegance. His style in writing was more impassioned, and although often incorrect, was too glowing not to be acquitted as venial to departures from rigid rules. Without being an overwhelming orator, he was an impressive speaker, who fixed the attention. On two signal arguments before the General Court, in which Mr. Henry and himself were coadjutors, each characterized himself—Mr. Jefferson drew copiously from the depths of the law. Mr. Henry from the recesses of the human heart.

When Mr. Jefferson first attracted notice, Christianity was directly denied in Virginia only by a few. He was adept, however, in the ensnaring subtleties of deism and gave it, among the rising generation, a philosophical patronage, which repudiates as falsehoods things unsusceptible of strict demonstration. It is believed that while such tenets as are in contempt of the Gospel inevitably terminate in espousing the fullest latitude in religious freedom, Mr. Jefferson's love of liberty would itself have produced the same effects. But his opinions against restraints on conscience ingratiated him with the enemies of the establishment, who did not stop to inquire how far those opinions might border on skepticism or infidelity. Parties in religion and politics rarely scan with nicety the peculiar private opinions of their adherents.

When he entered upon the practice of the law, he chose a residence, and traveled to a distance, which enabled him to display his great literary endowments and to establish advantageous connections among those classes of men who were daily rising in weight.

Nathaniel Cutting, Diary, Cowes, England,
October 12, 1789

I have found Mr. Jefferson a man of infinite information and sound Judgment, becoming gravity, and engaging affability mark his deportment. His general abilities are such as would do honor to any age or Country.

Benjamin Rush, Commonplace Book,
March 17, 1790

Visited Mr. Jefferson on his way to New York. It was the first time I saw him since his return from France. He was plain in his dress and unchanged in his manners. He still professed himself attached to republican forms of government, and deplored the change of opinion upon this subject in John Adams, of whom he spoke with respect and affection as a great and upright man.

Abigail Adams to Mary Cranch, New York,
April 3, 1790

Mr. Jefferson is here, and adds much to the social
circle.

James Madison to Edmund Randolph, New York,
May 6, 1790

Mr. Jefferson has been laid up near a week with his
periodical head-Ache which has been very severe.

William Maclay, Journal, *May 24, 1790*

Jefferson is a slender Man. Has rather the Air of
Stiffness in his Manner. His clothes seem too small
for him. He sits in a lounging Manner on One hip,
commonly, and with one of his shoulders elevated
much above the other. His face has a scrawny aspect.
His Whole figure has a loose shackling Air. He had a
rambling Vacant look & nothing of that firm collected
deportment which I expected would dignify the presence of a Secretary or Minister. I looked for gravity,
but a laxity of Manner, seemed shed about him. He
spoke almost without ceasing. But even his discourse
partook of his personal demeanor. It was lax & rambling and Yet he scattered information wherever he
went, and some even brilliant sentiments sparkled
from him. The information which he gave Us respecting foreign Ministers &ca. was all high Spiced.
He has been long enough abroad to catch the tone of
European folly. He gave Us a sentiment which seemed

to Savor rather of quaintness. "It is better to take the highest of the lowest, than the lowest of the highest." Translation. It is better to appoint a chargé des affaires with an handsome Salary, than a Minister Plenipotentiary with a small One. He took leave, and the Committee agreed to strike out, the Specific Sum to be given to any foreign appointment, leaving it to the President to account, and appropriated $30,000 generally for the purpose.

Benjamin Rush, Sketches

He possessed a genius of the first order. It was universal in its objects. He was not less distinguished for his political, than his mathematical and philosophical knowledge. The objects of his benevolence were as extensive as those of his knowledge. He was not only the friend of his country, but of all nations and religions. While Congress were deliberating upon the measure of sending commissioners to France I asked him what he thought of being one of them. He said "he would go to hell to serve his country." He was afterwards elected a commissioner, but declined at that time on account of the sickness of his wife. He seldom spoke in Congress, but was a member of all the important committees. He was the penman of the Declaration of Independence. He once showed me the original in his own hand writing. It contained a noble testimony against negro slavery which was struck out in its passage through Congress. He took notes of all the debates upon the

Declaration of Independence, and the first Confederation. He was said, at the time alluded to, to be unfriendly to Christianity. It is possible this may be true. His notes contain some expressions which favour that opinion. In my conversation with him in Philadelphia while he was Vice President he denied the charge, and said he believed in the divine mission of the Saviour of the World, but he did not believe that he was the Son of God in the way in which many Christians believed it. He said he believed further in the divine institution of the Sabbath, which he conceived to be a great blessing to the world, more especially to poor people and slaves. He believed likewise in the resurrection, and a future state of rewards and punishments.

Ezra Stiles to Thomas Jefferson, Yale College,
August 27, 1790

I am rejoiced that the United States are honored with your Counsels and Abilities in the high Department of the Secretary of State. This I say without Adulation, who am a Spectator only and a most cordial Friend to the Liberties and Glory of the American Republic, though without the least Efficiency or Influence in its Councils. There are four Characters which I cannot flatter; their Merit is above it. Such are those of a Franklin, an Adams, an Ellsworth, a Jefferson and a Washington. I glory in them all; I rejoice that my Country is happy in their useful Labors. And for yourself I can only wish, that when that best of Men, the present President [George Washington], shall be translated to the World of Light, a Jefferson may succeed him in the Presidency of the United States. Forgive me this Effusion of the Sentiments of sincere Respect and Estimation.

Oliver Wolcott, Jr. to Oliver Wolcott, Sr.,
Philadelphia, February 14, 1792

Mr. J. appears to have shown rather too much of a disposition to cultivate vulgar prejudice; accordingly he will become popular in ale houses, and will do much mischief to his country by exciting apprehensions that the government will operate unfavorably.

Alexander Hamilton to Edward Carrington,
Philadelphia, May 26, 1792

If I were disposed to promote Monarchy & overthrow State Governments, I would mount the hobby horse of popularity—I would cry out usurpation—danger to liberty &c. &c.—I would endeavor to prostrate the National Government—raise a ferment—and then "ride in the Whirlwind and direct the Storm." That there are men acting with Jefferson & Madison who have this in view I verily believe. I could lay my finger on some of them. That Madison does not mean it I also verily believe, and I rather believe the same of Jefferson; but I read him upon the whole thus—"A man of profound ambition & violent passions."

"Catullus" No. III (Alexander Hamilton),
Gazette of the United States,
September 29, 1792

Mr. Jefferson has hitherto been distinguished as the quiet modest, retiring philosopher—as the plain simple unambitious republican. He shall not now for the first time be regarded as the intriguing incendiary— the aspiring turbulent competitor.

How long it is since that gentleman's real character may have divined, or whether this is only the first time that the secret has been disclosed, I am not sufficiently acquainted with the history of his political life to determine; But there is always "a first time," when characters studious of artful disguises are unveiled; When the visor of stoicism is plucked from the brow of the Epicurean; when the plain garb of Quaker simplicity is stripped from the concealed voluptuary; when Caesar coyly refusing the proffered diadem, is seen to be Caesar rejecting the trappings, but tenaciously grasping the substance of imperial domination.

Alexander Hamilton to Charles Cotesworth
Pinckney, Philadelphia, October 10, 1792

[It would be unfortunate if Jefferson would defeat Adams as Vice President.] That Gentleman [Jefferson] whom I once very much esteemed, but who does not permit me to retain that sentiment for him, is certainly a man of sublimated and paradoxical imagination—entertaining & propagating notions inconsistent with dignified and orderly Government.

Alexander Hamilton to John Steele, Philadelphia, October 15, 1792

There was a time when I should have balanced between Mr. Jefferson & Mr. Adams; but I now view the former as a man of sublimated & paradoxical imagination—cherishing notions incompatible with regular and firm government.

Benjamin Rush, Commonplace Book, 1793

The whole of Mr. Jefferson's conversation on all subjects is instructing. He is wise without formality, and maintains a consequence without pomp or distance.

James Madison to James Monroe, Orange, Va., September 29, 1796

His enemies are as indefatigable as they are malignant.

From Alexander Hamilton to Unknown, New York, November 8, 1796

Our excellent President, as you have seen, has declined a reelection. 'Tis all-important to our country that his successor shall be a safe man. But it is far less important who of many men that may be named shall be the person, than that it shall not be Jefferson. We have every thing to fear if this man comes in, and from what I believe to be an accurate view of our political map I conclude that he has too good a chance of success, and that good calculation, prudence, and exertion were never more necessary to the Federal cause than at this very juncture. All personal and partial considerations must be discarded, and every thing must give way to the great object of excluding Jefferson.

John Nicholas to George Washington,
Charlottesville, Va., February 22, 1798

I do now know him to be one of the most artful, intriguing, industrious and double-faced politicians in all America.

Tadeuz Kosciuszko to Thomas Jefferson
[July 15–August 5, 1798]

You may rely upon my partiality towards America that I will do everything in my power to prevent a war so injurious to both republics, and in that respect you will be my Star that will guide my endeavors as you are a True American Patriot, and so disinterested a man who chose only the happiness of your own Country.

Robert Troup to Rufus King, New York,
October 2, 1798

On his return home from the last sitting of Congress, [Jefferson] was indiscreet enough to accept of the honor of a public entertainment in Virginia on a Sunday. This fact has been trumpeted from one end of the continent to the other as an irrefragable proof of his contempt for the Christian religion and his devotion to the new religion of France. It has made an impression much to his prejudice in the Middle and Eastern States.

Charles Carroll of Carrollton to Alexander Hamilton, Annapolis, April 18, 1800

We have strange reports circulated among us respecting the prevalence of Jacobinical principles in your State; it is asserted with confidence by the antifederal party here, that all your electors will vote for Mr. Jefferson as President; if such an event should really happen, it is probable he will be chosen; of such a choice the consequences to this country may be dreadful. Mr. Jefferson is too theoretical & fanciful a statesman to direct with steadiness & prudence the affairs of this extensive & growing confederacy; he might safely try his experiments, without much inconvenience, in the little Republic of St. Marino, but his fantastic tricks would dissolve this Union. Perhaps the miseries of France & more especially the Government of Buonaparte may have weaned him from his predilection for revolutions. I once saw a letter of his, in which among several others was contained this strange sentiment "that to preserve the liberties of a people, a revolution once in a century was necessary." A man of this way of thinking, surely may be said to be fond of revolutions; yet possibly were he the chief Magistrate he might not wish for a revolution during his presidency.

*Alexander Hamilton to Governor John Jay,
New York, May 7, 1800*

[Proposing a new method of electing New York's presidential electors that would divide them between Jefferson and Adams] In observing this, I shall not be supposed to mean that any thing ought to be done which integrity will forbid—but merely that the scruples of delicacy and propriety, as relative to a common course of things, ought to yield to the extraordinary nature of the crisis. They ought not to hinder the taking of a legal and constitutional step, to prevent an Atheist in Religion and a Fanatic in politics from getting possession of the helm of the State.

*Timothy Pickering to George Cabot, Philadelphia,
June 16, 1800*

[In a conversation between President Adams and James McHenry, Adams said] "Mr. Jefferson is an infinitely better man, a wiser one I am sure; and, if President, will act wisely. I know it, and would sooner be Vice-President under him, or even minister resident at the Hague, than be indebted to such a being as Hamilton for the Presidency." . . .

[In another conversation between President Adams and Timothy Pickering, Pickering] remarked that I supposed Mr. Jefferson to be a very learned man, "but certainly he is a very visionary man." The President answered, "Why, yes, he has a certain kind of learning in philosophy, &c., but very little of that which is necessary for a statesman."

Arthur Fenner's Report of a Conversation with Alexander Hamilton, Newport, R.I., June 25–26, 1800

[Hamilton said] Mr. Jefferson was a man of no judgment; he could write a pretty book.

Oliver Wolcott, Jr., to Fisher Ames, Washington, August 10, 1800

It is probable that Mr. Jefferson's conduct would be frequently whimsical and undignified; that he would affect the character of a philosopher; that he would countenance quacks, impostors, and projectors; that he would cultivate and increase our national prejudices, and so relax the principles of government as greatly to impair its utility as a bond of internal union and bulwark against foreign influence. He would certainly change all the principal officers of government, or rather there is no one of the gentlemen now in office who would serve under him. How their places would be supplied I cannot conjecture, but I know of no individuals of his party in whom are united the indispensable qualifications of character, talents, industry, experience, and integrity.

*Chauncey Goodrich to Oliver Wolcott, Jr., Hartford,
August 26, 1800*

Among all the good people of the state, there is a
horrid idea of Mr. Jefferson. The clergy abominate
him on account of his atheistical creed.

*Fisher Ames to Rufus King, Dedham, Mass.,
September 24, 1800*

His irreligion, wild philosophy and gimmickery in
politics are never mentioned [by John Adams]. On
the contrary the great man has been known to speak
of him with much regard, and an affected indignation at the charge of irreligion, asking what has that
to do with the public and adding that he is a good
patriot, citizen and father.

*George Cabot to Alexander Hamilton, Brookline,
Mass., October 11, 1800*

Dr. [Timothy] Dwight is here stirring us up to oppose the Demon of Jacobinism.

Gouverneur Morris, Diary, December 11, 1800

It seems to be the general opinion that Colonel Burr
will be chosen President by the House of Representatives. Many of them think it highly dangerous
that Mr. Jefferson should, in the present crisis, be
placed in that office. They consider him as a theoretic man, who would bring the National Government back to something like the old Confederation.

Mr. Nicholay comes today, and to him I state it as the opinion, not of light and fanciful but of serious and considerable men, that Burr must be preferred to Jefferson. He is, as I supposed, much wounded at this information.

John Marshall to Alexander Hamilton, Washington, January 1, 1801

I received this morning your letter of the 26th of December. It is I believe certain that Jefferson & Burr will come to the house of representatives with equal votes. The returns have been all received & this is the general opinion.

Being no longer in the house of representatives & consequently compelled by no duty to decide between them, my own mind had scarcely determined to which of these gentlemen the preference was due. To Mr. Jefferson whose political character is better known than that of Mr. Burr, I have felt almost insuperable objections. His foreign prejudices seem to me totally to unfit him for the chief magistracy of a nation which cannot indulge those prejudices without sustaining debt & permanent injury. In addition to this solid & immovable objection Mr. Jefferson appears to me to be a man who will embody himself with the house of representatives. By weakening the office of President he will increase his personal power. He will diminish his responsibility, sap the fundamental principles of the government & become the leader of that party which is about to constitute the majority of the legislature. The morals of the Author of the letter to Mazzei cannot be pure.

William Fitzhugh to Samuel Blachley Webb, Geneva, January 12, 1801

I will, nevertheless, venture to observe that as the issue of this late electioneering struggle has been the choice of Thomas Jefferson for our President, and as this choice is made by a majority of our countrymen, I am content, the more so, as I believe he will make a good President, and grievously disappoint the most violent of his partisans. Mr. Jefferson is a man of too much virtue and good sense to attempt any material change in a system which was adopted by our late beloved Washington, and has been since steadily pursued by Mr. Adams, and which has preserved our country in peace and prosperity for 12 years, during which period almost the whole civilized world has been deluged in blood, and this too in defiance of the repeated attempts of France & England by open threats and secret intrigues to draw us into the vortex of their ruinous convulsions.

Alexander Hamilton to James A. Bayard, New York, January 16, 1801

Perhaps myself the first, at some expense of popularity, to unfold the true character of Jefferson, it is too late for me to become his apologist. Nor can I have any disposition to do it. I admit that his politics are tinctured with fanaticism, that he is too much in earnest in his democracy, that he has been a mischievous enemy to the principal measures of our past administration, that he is crafty & persevering in his objects, that he is not scrupulous about the means of success, nor very mindful of truth, and that he is a contemptible hypocrite. But it is not true as is alleged that he is an enemy to the power of the Executive, or that he is for confounding all the powers in the House of Representatives. It is a fact which I have frequently mentioned that while we were in the administration together he was generally for a large construction of the Executive authority, & not backward to act upon it in cases which coincided with his views. Let it be added, that in his theoretic Ideas he has considered as improper the participation of the Senate in the Executive Authority. I have more than once made the reflection that viewing himself as the reversioner, he was solicitous to come into possession of a Good Estate. Nor is it true that Jefferson is zealot enough to do anything in pursuance of his principles which will contravene his popularity, or his interest. He is as likely as any man I know to temporize—to calculate what will be likely to promote his own reputation and advantage; and the probable result of such a temper is the preservation of systems, though originally opposed, which being once established, could not be overturned without danger to the person who did it. To my mind a true estimate of Mr. J's character warrants the expectation of a temporizing rather than a violent system. That Jefferson has

manifested a culpable predilection for France is certainly true; but I think it a question whether it did not
proceed quite as much from her popularity among us,
as from sentiment, and in proportion as that popularity is diminished his zeal will cool. Add to this that
there is no fair reason to suppose him capable of being corrupted, which is a security that he will not go
beyond certain limits. It is not at all improbable that
under the change of circumstances Jefferson's Galli-
cism has considerably abated.

Gouverneur Morris to Alexander Hamilton,
Washington, January 26, 1801

They [the Federalist members of the House of Repre-
sentatives] consider Mr. J. as infected with all the cold
blooded Vices and as particularly dangerous from the
false Principles of Government which he has imbibed.

Abigail Adams to Mary Cranch, Washington,
February 7, 1801

Have we any claim to the favour or protection of
Providence, when we have against warning admonition and advice Chosen as our chief Magistrate a
man who makes no pretensions to the belief of an all
wise and supreme Governor of the World, ordering
or directing or overruling the events which take
place in it? I do not mean that he is an Atheist, for I
do not think he is—but he believes Religion only
useful as it may be made a political Engine, and that
the outward forms are only, as I once heard him

express himself—mere Mummery. In short, he is not a believer in the Christian system—The other [i.e., Aaron Burr] if he is more of a believer, has more to answer for, because he has grossly offended against those doctrines by his practice.

Such are the Men whom we are like to have as our Rulers. Whether they are given us in wrath to punish us for our sins and transgressions, the Events will disclose—But if ever we saw a day of darkness, I fear this is one which will be visible until kindled into flames.

Manasseh Cutler to his son Ephraim Cutler, Beverly, Mass., March 21, 1801

What events are to follow the new order of things time will disclose. Jefferson's speech, though a mixed medley of Jacobinism, Republicanism, and Federalism, of religion and atheism, of sentiments consistent and inconsistent with the constitution of an energetic government, yet it is extremely smooth, and must be highly popular with the people at large. There is a fair opening, and I think a hope, that he may prove a prudent man, and, though the next Congress will have a majority of Jacobins, the administration may not be greatly changed. I did wish that Burr might be elected, I now think it fortunate that Jefferson is chosen. If he pursues a wise and prudent tone of conduct, he will have a hornet's nest of Jacobins about his ears, and be stung by the insects he has been so long hatching. He will never make a Bonaparte; but Burr's unbounded ambition, courage and perseverance would prompt him to be a Bonaparte, a King, and an Emperor, or any thing else which might place him at the head of the nation. Nothing but a revolution can effect this, and nothing will produce a revolution at present unless Jefferson abandons the Federalists, and pursues all the wild, demoralizing schemes of the Jacobins. I spent a considerable time lately with Timothy Pickering, Esq. It is his decided opinion, who knows Jefferson well, that he will make no great strides from the old administration, and will look more to the Federalists than to Jacobins for his support.

Theodore Sedgwick to Rufus King, Stockbridge, Mass., May 24, 1801

Jefferson was believed to be a sincere Democrat—hostile to the principles of our Constitution, and the measures of the administration—desirous of conforming in practice to the imbecile principles of the old confederation, a confederation whose measures would be directed by the arrogance of Virginia aided by those states which looked up to her with servile submission. It was believed that he had given evidence of an entire devotion to France under every form of her government, and that under the dominion of this political passion, aided by a rancorous hatred to Great Britain, he might involve the country in war with the latter, & what is worse form an intimate and subordinate connection with the former.

Robert Troup to Rufus King, New York,
May 27, 1801

Jefferson's inaugural speech has had a wonderful lullaby effect. I do not apprehend the serious mischiefs from his administration that have been foretold; but my opinion is, that it will be the little contemptible thing that grows of a trimming system and a studied adherence to popular notions. Hamilton is persuaded that neither Jefferson nor his friends have sufficient skill or patriotism to conduct the political vessel in the tempestuous sea of liberty.

Fisher Ames to John Rutledge, Dedham, Mass.,
July 30, 1801

Mr. Jefferson's removals and appointments afford proof enough of the quo animo* he administers the government. They present a most singular confutation of the puritanism with which his party sought office, and a noiseless efficient instrument of exposing the party to the world. A prevailing party should forbid their chief pen & ink, especially if he is a scribbler by trade and vain of his writing. Tom Payne has said that nobody could write a man down who was up but himself. The two Toms are strong illustrations that the fellow, so often in the wrong, was for once in the right.

*the real intentions

Robert Troup to Rufus King, New York, April 9, 1802

Jefferson is the supreme director of measures—he has no levee days—observes no ceremony—often sees company in an undress, sometimes with his slippers on—always accessible to, and very familiar with, the sovereign people.

William Plumer, Memorandum, November 10, 1804

I found the President dressed better than I ever saw him at any time when I called on a morning visit. Though his coat was old & threadbare, his scarlet vest, his corduroy small cloths, & his white cotton hose, were new & clean—but his linen was much soiled, & his slippers old—His hair was cropt & powdered.

John Quincy Adams, Diary, March 4, 1805

The President previously delivered an inaugural address, in so low a voice that not half of it was heard by any part of the crowded auditory.

Manasseh Cutler to Jonathan Stokes, Hamilton, Mass., May 15, 1805

The democratic notions which have so unfortunately divided the people in this country, and led them off from the true federal principles (the only principles on which a free government can exist), threaten us with the same issue as in France. We are progressing rapidly to a despotic government, and the democratic Mr. Jefferson will probably be our first Emperor. The plant of freedom is withering in this country, and "Crown Imperial" will occupy the ground.

Timothy Pickering to Manasseh Cutler, Washington, March 8, 1806

John Randolph has repeated in public the reproaches which, with closed doors, he had uttered against our noble President, who is, indeed, a most miserable visionary in politics, and ridiculously credulous in all things, even in his favorite pursuit, Natural History. I do not think any Federalists view him with more contempt than many of his own adherents.

He is evidently fast sinking into contempt; and, before his term expires (going on as of late), he will be glad to seek refuge in Carter's or any other mountain, not from an enemy, but from the scorn of the whole American world.

William Plumer, Memorandum, March 16, 1806

The more critically & impartially I examine the character & conduct of Mr. Jefferson the more favorably I think of his integrity. I am really inclined to think I have done him injustice in not allowing him more credit for the integrity of heart that he possesses.

A city appears very different when viewed from different positions—& so it is with man. Viewed in different situations—different times—places—circumstances—relations & with different dispositions, the man thus examined appears unlike himself. My object is truth—I write for myself—I wish not—I am determined not—to set down ought in malice, or to diminish anything from the fact.

The result of my investigation is that Mr. Jefferson has as much honesty & integrity as men in the higher grades of society usually have—& indeed I think more. He is a man of science. But he is very credulous—he knows little of the nature of man—very little indeed. He has travelled the tour of Europe—he has been Minister at Versailles. He has had great opportunities to know man. He has much knowledge of books—of insects—of shells & of all that charms a virtuoso—but he knows not the human heart. He is a closet politician—but not a practical statesman. He has much fine sense but little of that plain common sense so requisite to business—& which in fact governs the world.

These observations on his character are founded on facts that have fallen within my own View.

An infidel in religion—but in every thing else credulous to a fault!

Alas man is himself a contradiction! I do not however mean to insinuate that Mr. Jefferson is a model of goodness. He has too much cunning. Still I repeat the errors of his administration proceed more often from the head than the heart. They partake more of credulity than of wickedness. Examine his whole life with a view to this fact & you will meet with proof in almost every official act.

Permit me to mention that no one circumstance tended so much to his elevation as the great confidence General Washington reposed in him. Washington did this with a full & perfect knowledge of him. They were both Virginians. His conduct during & after the Revolution was known to Washington. And although Jefferson was publicly opposed to the adoption of the Constitution of the United States yet Genl. Washington when called to administer the government gave to Mr. Jefferson the most important confidential office under him, that of Secretary of State. This office Mr. Jefferson held as long as he wished. Mr. Washington did not withdraw his confidence from him while in office. The approbation of Washington, under these circumstances, is honorable.

I do not myself so implicitly yield to the opinion of Mr. Washington as some men do. Still I think his approbation is worthy of great notice. It renders popular, the man on whom it has been conferred, to a certain extent. . . .

Mr. Jefferson is too timid—too irresolute—too fickle—he wants nerve—he wants firmness & resolution. A wavering doubtful hesitating mind joined with credulity is oftentimes as injurious to the nation as a wicked depraved heart.

William Plumer, Memorandum,
December 11, 1806

General [Stephen R.] Bradley, of the State, said to me this day, "That it was time to have some other man president—That Mr. Jefferson's influence in Congress was irresistible—that it was alarming—That if he should recommend to us to repeal the Gospels of the Evangelist, a majority of Congress would do it."

William Plumer, Memorandum,
December 27, 1806

It appears to me that Mr. Jefferson is growing hard of hearing—that deafness is approaching upon him. I observed him several times to bend his head to listen—& he inquired what I had said. Age has some effect upon him.

He always renders his company easy & agreeable. His table was well furnished—good dinner—rich & various dessert—but his wine, except Madeira & Hermitage, not good.

Joseph Story to Samuel P. P. Fay,
Washington, May 30, 1807

Jefferson is tall and thin, of a sallow complexion, with a fine, intelligent eye. Dr. M. yesterday introduced me, and we spent a half hour with him, in which time he conversed in a very easy, correct, and pleasant style. His language is peculiarly appropriate, and his manner very unaffected. The negligence of his dress a little surprised me. He received us in his slippers, and wore old-fashioned clothes, which were not in the nicest order, or of the most elegant kind; a blue coat, white worked cassimere waistcoat and corduroy breeches (I beg your pardon, I mean small clothes) constituted his dress. You know Virginians have some pride in appearing in simple habiliments, and are willing to rest their claim to attention upon their force of mind and suavity of manners. The President is a little awkward in his first address, but you are immediately at ease in his presence. His manners are inviting and not uncourtly; and his voice flexible and distinct. He bears the marks of intense thought and perseverance in his countenance. . . . I visited him again this morning in company with Mr. Madison, at whose house I breakfasted, and conversed with him upon politics in a perfectly familiar manner. His smile is very engaging and impresses you with cheerful frankness. His familiarity, however, is tempered with great calmness of manner and with becoming propriety. Open to all, he seems willing to stand the test of inquiry, and to be weighed in the balance only by his merit and attainments. You may measure if you please, and cannot easily misjudge. On the whole, I confess he appears to me a clear and intelligent man, ready and discriminating, but more formed by philosophical reflection, than by rapid, enterprising, overbearing genius. If he chooses, he cannot fail to please. If he cannot awe, he will not sink into neglect. The current of his thoughts is gentle and uniform, unbroken by the torrent of eloquence, and unruffled by the fervor of vivid internal flame. Take this passing sketch and color it to your own fancy.

Joseph Story, Autobiography

Mr. Jefferson has imputed mainly to me the repeal of the embargo, in a letter to which I have already alluded, and has stigmatized me on this account with the epithet of "pseudo-republican." "Pseudo-republican" of course, I must be; as every one was in Mr. Jefferson's opinion, who dared to venture upon a doubt of his infallibility.

John Adams to Benjamin Rush, September 1807

Jefferson resigned his office as Secretary of State and retired, and his friends said he had struck a great stroke to obtain the presidency. . . . The whole anti-Federal party at that time considered this retirement as a sure and certain step towards the summit of the pyramid and, accordingly, represented him as unambitious, unavaricious, and perfectly disinterested in all parts of all the states in the union. When a man has one of the two greatest parties in a nation interested in representing him to be disinterested, even those who believe it to be a lie will repeat it so often to one another that at last they will seem to believe it to be true. Jefferson has succeeded; and multitudes are made to believe that he is pure benevolence; that he desires no profit; that he wants no patronage; that if you will only let him govern, he will rule only to make the people happy. But you and I know him to be an intriguer.

John Adams to Benjamin Rush,
April 18, 1808

Mr. Jefferson has reason to reflect upon himself. How he will get rid of his remorse in his retirement, I know not. He must know that he leaves the government infinitely worse than he found it, and that from his own error or ignorance. I wish his telescopes and mathematical instruments, however, may secure his felicity. But if I have not mismeasured his ambition, he will be uneasy and the sword will cut away the scabbard. As he has, however, a good taste for letters and an ardent curiosity for science, he may, and I hope will, find amusement and consolation from them; for I have no resentment against him, though he has honored and salaried almost every villain he could find who had been an enemy to me.

The General Republican Committee of the City and
County of New York to Thomas Jefferson,
September 16, 1809

We reluctantly parted with you as President. In the difficult situation of our Country, it was honestly wished to continue the aid of your wisdom, experience and tried integrity. We felt towards you the affection of a child to a parent, and, the moment of political separation was painful in the extreme. Your reasons nevertheless convinced us of the propriety of your retirement, and the election of your friend as a successor, produces at this moment our greatest consolation.

John Adams to Benjamin Rush,
October 25, 1809

There has never been the smallest interruption of the personal friendship between me and Mr. Jefferson that I know of. You should remember that Jefferson was but a boy to me. I was at least ten years older than him in age and more than twenty years older than him in politics. I am bold to say I was his preceptor in politics and taught him everything that has been good and solid in his whole political conduct. I served with him on many committees of Congress, in which we established some of the most important regulations of the army &c., &c., &c.

John Adams to Benjamin Rush,
June 21, 1811

[In speaking of the "masters of the theatrical exhibitions of politics"] We whigs attempted somewhat of the kind. The Declaration of Independence I always considered as a theatrical show. Jefferson ran away with all the stage effect of that . . . and all the glory of it.

James Madison to Albert Gallatin, Montpelier, Vt.,
September 14, 1811

We are just setting out on a visit for two or three
days to Monticello. Mr. Jefferson was with us a
week or two ago, and seemed to enjoy good health,
with the exception of a troublesome rheumatic affliction near the hip.

John Adams to Benjamin Rush,
December 25, 1811

[In speaking of Jefferson and Benjamin Rush] I believe you both to mean well to mankind and your
country. I might suspect you both to sacrifice a little to
the infernal gods, and perhaps unconsciously to suffer
your judgments to be a little swayed by a love of
popularity and possibly by a little spice of ambition.

Benjamin Rush to John Adams, Philadelphia,
February 17, 1812

I rejoice in the correspondence which has taken
place between you and your old friend Mr. Jefferson. I consider you and him as the North and South
Poles of the American Revolution. Some talked,
some wrote, and some fought to promote and establish it, but you and Mr. Jefferson thought for us all.

John Adams to Benjamin Rush,
December 27, 1812

On the 16th January 1804, I wrote to a correspondent, "I wish Jefferson no ill; I envy him not. I

shudder at the calamities which I fear his conduct is preparing for his country, from a mean thirst of popularity, an inordinate ambition, and a want of sincerity."

John Marshall to Joseph Story, Richmond, Mass., July 13, 1821

For Mr. Jefferson's opinion as respects this department [the judiciary] it is not difficult to assign the cause. He is among the most ambitious, & I suspect among the most unforgiving of men. His great power is over the mass of the people & this power is chiefly acquired by professions of democracy. Every check on the wild impulse of the moment is a check on his own power, & he is unfriendly to the source from which it flows. He looks, of course, with ill will at an independent judiciary.

That in a free country with a written constitution, any intelligent man should wish a dependent judiciary, or should think that the constitution is not a law for the court as well as the legislature, would astonish me if I had not learnt from observation that, with many men, the judgment is completely controlled by the passions.

John Marshall to Joseph Story, Richmond, September 18, 1821

[Jefferson is referred to as] the great Lama of the mountains.

John Adams to Thomas Jefferson, Quincy,
Mass., July 12, 1822

I hope one day your letters will be all published in
volumes; they will not always appear Orthodox, or
liberal in politics; but they will exhibit a Mass of
Taste, Sense, Literature and Science, presented in a
sweet simplicity and a neat elegance of Style, which
will be read with delight in future ages.

John Quincy Adams, Diary, May 23, 1824

Mr. Hay spoke, as he always does, with extreme bitterness of Mr. Jefferson, whom he declares to be one
of the most insincere men in the world.

Daniel Webster, Notes of Conversation with
Thomas Jefferson, 1824

Mr. Jefferson is now between eighty-one & eighty-
two, above six feet high, of an ample long frame,
rather thin & spare. His head, which is not peculiar
in its shape, is set rather forward on his shoulders,
& his neck being long, there is, when he is walking
or conversing, an habitual protrusion of it. It is still
well covered with hair, which having been once
red, & now turning grey, is of an indistinct sandy
color. His eyes are small, very light, & now neither
brilliant, nor striking. His chin is rather long, but
not pointed, his nose small, regular in its outline, &
the nostrils a little elevated. His mouth is well
formed, & still filled with teeth; it is generally

strongly compressed, bearing an expression of contentment & benevolence. His complexion formerly light, & freckled, now bears the marks of age & cutaneous affection. His limbs are uncommonly long, his hands & feet very large, & his wrists of a most extraordinary size. His walk is not precise & military, but easy & swinging; he stoops a little, not so much from age, as from natural formation. When sitting he appears short, partly from a rather lounging habit of sitting, & partly from the disproportionate length of his limbs. His dress when in the house, is a grey surtout coat, kerseymere buff waistcoat, with an under one faced with some material of a dingy red. His pantaloons are very long, loose, & of the same color as his coat. His stockings are woolen, either white or grey, & his shoes of the kind that bear his name. His whole dress is neglected but not slovenly. He wears a common round hat. He wears when on horseback a grey strait bodiced coat, & a spencer of the same material, both fastened with large pearl buttons. When we first saw him he was riding, & in addition to the above, wore round his throat a knit white woolen tippet, in the place of a cravat, & black velvet gaiters under his pantaloons.

His general appearance indicates an extraordinary degree of health, vivacity, & spirit. His sight is still good, for he needs glasses only in the evening, his hearing is generally good, but a number of voices in animated conversation, confuses it.

Mr. J. rises in the morning, as soon as he can see the hands of his clock (which is directly opposite his bed) & examines his thermometer immediately, as he keeps a regular meteorological diary. He employs himself chiefly in writing till breakfast, which is at nine. From that time till dinner, he is in his library, excepting that in fair weather he rides on horseback from seven to fourteen miles. Dines at four, returns to the drawing room at six, when coffee is brought in, & passes the evening, *till nine* in conversation. His habit of retiring at that hour is so strong, that it has become essential to his health & comfort. His diet is simple, but he seems restrained only by his tastes. His breakfast is tea & coffee, bread, of which he does not seem afraid, although it is always fresh from the oven, with sometimes a slight accompaniment of cold meat.

He enjoys his dinner well, taking with meat a large proportion of vegetables. He has a strong preference for the wines of the Continent, of which he has many sorts of excellent quality, having been more than commonly successful in his mode of importing, & preserving them. Among others we found the following, which are very rare in this country, & apparently not at all injured by transportation. L'Ednau, Muscat, Samian, & Blanchette de Limoux. Dinner is served in half Virginian, half French style, in good taste & abundance. No wine is put on the table till the cloth is removed.

In conversation, Mr. J. is easy & natural, & apparently not ambitious; it is not loud as challenging general attention, but usually addressed to the person next him. The topics when not selected to suit the character & feelings of his auditor, are those subjects with which his mind seems particularly occupied, & these at present, may be said to be Science & Letters, & especially the University of Virginia, which is coming into existence almost entirely from his exertions, & will rise it is to be hoped, to usefulness & credit under his continued care. When we were with him, his favorite subjects were Greek & Anglo-Saxon, & historical recollections of the times & events of the Revolution & of his residence in France, from 1783–4 to 89.

Daniel Webster to Jeremiah Mason, Washington, December 29, 1824

At Mr. Jefferson's, we remained five days. This was something longer than our intention, but there came rains, which prevented our departure. Mr. Jefferson is a man of whom one may form a very just account, as to person & manners, from description, & pictures. We met him in the road, & I knew him at once, although he was on horseback, & something straighter, & freer from the debility of age, than I had expected. We found him uniformly pleasant, social & interesting. He talked less of present things than might be expected, although in the intercourse with gentlemen under his own roof, he did not keep back his opinions, on men or things. But if I were to say what appeared to be the leading topics, with him, & those to which his mind habitually turned itself, I should mention three—early anecdotes of

Revolutionary times—French society—politics—& literature, such as they were when he was in France—and Genl. Literature, & the Va. University.

On these three general topics he has much to say & he says it all well.

Daniel Webster to Joseph Hopkinson, Washington, December 31, 1824

My visit to Virginia was not unpleasant. Mr. Jefferson is full of conversation, & as it relates, pretty much, to by-gone times, it is replete with information & useful anecdote. All the great men of our Revolutionary epoch necessarily had a circle of which they were, severally, the center. Each, therefore, has something to tell not common to all. Mr. Adams & Mr. Jefferson, for example, though acting together, on a common theater, at Philadelphia, were nevertheless far apart, when in Massachusetts & Virginia, & each was at home, in the midst of men & of events, more or less different from those which surrounded the other. I heard Mr. Jefferson talk over the events of his early life, as your friend [David] Hunter represents the young Indians to listen to the tales of the age-stricken warriors; not without occasionally feeling, like them, an impulse to raise the war song, & grasp the tomahawk. Mr. Jefferson's conversation is little on present things; partly perhaps from the prudence of forbearing to engage in questions which now divide the community, but mostly from a greater love for other topics.

Early Revolutionary events, political occurrences, in both Hemispheres, about the time he was in France, & general literature & the University of Virginia would seem to be his favorite subjects.

James Kent, Journal to his son,
April 30, 1833

He [Egbert Benson in 1833] spoke of Jefferson as one of the most unprincipled, malignant, false & visionary Men that ever lived, & that it was he who on his return to the U. States converted Madison to democracy & subdued, perverted & corrupted his mind & Principles.

James Madison to George Tucker, Montpelier,
June 27, 1836

Apart from the value put on such a mark of respect from you in a dedication of your "Life of Mr. Jefferson" to me, I could only be governed in accepting it by my confidence in your capacity to do justice to a character so interesting to his country and to the world; and, I may be permitted to add, with whose principles of liberty and political career mine have been so extensively congenial.

Thomas Jefferson
Describes Himself

To Elizabeth Wayles Eppes, October 3, 1782

This miserable kind of existence* is really too bur-
thensome to be borne, and were it not for the infidelity of deserting the sacred charge left me [i.e., his
three daughters], I could not wish its continuance a
moment. For what could it be wished? All my plans
of comfort and happiness reversed by a single event
and nothing answering in prospect before me but a
gloom unbrightened with one cheerful expectation.
The care and instruction of our children indeed affords some temporary abstractions from wretchedness and nourishes a soothing reflection that if there
be beyond the grave any concern for the things of
this world there is one angel at least who views
these attentions with pleasure and wishes continuance of them while she must pity the miseries to
which they confine me.

> *A distraught Jefferson refers to his wife's recent
> death.

To William Short, Annapolis, March 1, 1784

Having to my habitual ill health, had lately
added an attack of my periodical headache, I am
obliged to avoid reading, writing and almost
thinking.

To Abigail Adams, Paris, September 25, 1785

I do not love difficulties. I am fond of quiet, willing to do my duty, but irritable by slander & apt to be forced by it to abandon my post. These are weaknesses from which reason & your counsels will preserve Mr. Adams.

To George Gilmer, Paris, August 12, 1787

My own health has been as good as ever, after the first year's probation. The accident of a dislocated wrist, badly set, has I fear deprived me for ever of almost every use of my right hand. Nor is the extent of the evil as yet known, the hand withering, the fingers remaining swelled & crooked, & losing rather than gaining in point of suppleness. It is now eleven months since the accident. I am able however to write, tho for a long time I was not so.

To Francis Hopkinson, Paris, March 13, 1789

You say that I have been dished up to you as an antifederalist, and ask me if it be just. My opinion was never worthy enough of notice to merit citing: but since you ask it I will tell you. I am not a Federalist, because I never submitted the whole system of my opinions to the creed of any party of men whatever in religion, in philosophy, in politics, or in any thing else where I was capable of thinking for myself. Such an addiction is the last degradation of a free and moral agent. If I could not go to heaven but with

a party, I would not go there at all. Therefore I
protest to you I am not of the party of federalists.
But I am much farther from that of the Antifederalists. I approved from the first moment, of the great
mass of what is in the new constitution, the consolidation of the government, the organization into Executive, legislative & judiciary, the subdivision of the
legislative, the happy compromise of interests between the great & little states by the different manner of voting in the different houses, the voting by
persons instead of states, the qualified negative on
laws given to the Executive which however I should
have liked better if associated with the judiciary also
as in New York, and the power of taxation. I thought
at first that the latter might have been limited. A little reflection soon convinced me it ought not to be.
What I disapproved from the first moment also was
the want of a bill of rights to guard liberty against
the legislative as well as executive branches of the
government, that is to say to secure freedom in religion, freedom of the press, freedom from monopolies, freedom from unlawful imprisonment, freedom
from a permanent military, and a trial by jury in all
cases determinable by the laws of the land. I disapproved also the perpetual reeligibility of the President. . . . These, my dear friend, are my sentiments,
by which you will see I was right in saying I am neither federalist nor antifederalist; that I am of neither
party, nor yet a trimmer between parties. These my
opinions I wrote within a few hours after I had read
the constitution, to one or two friends in America. I

had not then read one single word printed on the subject. I never had an opinion in politics or religion which I was afraid to own. A costive reserve on these subjects might have procured me more esteem from some people, but less from myself. My great wish is to go on in a strict but silent performance of my duty: to avoid attracting notice & to keep my name out of newspapers, because I find the pain of a little censure, even when it is unfounded, is more acute than the pleasure of much praise.

To Charles Rose, Monticello, April 17, 1794

A twenty years' desuetude in matters of law, has produced a rust which will never be attempted to be rubbed off again. I rarely therefore permit myself to give opinions on the subject even in conversation.

To George Wythe, Monticello, April 18, 1795

I live on my horse from an early breakfast to a late dinner, & very often after that till dark.

To Alexander Donald, Monticello,
May 30, 1795

When I left public office I expected to be so much at leisure that I should keep up a very animated correspondence with my friends. On my return home I found my farms in a ruinous condition, which made it necessary for me to undertake their recovery and culture myself. Forced to make myself acquainted both with the theory and practice, I at length became so fascinated with the occupation that I am now the most ardent farmer in the state. I live on my horse nearly the whole day, and when in the house it is in a state of fatigue which admits neither thought nor action. I rarely take up a book, and never a pen if I can help it. Hence instead of the animated correspondence I had calculated on, I have kept no correspondence but where pressing business called for it.

To John Adams, December 28, 1796

I have no ambition to govern men. It is a painful and thankless office.

To Thomas Willing, Philadelphia,
February 23, 1798

Th: Jefferson presents his respects to Mr. Willing, and other gentlemen managers of the ball of this evening [honoring Washington's birthday]. He hopes his non-attendance will not be misconstrued. He has not been at a ball these twenty years, nor for a long time permitted himself to go to any entertainments of the evening, from motives of attention to health. On these grounds he excused to Genl. Washington when living in the city his not going to his birthnights, to Mrs. Washington not attending her evenings, to Mrs. Adams the same, and to all his friends who have been so good as to invite him to tea & card parties, the declining to go to them. It is an indulgence which his age and habits will he hopes obtain and continue to him. He has always testified his homage to the occasion by his subscription to it.

To Benjamin Hawkins, Washington, February 18, 1803

I retain myself very perfect health, having not had 20 hours of fever in 42 years past. I have sometimes had a troublesome headache, and some slight rheumatic pains, but now sixty years old nearly, I have had as little to complain of in point of health as most people.

To Albert Gallatin, Washington, January 13, 1807

The appointment of a woman to office is an innovation for which the public is not prepared, nor am I.

To Tadeusz Kosciusko, Monticello, February 26, 1810

I am retired to Monticello, where, in the bosom of my family, & surrounded by my books, I enjoy a repose to which I have been long a stranger. My mornings are devoted to correspondence. From breakfast to dinner, I am in my shops, my garden, or on horseback among my farms; from dinner to dark I give to society & recreation with my neighbors & friends; & from candlelight to early bed-time, I read. My health is perfect; and my strength considerably reinforced by the activity of the course I pursue; perhaps it is as great as usually falls to the lot of near 67 years of age. I talk of ploughs & harrows, of seedings & harvesting, with my neighbors, & of politics too, if they choose, with as little reserve as the rest of my fellow citizens, & feel at length the blessing of being free to say & do what I please, without being responsible for it to any mortal.

To Benjamin Rush, Poplar Forest,
August 17, 1811

I write to you from a place 90 miles from Monticello, near the New London of this state, which I visit three or four times a year, & stay from a fortnight to a month at a time. I have fixed myself comfortably, keep some books here, bring others occasionally, am in the solitude of a hermit, and quite at leisure to attend to my absent friends.

To Caesar A. Rodney, Monticello,
March 16, 1815

Come as you will, or as you can, it will always be joy enough to me. Only you must give me a month's notice; because I go three or four times a year to a possession 90 miles Southwestward, and am absent a month at a time, and the mortification would be indelible of losing such a visit by a mistimed absence. You will find me in habitual good health, great contentedness, enfeebled in body, impaired in memory, but without decay in my friendships.

To Charles Thomson, Monticello, January 9, 1816

I retain good health, am rather feeble to walk much, but ride with ease, passing two or three hours a day on horseback, and every three or four months taking in a carriage a journey of 90 miles to a distant possession, where I pass a good deal of my time. My eyes need the aid of glasses by night, and with small print in the day also; my hearing is not quite so sensible as it used to be; no tooth shaking yet, but shivering and shrinking in body from the cold we now experience, my thermometer having been as low as 12° this morning. My greatest oppression is a correspondence afflictingly laborious, the extent of which I have been endeavoring to curtail. This keeps me at the drudgery of the writing table all the prime hours of the day, leaving for the gratification of my appetite for reading only what I can steal from the hours of sleep. Could I reduce this epistolary corvée within the limits of my friends, and affairs, and give the time redeemed from it to reading and reflection, to history, ethics, mathematics, my life would be as happy as the infirmities of age would admit, and I should look on its consummation with the composure of one "qui summum nec me tuit diem nec optat."*

      *Who neither fears the final day nor hopes for it

*To Benjamin Waterhouse, Monticello,
March 3, 1818*

I am much debilitated in body, and my memory sensibly on the wane. Still however I enjoy good health and spirits, and am as industrious a reader as when a student at College. Not of newspapers. These I have discarded. I relinquish, as I ought to do, all intermedling with public affairs, committing myself cheerfully to the watch and care of those for whom, in my turn, I have watched and cared.

To Vine Utley, Monticello, March 21, 1819

Your letter of Feb 18 came to hand on the 1st instant; and the request of the history of my physical habits would have puzzled me not a little, had it not been for the model, with which you accompanied it, of Dr. Rush's answer to a similar inquiry. I live so much like other people, that I might refer to ordinary life as the history of my own. Like my friend the Doctor, I have lived temperately, eating little animal food, & that, not as an aliment so much as a condiment for the vegetables, which constitute my principal diet. I double however the doctor's glass and a half of wine, and even treble it with a friend; but halve its effects by drinking the weak wines only. The ardent wines I cannot drink, nor do I use ardent spirits in any form. Malt liquors & cyder are my table drinks, and my breakfast, like that also of my friend, is of tea & coffee. I have been blest with organs of digestion which accept and concoct, without ever murmuring, whatever the palate chooses to consign to them, and I have not yet lost a tooth by age. I was a hard student until I entered on the business of life, the duties of which leave no idle time to those disposed to fulfill them; & now, retired, and at the age of 76, I am again a hard student. Indeed, my fondness for reading and study revolts me from the drudgery of letter writing, and a stiff wrist, the consequence of an early dislocation, makes writing both slow and painful. I am not so regular in my sleep as the Doctor says he was, devoting to it from 5 to 8 hours, according as my company or the book I am reading interests me; and I never go to bed without an hour, or half hour's previous reading of something moral, whereon to ruminate in the intervals of sleep. But whether I retire to bed early or late, I rise with the sun. I use spectacles at night, but not necessarily in the day, unless in reading small print. My hearing is distinct in particular conversation, but confused when several voices cross each other, which unfits me for the society of the table. I have been more fortunate than my friend in the article of health. So free from catarrhs that I have not had one, (in the breast, I mean) on an average of 8 or 10 years thro' life. I ascribe this exemption partly to the habit of bathing my feet in cold water every morning, for 60 years past. A fever of more than 24 hours I have not had above 2 or 3 times in my life. A periodical head ache has afflicted me occasionally, once perhaps, in 6 or 8 years, for 2 or 3 weeks at a time, which seems now to have left me; and except on a late occasion of indisposition, I enjoy good health; too feeble indeed, to walk much, but riding without fatigue 6 or 8 miles a day, and sometimes 30 or 40. I may end these egotisms therefore, as I began, by saying that my life has been so much like that of other people, that I might say, with Horace, to every one "Nomine mutato, narratur fabula de te."*

> *Just change the name and the story could be told about you.

To John Adams, Monticello, June 1, 1822

I have ever dreaded a doting old age; and my health has been generally so good, and is now so good, that I dread it still. The rapid decline of my strength during the last winter has made me hope sometimes that I see land. During summer I enjoy its temperature, but I shudder at the approach of winter, and wish I could sleep through it with the Dormouse, and only wake with him in spring, if ever. They say that [General John] Starke could walk about his room. I am told you walk well and firmly. I can only reach my garden, and that with sensible fatigue. I ride however daily. But reading is my delight. I should wish never to put pen to paper; and the more because of the treacherous practice some people have of publishing one's letters without leave.

Jefferson's Correspondents

Adams, Abigail (Mass.): friend; wife of John Adams

Adams, John (Mass.): revolutionary; member of Continental Congress; American diplomat; first U.S. vice president; second U.S. president

Adams, Samuel (Mass.): revolutionary; member of Continental Congress; lt. governor and governor of Mass.

Amelot de la Croix (France): author of books on travel in China

Armstrong, John (Pa.): military officer; diplomat; Madison's secretary of war

Arnound, L'Abbé (France): philosophe

Arnoux, L'Abbé (France): philosophe

Austin, Benjamin (Mass.): merchant; revolutionary; essayist; Anti-Federalist; state representative; U.S. senator

Bailey, Theodorus (N.Y.): Republican; U.S. Congressman

Banister, John, Jr. (Va.): traveler of Europe

Banister, John, Sr. (Va.): member of Virginia House of Delegates; absolved TJ of misconduct as governor

Banneker, Benjamin (Md.): free black; astronomer; mathematician; almanac maker

Barbé-Marbois, Pierre François de (France): diplomat; minister of finance; negotiated Louisiana Purchase

Barclay, Thomas: diplomat

Barlow, Joel (Conn.): poet; diplomat

Barnes, John (Pa.): Phila. tea merchant; grocer

Barton, Benjamin Smith (Pa.): professor of medicine at Univ. of Pennsylvania; naturalist

Bell, Thomas (Va.): planter, neighbor

Bellini, Charles (Carlo) (Florence, Va.): professor of modern languages at William and Mary College

Carr, Peter (Va.): TJ's nephew; studied law with TJ

Carrington, Edward (Va.): soldier; member of
  Confederation Congress; U.S. marshal

Cartwright, John (Eng.): supported American colonies;
  Parliamentary reformer

Cary, Wilson Miles (Va.): TJ's great-great-nephew

Chapman, Dr. Nathaniel (Pa.): physician; studied under
  Rush; professor of theory and practice of medicine at
  Univ. of Pennsylvania

Chastellux, François J. de (France): philosophe

Church, Angelica Schuyler (N.Y. and Eng.): in TJ's social
  circle; sister-in-law of Alexander Hamilton

Claiborne, Richard (Va.): soldier

Clark, George Rogers (Va.): Revolutionary War general;
  TJ asks to lead expedition to the West

Clay, Charles (Va.): clergyman

Clinton, George (N.Y.): revolutionary; soldier; governor;
  TJ's second vice president; Madison's first vice
  president

Cocke, William (Tenn.): U.S. senator

Coles, Edward (Va. and Ill.): Madison's secretary; freed
  his slaves

Cooper, Thomas (Eng.): professor of chemistry,
  mineralogy, and natural philosophy

Coray, Adamantios (Greece and France): scholar of
  ancient Greece

Corny, Madame de (France): in TJ's social circle

Correa da Serra, Abbé José (Portugal): botanist

Coste, Jean de la (France): wine merchant

Cosway, Maria (Italy and Eng.): painter; singer;
  musician; TJ's love

Coxe, Tench (Pa.): Federalist pamphleteer; asst. secretary
  of the Treasury under Washington; becomes
  Republican

Crawford, William H. (Ga.): minister to France, secretary
  of the Treasury (1816–25); presidential candidate

Crèvecoeur, St. John de (France and N.Y.): French
   diplomat
Currie, Dr. James (Va.): physician
Cutting, Nathaniel (Mass.): merchant

Dearborn, Henry (Mass.): soldier; TJ's secretary of war
Delaplaine, Joseph (Pa.): publisher
Démeunier, Jean Nicolas (France): encyclopedist
Derieux, J.P.P. (France): merchant; money exchanger
Destutt de Tracy (France): philosophe
Dickinson, John (Pa. and Del.): revolutionary; member of
   Continental Congress; delegate to Constitutional
   Convention
Digges, Thomas Attwood (London and Md.): friend of
   United States; novelist
Donald, Alexander (Va.): TJ's schoolmate
Drayton, William (S.C.): sent rice and olives by TJ
Duane, William (Pa.): newspaper editor
Dumas, C.W.F. (Netherlands): Am. diplomat resident in
   the Netherlands
Dunbar, William (Mississippi Territory): explorer
Dupont, P. S. de Nemours (France): philosophe

Emmet, John P. (Va.): professor of natural history Univ.
   of Virginia
Eppes, Elizabeth Wayles (Va.): TJ's sister-in-law
Eppes, Francis (Va.): TJ's brother-in-law
Eppes, John Wayles (Va.): TJ's son-in-law
Eppes, Mary Jefferson (Polly) (Va.): TJ's daughter
Eustis, William (Mass.): physician; soldier; state
   representative; U.S. congressman; Madison's
   secretary of war; diplomat
Everett, Edward (Mass.): scholar of ancient Greece

Fabbroni, Giovanni (Italy): naturalist; chemist; engineer
Fairfax, Ferdinando (Va.): planter

Fishback, James (Ky.): physician; lawyer; newspaper
    editor
Fitzhugh, Peregrine (Md.): planter
Franklin, William Temple (Pa.): diplomat; Benjamin
    Franklin's grandson
Fulton, Robert (N.Y.): steamship inventor

Gallatin, Albert (Pa.): TJ's and Madison's secretary of
    the Treasury
Galloway, Benjamin (Md.): lawyer; planter; state
    assemblyman; state attorney general
Gates, Horatio (Va. and N.Y.): soldier
Gérard de Rayneval, Joseph Matthais (France): diplomat
Gerry, Elbridge (Mass.) member of Confederation
    Congress; representative to Constitutional
    Convention; Anti-Federalist; governor of Mass.;
    Madison's second vice president
Giles, William Branch (Va.): radical Republican leader in
    U.S. House of Representatives; U.S. senator
Gilmer, Francis W. (Va.): professor of law at Univ. of
    Virginia
Gilmer, Dr. George (Va.): old friend
Girardin, Louis H. (Norway and Va.): professor of
    history, etc. at William and Mary College
Giroud, Alexandre (France): artillery foundry
Granger, Gideon (Conn.): TJ's postmaster general
Gray, Francis C. (Mass.): visitor to Monticello; lawyer
Gregoire, Abbé Henri (France): author of equal rights for
    Jews and Blacks

Hamilton, Alexander (N.Y.): soldier; secretary of the Trea-
    sury; TJ's political opponent; shot and killed by Burr
Harrison, Benjamin (Va.): member of Virginia House of
    Delegates; governor of Va.
Hartley, David (Eng.): diplomat; signed peace treaty
    ending American Revolution

Hawkins, Benjamin (N.C.): U.S. Indian agent

Hay, George W. (Va.): Monroe's son-in-law; U.S. district attorney; prosecutes Burr

Hazard, Ebenezer (Pa. and N.Y.): Confederation's postmaster general

Henley, Samuel (Va.): clergyman

Henry, John (Md.): U.S. senator

Hilliard d'Auberteuil, Michel René (France): historian

Holmes, John (Maine): U.S. congressman

Hopkinson, Francis (Pa.): poet; musician; essayist; U.S. district judge

Hopkinson, Joseph: lawyer; defended Samuel Chase

Howell, David (R.I.): Confederation Congress

Humboldt, Alexander, Baron von (Germany): natural scientist; explorer; wrote on Latin and South America

Humphreys, David (Conn.): poet; soldier; diplomat

Ivernois, François D' (France): historian

Izard, Ralph (S.C.): diplomat

Jackson, Andrew (Tenn.): soldier; presidential candidate

Jackson, James (Ga.): U.S. congressman; U.S. senator

Jackson, William (Pa. and Ga.): secretary for Constitutional Convention

Jarvis, William Charles: U.S. consul to Lisbon

Jay, James (Eng. and N.Y.): physician; American spy

Jay, John (N.Y.): revolutionary; diplomat; peace commissioner; secretary for foreign affairs; U.S. chief justice; negotiated Jay Treaty; governor of N.Y.

Jefferson, John Garland (Va.): studied law with TJ

Jefferson, Martha (Patsy) (Va.): daughter

Jefferson, Mary (Polly) (Va.): daughter

Jefferson, Randolph (Va.): brother

Johnson, Chapman (Va.): on Board of Visitors of Univ. of Virginia

Johnson, Richard M. (City of Washington): clerk in State Dept.

Johnson, William (S.C.): TJ's first appointment to U.S. Supreme Court

Jones, Joseph (Va.): member of Confederation Congress; member of Virginia House of Delegates

Jones, Dr. Walter (Va.)

Jullien, Marc Antoine (France): revolutionary; liberal; fought for revolution of colonies against Spain

Kent, James (N.Y.): lawyer; judge; chancellor

Kercheval, Samuel (Va.): Stephensburg innkeeper

Knox, Henry (Mass.): Revolutionary War general; Confederation and U.S. secretary at war

Kosciusko, Tadeusz: Polish revolutionary; engineer of West Point during Revolutionary War

Lafayette, Marquis de (France): general in Am. Revolutionary War; aided TJ in France

Lambert, William (Va.): astronomer; clerk in State Dept; clerk in U.S. House of Reps.

Langdon, John (N.H.): merchant; Revolutionary War leader; member of Confederation Congress; delegate to Constitutional Convention; governor of N.H.

Lasteryrie-du Saillant, Charles Philbert de (France): journalist; founded lithographic practice in Paris

Latrobe, Benjamin Henry (Eng., Va., and Washington); architect

Law, Thomas (Eng. and Va.): married Martha Washington's granddaughter; advocate for national currency

Lee, Henry (Va.): soldier; governor of Va.

Lee, Richard Henry (Va.): revolutionary; member of Continental and Confederation congresses; Anti-Federalist; U.S. senator

Leiper, Thomas (Pa.): TJ's landlord in Philadelphia

Lewis, James, Jr. (Va.): lawyer

Lewis, Meriwether (Va.): TJ's secretary; led expedition to the West

Lewis, Nicholas (Va.): neighbor; managed TJ's affairs

Lincoln, Levi (Mass.): lawyer; lt. governor of Mass.; TJ's attorney general

Livingston, Edward (N.Y.): district attorney; U.S. congressman; moved to Louisiana; Batture case against TJ

Livingston, Robert R. (N.Y.): revolutionary; secretary for Foreign Affairs for Confederation; N.Y. chancellor; member of Confederation Congress; U.S. minister to France

Logan, George (Pa.): Quaker, antiwar U.S. senator

Lomax, Thomas (Va.): lawyer and planter

Macon, Nathaniel (N.C.): U.S. senator; Speaker of the House of Representatives

Madison, James (Va.): TJ's close friend and political ally; representative to Continental and Confederation congresses; delegate to Constitutional Convention; U.S. congressman; TJ's secretary of state; fourth U.S. president

Madison, Rev. James (Va.): president of William and Mary College

Marks, Anna Jefferson (Va.): TJ's sister

Marshall, John (Va.): soldier; lawyer; diplomat; U.S. congressman; U.S. chief justice; personal and political enemy of TJ

Mason, George (Va.): planter; revolutionary; author of Virginia Declaration of Rights; delegate to Constitutional Convention; Anti-Federalist

Mason, Stevens Thomson (Va.): U.S. senator

Maury, James (Va.): minister; TJ's teacher

Mazzei, Philip (Italy and Va.): friend

Patterson, Robert (Pa.): mathematician; professor at Univ. of Pennsylvania; director of U.S. Mint

Peale, Charles Willson (Pa.): painter; inventor; museum director

Pendleton, Edmund (Va.): lawyer; chancellor; president of Va. convention that notified Constitution

Peters, Richard (Pa.): lawyer; U.S. district judge

Pickering, Timothy (Pa. and Mass.): U.S. postmaster general; U.S. secretary of state; TJ's political opponent

Pictet, Marc Auguste (Switzerland): lawyer; natural scientist; professor of natural philosophy at Academy of Geneva

Pigott, Robert (Eng.): vegetarian

Pinckney, Thomas: diplomat

Pleasants, Robert (Va.): Quaker merchant

Plumer, William (N.H.): U.S. senator; kept memorandum of Senate

Pope, Matthew (Va.): apothecary

Price, Richard (Eng.): pamphleteer; reformer; friend of United States

Priestley, Joseph (Eng. and Pa.): chemist; famous Unitarian clergyman and writer; TJ's close friend

Ramsay, David (S.C.): physician; pamphleteer; member of Confederation Congress; U.S. congressman; historian

Randolph, Edmund (Va.): attorney general for and governor of Va.; delegate to Constitutional Convention; U.S. attorney general; U.S. secretary of state

Randolph, John (Va.): lawyer; U.S. congressman; political opponent of TJ

Randolph, Martha (Patsy) Jefferson (Va.): daughter

Randolph, Thomas Jefferson (Va.): grandson

Randolph, Thomas Mann, Jr. (Va.): son-in-law; U.S. congressman; governor of Va.

Randolph, Thomas Mann, Sr. (Va.) plantation owner; TJ's friend

Remsen, Henry: chief clerk U.S. State Dept.

Ritchie, Thomas (Va.): newspaper editor

Rittenhouse, David (Pa.): inventor; treasurer; member of Am. Philos. Soc.

Roane, Spencer (Va.): judge

Robinson, Moses (Vt.): governor of Vt.; U.S. senator

Rodney, Caesar A. (Del.): U.S. attorney general during Burr case

Roscoe, William (Eng.): historian; poet; botanist

Ross, David (Va.): merchant; owner of iron works; bankrupt

Rush, Benjamin (Pa.): physician; revolutionary; signer of Declaration of Independence; delegate to Pa. convention that ratified U.S. Constitution; TJ's close friend; reconciled TJ and John Adams

Rush, Richard (Pa.): Benjamin Rush's son; diplomat

Rutledge, Edward (S.C.): signer of Declaration of Independence; member of Continental Congress

Rutledge, Edward, Jr. (S.C.): recipient of TJ's travel advice

Rutledge, John (S.C.): delegate to Constitutional Convention; governor of S.C.; U.S. supreme court justice; S.C. chief justice; U.S. chief justice (not confirmed)

Rutledge, John, Jr. (S.C.): recipient of TJ's travel advice

Sargeant, Ezra (N.Y.): publisher

Say, Jean Baptiste (France): political economist

Shee, John: soldier

Shippen, William, Jr. (Pa.): physician

Short, William (Va.): TJ's secretary and virtual adopted son; diplomat

Silvestre, Augustin François (France): scientist; public administrator

Sinclair, Sir John (Eng.): president of Natl. Board of Agriculture

Skipwith, Henry (Va.): TJ's brother-in-law; soldier; member of Va. House of Delegates; TJ's fellow executor of John Wayles's estate

Skipwith, Robert (Va.): TJ's brother-in-law

Smith, Abigail Adams (Mass. and N.Y.): daughter of John and Abigail Adams; wife of William Stephens Smith

Smith, Larkin (Va.): soldier; member of Va. House of Delegates; appointed customs collector for Norfolk and Portsmouth by TJ

Smith, Margaret Bayard (City of Washington): socialite

Smith, Robert (Md.): sec. of navy; attorney general; secretary of state; resigned after feud with Gallatin

Smith, Samuel (Md.): U.S. senator

Smith, Samuel Harrison (City of Washington): newspaper editor

Smith, William Stephens (N.Y.): soldier; son-in-law of John Adams

Smyth, Alexander: soldier

Spafford, Horatio Gates (Vt.): geographer; editor; inventor

Sparks, Jared: editor; historian

Stael, Madame de Holstein de (France): in TJ's social circle

Stiles, Ezra (Conn.): president of Yale College

Story, Joseph (Mass.): U.S. congressman; appointed by Madison to U.S. Supreme Court over TJ's objections

Stuart, Archibald (Va.): member of Virginia House of Delegates; judge

Sullivan, James (Mass.): revolutionary; pamphleteer; governor of Mass.

Sully, Thomas (N.Y. and Pa.): painter

Waterhouse, Benjamin (Mass.): professor at Harvard College; promoted inoculation for small pox; appointed by TJ as head physician to U.S. marine hospital in Charlestown, Mass.

Watterson, George (City of Washington): third librarian of Congress; bought Jefferson's library

Webster, Daniel (Mass.): lawyer; visitor to Monticello

Weightman, Roger C. (City of Washington): mayor

Wilkinson, James (Md. and New Orleans): soldier; intriguer

Willis, Francis, Jr. (Va.): physician

Wirt, William (Va.): lawyer; prosecutor in Burr case; author

Wistar, Dr. Caspar (Pa.): physician at the Univ. of Pennsylvania

Wright, Frances (Fanny) (Scotland): visitor to Monticello; reformer

Wyche, John (Va.): surveyor; justice of the peace

Wythe, George (Va.): lawyer; TJ's law mentor

Yancey, Charles (Va.): member of Virginia House of Delegates

Bibliography

Adams, William Howard. *The Paris Years of Thomas Jefferson*. New Haven, Conn., 1997.

Appleby, Joyce. *Thomas Jefferson*. New York, 2003.

Banning, Lance. *Jefferson and Madison: Three Conversations from the Founding*. Madison, Wis., 1995.

——. *The Jeffersonian Persuasion: Evolution of a Party Ideology*. Ithaca, N.Y., 1978.

Bear, James A., Jr., ed. *Jefferson at Monticello*. Charlottesville, Va., 1967.*

Bedini, Silvio. *Thomas Jefferson: Statesman of Science*. New York, 1990.

Bernstein, R. B. *Thomas Jefferson*. New York, 2004.

Boyd, Julian P., et al., eds. *The Papers of Thomas Jefferson*. Princeton, N.J., 1950–.*

Brodie, Fawn M. *Thomas Jefferson: An Intimate History*. New York, 1974.

Burstein, Andrew. *Jefferson's Secret: Death and Desire at Monticello*. New York, 2005.

——. *The Inner Jefferson: Portrait of a Grieving Optimist*. Charlottesville, Va., 1995.

Cappon, Lester J., ed. *The Adams-Jefferson Letters: The Complete Correspondence between Thomas Jefferson and Abigail and John Adams*. Chapel Hill, N.C., 1987.*

Cunningham, Noble E. *The Jeffersonian Republicans: The Formation of Party Organization, 1789–1801*. Chapel Hill, N.C., 1957.

——. *The Process of Government under Jefferson*. Princeton, N.J., 1978.

——. *In Pursuit of Reason: The Life of Thomas Jefferson*. Baton Rouge, La., 1987.

Elkins, Stanley, and Eric McKitrick. *The Age of Federalism: The Early American Republic, 1788–1800*. New York, 1993.

Ellis, Joseph J. *American Sphinx: The Character of Thomas Jefferson*. New York, 1998.

Ellis, Richard E. *The Jeffersonian Crisis: Courts and Politics in the Young Republic*. New York, 1971.

Ferling, John. *Adams vs. Jefferson: The Tumultuous Election of 1800*. New York, 2004.

Foley, John P. *Jefferson Cyclopedia*. New York, 1900.

Golden, James L., and Alan L. Golden. *Thomas Jefferson and the Rhetoric of Virtue*. Lanham, Md., 2002.

Gordon-Reed, Annette. *Thomas Jefferson and Sally Hemings: An American Controversy*. Charlottesville, Va., 1997.

Horn, James, Jan Ellen Lewis, and Peter S. Onuf, eds. *The Revolution of 1800: Democracy, Race, and the New Republic*. Charlottesville, 2002.

Kaminski, John P. *Citizen Jefferson: The Wit and Wisdom of an American Sage*. Madison, Wis., 1994.

———. *Jefferson in Love: The Love Letters between Thomas Jefferson and Maria Cosway*. Madison, Wis., 1999.*

———. *Thomas Jefferson: Philosopher and Politician*. Madison, Wis., 2005.

Kaplan, Lawrence S. *Jefferson and France: An Essay on Politics and Political Ideas*. New Haven, Conn., 1967.

Kennedy, Roger G. *Mr. Jefferson's Lost Cause: Land, Farmers, Slavery, and the Louisiana Purchase*. Oxford, 2003.

Levy, Leonard W. *Jefferson and Civil Liberties: The Darker Side*. Chicago, 1989.

Looney, J. Jefferson, et al., eds. *The Papers of Thomas Jefferson: Retirement Series*. Princeton, N.J., 2004–.*

Malone, Dumas. *Jefferson and His Time*. 6 vols. Boston, 1948–81.

Matthews, Richard K. *The Radical Politics of Thomas Jefferson: A Revisionist View*. Lawrence, Kan., 1984.

Mayer, David N. *The Constitutional Thought of Thomas Jefferson*. Charlottesville, 1994.

Mayo, Bernard. *Jefferson Himself: The Personal Narrative of a Many-Sided American.* Charlottesville, Va., 1942.

McCoy, Drew R. *The Elusive Republic: Political Economy in Jeffersonian America.* Chapel Hill, N.C., 1980.

McLaughlin, Jack. *Jefferson and Monticello: The Biography of a Builder.* New York, 1988.

Miller, Charles A. *Jefferson and Nature: An Interpretation.* Baltimore, 1988.

Miller, John Chester. *The Wolf by the Ears: Thomas Jefferson and Slavery.* Charlottesville, Va., 1991.

Onuf, Peter S. *Jefferson's Empire: The Language of American Nationhood.* Charlottesville, Va., 2000.

———. *Jeffersonian Legacies.* Charlottesville, Va., 1993.

Peterson, Merrill D. *The Jefferson Image in the American Mind.* New York, 1960.

———, ed. *Thomas Jefferson: Writings.* New York, 1984.*

———. *Thomas Jefferson and the New Nation: A Biography.* New York, 1970.

Randolph, Sarah N., comp. *The Domestic Life of Thomas Jefferson.* Charlottesville, Va., 1978 reprint of the 1871 ed.*

Risjord, Norman K. *Thomas Jefferson.* Madison, Wis., 1994.

Sheehan, Bernard W. *Seeds of Extinction: Jefferson Philanthropy and the American Indian.* New York, 1973.

Sheldon, Garrett Ward. *The Political Philosophy of Thomas Jefferson.* Baltimore, 1991.

Sheridan, Eugene R. *Jefferson and Religion.* Princeton, N.J., 1983.

Sloan, Herbert E. *Principle and Interest: Thomas Jefferson and the Problem of Debt.* New York, 1995.

Smith, James Morton, ed. *The Republic of Letters: The Correspondence between Thomas Jefferson and James Madison, 1776–1826.* 3 vols. New York, 1995.*

Sowerby, E. Millicent, ed. *Catalogue of the Library of Thomas Jefferson.* 5 vols. Washington, D.C., 1952–59.

Stuart, Reginald C. *The Half-Way Pacifist: Thomas Jefferson's View of War.* Toronto, 1978.

Tucker, Robert W., and David C. Hendrickson. *Empire of Liberty: The Statecraft of Thomas Jefferson.* New York, 1990.

Wallace, Anthony F. C. *Jefferson and the Indians: The Tragic Fate of the First Americans.* Cambridge, Mass., 1999.

Note: All asterisked items are documentary editions.

Index

—the softest pillow (ignorance), 89
—the softest pillow (tranquility), 225
—the sole depository of the sacred fire of freedom & self-government (U.S.), 16
—as a solitary trunk in a desolate field, lvii
—solitude of a hermit (TJ), 496
—a son of nature, 21
—son of science, 316
—a sore affliction, 176
—sovereign invigorator of the body (exercise), 176
—specimens of antiquity for the observation of the curious, 278
—the speck in our horizon which is to burst on us as a tornado, 388
—a spectacle for the pity of my friends, 287
—a splendid misery (the presidency), 155
—the sport of every wind (man without reason), 94
—stage of public affairs, 167
—a standing monument & example (republican government), 16
—the stillness of the grave, 137
—like a storm in the Atmosphere, 391
—as storms in the physical, 390
—stormy ocean of public life, 74

—subtle corps of sappers & miners, 259–60
—sucked in the principles of liberty as it were with their mother's milk, xxxvii, 374
—like a superannuated soldier, 288
—surest guide (good faith), 233
—surest road to affluence (agriculture), 6
—swaggering on deck as a passenger (retirement), 288
—the theatre of the Revolution, 423
—like a thief (the judiciary), 261
—threatened shipwreck, 295
—time and silence are the only medicines, 291, 325
—all tongue without either head or heart (Patrick Henry), 411
—torrent of our tears, 225, 325
—the tree of liberty, 391
—the true foundation of republican government (equality of the people), 160
—the true secret, the grand recipe, for felicity (employing the mind), 237
—deliver up our trust, 273
—voice of affection, 72
—vulgar vehicles of passion (English newspapers), 348
—a wall of separation between Church & State, 352
—what the wand is to the sorcerer (plow), 9